Archetypal Patterns
in Fairy Tales

Marie-Louise von Franz, Honorary Patron

**Studies in Jungian Psychology
by Jungian Analysts**

Daryl Sharp, General Editor

Archetypal Patterns
in
FAIRY TALES

MARIE-LOUISE VON FRANZ

Also by Marie-Louise von Franz in this Series:
The Psychological Meaning of Redemption Motifs in Fairy Tales
On Divination and Synchronicity: The Psychology of Meaningful Chance
Alchemy: An Introduction to the Symbolism and the Psychology

Canadian Cataloguing in Publication Data

Franz, Marie-Louise von, 1915-1998
　　　Archetypal patterns in fairy tales

(Studies in Jungian psychology by Jungian analysts; 76)

Includes bibliographical references and index.

ISBN 9780919123779

1. Fairy tales—Psychological aspects.
2. Archetype (Psychology).
3. Psychoanalysis and folklore.
4. Fairy tales—History and criticism.
I. Title. II. Series.

GR550.F68 1997　　　398'.2'01'9　　　C97-930675-2

INNER CITY BOOKS
53 Alvin Avenue, Toronto, ON M4T 2A8, Canada.
Telephone 416-927-0355
Toll-free in Canada and U.S.: 1-888-927-0355
www.innercitybooks.net / booksales@innercitybooks.net

Honorary Patron: Marie-Louise von Franz.
Publisher and General Editor: Daryl Sharp.
Senior Editor: Victoria B. Cowan.
Office Manager: Scott Milligen.
IT Manager: Sharpconnections.com.
Editorial Assistance: David Sharp, J. Morgan, E. Jefferson.

INNER CITY BOOKS was founded in 1980 to promote the
understanding and practical application of the work of C.G. Jung.

Cover: "Table-top Globe," monoprint by Vicki Cowan, © 1997.

Index by Daryl Sharp.

Printed and bound in Canada by Thistle Printing
Reprinted 2020

CONTENTS

See final page for descriptions of other Inner City Books

Marie-Louise von Franz
(photo by Edwin Snyder)

Preface

This book is a collection of fairy tale interpretations which I presented in a series of lectures in 1974 at the C.G. Jung Institute in Zürich. I did not want to focus around a specific theme but rather to wander through many countries and many types of fairy tales. I chose some that challenged me because they were not the usual type. I wanted to show their diversity and also their underlying similar trends, so that one could appreciate what is nationally or racially specific and what is common to all civilizations and all human beings. I wanted to show how Jung's method of interpreting archetypal fantasy material could be applied to these diverse tales. This approach applied especially to the "little joke" story ("The Blade of Straw, the Coal, and the Bean") but it was also true for the others. It is up to the reader to judge if it works or not.

The bases of the text are tapes. Only with the invaluable help of Dr. Vivienne Mackrell was I able to make it a readable text. My heartiest thanks go to her and to Barbara Smith who typed the first text from the tapes.

Marie-Louise von Franz, Küsnacht
February 1997

1

The Princess with the Twelve Pairs of Golden Shoes
(Danish)

The first fairy tale, from Denmark, is called "The Princess with the Twelve Pairs of Golden Shoes."[1] It goes like this:

There was once a young man who went out into the world to find his luck. On his way he met an old man who begged him for some money. The young man said, "I have no money, but I will certainly share my food with you." And the old man accepted, so they sat under a tree and the young man distributed his food. When they had eaten, the old man said, "You have shared with me what you have; now I will give you in return this stick and this ball which will bring you luck. If you lift the stick before you, you will become invisible. And when you hit the ball with the stick, the ball will roll before you and show you where you should go."

The young man thanked him for the gift, threw the ball to the ground and hit it with the stick, and the ball quickly rolled ahead of him. It rolled and rolled until he came to a big town. Here he discovered that on the wall surrounding the town, there were many heads stuck up on display—cut-off human heads! He asked a man he met what the matter was. The man told him that there a great worry in this country because every night the princess of the country was tearing twelve pairs of golden shoes to bits. Nobody knew how it happened. The old king was sick of this affair and had sworn to find out what was the matter. Whoever would find out would get the princess and half of the empire, but if he could *not* find out what was the matter he would be killed. Many noble men had come already and tried, because the princess was very beautiful, but they had all been killed, and the old king was very sad about it.

When the young man heard this, he felt a great desire to try this adventure, and he went to the castle and said he would try the next night. The old king was very sorry for him and told him not to do it, for he would succumb like all the others. But the young man insisted, so the king said he must sleep for three nights in the bedroom of the princess and find out if he could discover something. If he hadn't discovered anything by the third day, he must be killed. The young man was satisfied. In the evening a servant led him to the room of the princess where there was a bed for him. He put his stick against the bed, put his rucksack next to it and climbed into bed, determined not to close an eye. For a long time he didn't sleep,

---

[1] MDW, *Nordische Volksmärchen*, vol. 1, Dänemark, no. 8 (Jena: Diederichs, 1922). [MDW refers to *Die Märchen der Weltliteratur* (Fairy Tales of World Literature)]

but still he didn't notice anything. Finally he slept. When he woke up suddenly, he found it was morning, and he was furious because he had missed seeing anything. He swore he would be more attentive the next night.

The next night it went the same way, and now the young man had only one night left to save his life. The third evening he pretended to sleep, and before long he heard a voice asking the princess if he was asleep. The princess said yes, and a girl in white clothes came to the bed of the princess and said, "I must still try to see if he really sleeps." She took a golden needle and pricked him in the heel. He did not move, though it hurt, and she left the golden needle in his foot. Then he saw how the princess and the girl pushed the bed aside and a stair appeared in the wall and they went down. So he quickly took the needle out and put it into his rucksack. Then he took the stick that made him invisible, and the ball, and followed them down the stairs until they came to a forest where everything was made of silver: the trees, the flowers and the grass. When they came to the end of the silver forest, he broke off a twig and put it too into his rucksack. The princess heard some noise in the trees and looked around but couldn't see anybody. She said to the white girl, "I think somebody is behind us." "Oh, that's only the wind," the white girl said. Then they came to a wood where everything was made of gold: the trees, the flowers and everything. Again he broke off a twig, and again the princess had a feeling somebody was behind them, but again the girl said it was only the wind. Next they came to a wood where everything was made from diamonds, and again he broke off a twig.

Then they came to a lake, where there was a little boat. The princess and the girl went into it, but when they pushed away from the land, the young man quickly jumped into the boat. But the boat wobbled so badly that the princess became terrified; this time she was sure that somebody was behind them, but again the white girl said, "Oh no, that's only the wind." And then they went over the lake and came to a big castle. When they arrived at the door, a very ugly troll received the princess and asked why she came so late. She said she had a terrible fear that somebody was behind them and had been spying, but she couldn't see anybody. They sat at a table and the young man stood behind the chair of the princess. When they had eaten, he took her golden plate and also her golden knife and fork. These he also put into his baggage. The troll and the princess couldn't explain how these things had disappeared, but the troll didn't bother about it any more, and they began to dance with each other. They danced twelve dances, and in every dance the princess tore or used up a pair of golden shoes. And when they had danced the last dance, and she had thrown the last pair of golden shoes in a corner, the young man took them and put them in his baggage. Then the troll accompanied the princess back to the boat, and the young man came along and jumped first on land. He quickly ran back to his bed so that when the princess arrived in her room he was already seemingly sleeping.

The next morning the old king asked if he had seen something, and he said no, he hadn't discovered anything. The old king was very unhappy, but the princess was triumphant and wanted to see his execution. So the young man was led to the gallows, and the king and the princess and the whole court went along. When he was standing on the gallows, he asked the king for permission to tell a strange dream which he had had the previous night, and the king agreed. So he told that he dreamt a white girl had come to the princess and asked if he slept, and then had pricked this golden needle into his foot to find out. Then he said, "I think it is *that* golden needle," and he showed it. He continued: "I dreamt how I went down the stairs, and we went through a silver forest, and I think *this* is the twig from the silver forest." He did the same with the golden forest and the diamond forest. Then he told about the dinner party with the troll, and then he said, "I think *this* was the plate she ate on," and he showed the plate and the fork as proof. Then he told about her dance, and showed the golden shoes. "And then I dreamt that the princess came home again but that I had come home earlier and was already in bed when she arrived." When the king heard all this he was terribly happy, but the princess was half dead from fright and couldn't understand how it had happened.

Now the king wanted the young man and the princess to marry, but the young man wanted first to find the troll. He asked the princess to lend him a golden thimble. She gave it to him. He went out to seek the troll. When he found him, he took the golden needle and pricked it into his heart and killed him. Then he extracted from his heart three drops of blood and collected them in the thimble. On his way back, he went through the diamond forest. Here he dropped one drop of the troll's blood on the earth, and all trees and flowers and grass became men and women and children who were terribly happy that they were redeemed from their curse. They said he should now become their king, for the forest was a whole kingdom. Then he went to the golden wood, and there again, with a drop of the troll's blood, he redeemed all the people of this kingdom who had been turned by the troll into those golden trees, flowers and grass, and they also elected him king. Then he went to the silver wood and did the same thing, and the same thing happened.

All the people thanked him for having been freed, and they wanted him to be king. Then they went to the old king and told him about it, and the princess was now very happy that she was also now redeemed from her curse. The young man married the princess in great pomp, and he became king over all three kingdoms.

We have a parallel to this story which is a bit more complicated, a Grimm fairy tale that in German is called "Die Zertanzten Schuhe,"[2] which means "the shoes ruined by dancing" or "the shoes danced to bits." There are certain differ-

2 MDW, *Kinder und Hausmärchen,* Die Gebrüder Grimm, vol. 2, no. 166 (Jena: Diederichs, 1922). The English version is called "The Shoes That Were Danced to Pieces," in *The Complete Grimm's Fairy Tales* (New York: Pantheon Books, 1944), p. 596.

ences, but the German version is more difficult to understand than this one, which is simpler and clearer. Therefore I will take the Danish story I just told you as the basis, and use the other only for amplifications.

I will tell you the main difference. In the German story there are twelve princesses who dance every night. They dance not with a troll in the beyond, but with twelve princes who are under a curse. After they dance with the princesses, these princes are cursed again in the end. There are a few other variations. The main one is that the hero is an old soldier who is dismissed from the army and goes out for adventure.

One motif we find in the Danish story, which I think is essential here, has really given me the clue about what I never understood very well in the German version: here the silver, golden and diamond forests are cursed kingdoms which are turned back into human kingdoms with a drop of the troll's blood. That motif is completely missing in the German version. It is very advisable, therefore, to persist whenever you meet a fairy tale with motifs you can't figure out. You should ask yourself, "Now how does that fit in?" And if you get into difficulties, it is very important to look up parallels, because sometimes in the parallel it becomes clear. Then you will also understand the more complicated version.

This is important advice: whenever you get stuck, don't only look up amplifications of the motifs, but also look up parallel stories, because when you do this you may discover not only amplifications of single motifs, but also amplifications of a *sequence* of motifs. Parallel stories very often provide a clue you would not be able to find any other way. With the German version of this story I was mystified until I discovered the Danish one.

The first sentence is simply, "There was once a young man who went out into the world to find his luck"—to find adventure. It is as impersonal and just so as all that. Or you can begin with the three-and-a-half kingdoms. If you are a thinking type, and that kind of approach amuses you, then it is quite advisable to make a scheme in which you will have four kingdoms. First you have the kingdom of the king and the princess. And then you have the three other kingdoms: the silver, the gold and the diamond. Of these three the young man becomes king. In the beginning, the king had promised also that the young man would get half of the first kingdom, but that is not mentioned at the end, where it merely says he becomes king of the other three kingdoms. It is probably assumed as self-evident that he gets half of that first kingdom.

So, a young man begins nowhere—just, "There was a young man . . ." He has no parents, not even a name. He achieves the whole opus with the help of an old man. The silver, diamond and gold kingdoms were under the curse of the troll, but the young man kills the troll and wins the three kingdoms in the end.

We also have the white girl. She and the troll must have something in common because she comes, so to speak, as a messenger to fetch the princess. She doesn't go back with her, just fetches her. They have something else in common: the princess is always terribly nervous when she feels somebody is behind her, but the white girl and the troll always say, "Oh, that's nothing." They are insensitive to the danger; they aren't aware of what's going on. Also, the golden needle with which the hero kills the troll comes from the white girl.

If you are a sensation type, it is better to start not by trying to use your inferior function, but by just sticking to the facts, beginning sentence by sentence: "A young man without a name . . ."; "What does the hero represent?" and so on, step by step.

If you are intuitive, you might have a flash of insight by looking at the general structure or at the whole. And, if you are a feeling type, you must first say to yourself, "How does this story affect me? . . . What a strange story!"

This *is* a strange story. From the feeling standpoint, for many years I never liked it very much. I had a kind of uncanny feeling of something not agreeable about it. And now I know why, but I will tell you that only later.

A story is only really properly interpreted if you circumambulate it as much as possible with all your functions. You must consider the structure. You must consider how it affects you from the feeling standpoint—whether it is an agreeable or disagreeable story, or whether it conveys something redeeming to you or leaves a sort of uncanny malaise. And then, of course, you must consider all scientific interpretations: facts, facts first, and facts again! You have to stick to the text and not put your subjective fantasy into it. But you sometimes also have to use your intuition to perceive the overall structure and to pick the right amplifications. There you must have the lucky eye of the intuitive.

Now, if you have some experience with fairy tales, you will see that very often you have either heroes like princes and princesses or you have anonymous nobodies as in our story, or socially underprivileged people, a poor devil, a soldier who has deserted, or someone stupid whom everyone despises, a Dummling, or a dwarflike, crippled person. So it's either the prince and the elite, so to speak, or the underprivileged. A third class which also appears sometimes is that of the more "ordinary" sort of person: a peasant or a peasant's son, or sometimes a fisherman or a hunter. These make up about ninety-eight per cent of all fairy tale heroes. Sometimes you have a businessman, but that is very, very rare.

Therefore, we have to look really closely at this angle: What is the difference in meaning if we have a peasant or a fisher-hunter, or an underprivileged person? In most cases, that person becomes the next king by marrying a princess, so the story describes the hero's ascent from a very low or anonymous collective personality into the leading position at the king's court. Naturally, the implication is always that after the old king's death, he will become the future king. Sometimes we have a prince who becomes the future king, but generally he has some trouble. For instance, he might be the third of three brothers, the one everybody despises. He would be the one who wouldn't get the throne in his home country, being the youngest, but can only achieve sovereignty in another kingdom. Or, he might become king in his own kingdom quite unexpectedly. Sometimes what happens is that a simple, socially underprivileged person just marries the daughter of a very rich man and becomes a rich ruler but not a king. Yet this is also a major social ascent.

Now, the great temptation, and a kind of half-legitimate thing to do, is to identify the hero of the story with the human ego. This is legitimate only insofar as the naive hearer does that very often. I once tried an experiment with a school teacher. She was to tell our fairy tale to her drawing class, and then have the children paint one scene from it, any scene of their choice. It became quite clear that the girls identified with the female figure of the story, even though she was not the heroine. They would paint the princess going in the boat over the lake, not the young man sharing his bread with the old man under a tree. On the other hand, the boys would choose the scenes where the young man, the real hero, was in the center, clearly with an underlying tone of identifying with him. And I am sure, if you men remember your childhood, you would have probably identified with the hero quite naturally. And then, you see, doing that, you will go on to take Jungian concepts like anima and shadow and tack them on to the fairy tale figures—and you will be all wet! If you start by saying, "This is a man who is looking for the anima, and the white girl is the anima's shadow, and the troll is his or the king's shadow," and so on, you are off the track completely. Because I could just as well say, "No, excuse me, the princess is the old king's anima, that's a girl with a father complex." Or I could just as well say, . . . Ah, you see?—we just get stuck in projection!

You must never forget that Jung built up his concepts of shadow, animus and anima, and Self from looking at the single individual—an individual Mr. Meier or a Mrs. Miller—experiencing the unconscious. But a fairy tale is *not* that. A fairy tale is *not* simply the tale of a personal experience. Fairy tales normally come into existence in one of two ways. Some fairy tales, as far as we can trace them, are created by people who had parapsychological or dreamlike or visionary experiences. They relate these again and again, and then these experiences become enlarged in the community into stories. The other way fairy tales come into existence is the same way as literature does: among those of the population who are not writers, some people are gifted with a strong imagination. The tales originate in what you could call the active imaginations of certain individuals in the folk population. In both cases, whether the nucleus of a fairy tale was a visionary experience, a big dream or a parapsychological experience, or whether it came originally from some folk poet or storyteller, it was something that had to fit the psyche of the whole collective. Otherwise it would not have endured.

In primitive tribes there is still generally a storyteller. When you gather round a fire in the evening, they pick one person and say, "Come on, tell us a story." And then the teller relates stories heard in childhood. Sometimes, a poetic storyteller invents, adding new details or whole stories. In primitive societies, stories were even sold, and that was still so until the eighteenth century in Alsace-Lorraine and other countries. You weren't even allowed free access to them, much less freedom to alter them according to your own whim! Certain peasants owned certain stories, and they lent them to certain friends. No one else was allowed to tell the story. Or if so, they had to pay a lot of beer and wine or even money for official permission to retell that story. It was the possession of a certain group or individual.

For instance, in the introduction to the volume of Austrian fairy tales collected by Father Bramberger,[3] a Catholic father, you will find that he got about a fourth of the beautiful fairy tales he collected from the so-called "old dog girl," a beggar woman who went up and down the country selling shoe laces and the like. Wherever she went, she called the children and took them aside and told them stories, and no adult was ever allowed to listen. But in return for telling the stories to the children, she asked for a meal. That's how she earned her living. The parents paid the meal and then she took the children aside and told them stories. Father Bramberger himself had to pay her with many sausages before he was allowed into the presence of the children to write down those stories.

So, when you see how they originate and understand the way they are handed on, you realize that anything *personal*—which might come from the complexes of the person who had the vision or invented the tale from an active imagination, and which would make the story deviate from the archetypal pattern—these things would be discarded or corrected by retelling, because what does not fit the psyche of the collective doesn't stick.

We were visited here once by a young American school teacher who tried an

---

3 MDW, *Märchen aus dem Donaulande* (Jena: Diederichs, 1926).

experiment. One day he read to his class a novel—a good, short novel by a modern writer—and then he also read them a fairy tale. A few days later, he made them write down by heart what they remembered. There was absolutely no comparison between how well the students remembered the fairy tale as opposed to the novel, although the novel was a good, real and poignant one.

This shows that in fairy tales there is a pattern which fits into the unconscious of everybody and is therefore retained more securely. We know now that memory formation has to do with emotion. The more emotionally impressive something is, the more it sticks in the memory. And therefore, because the kind of fairy tale that expresses collective structures touches the emotions more deeply, it stays better in one's memory. Also, this happens naturally in the autonomous retelling process; only those things which express a generally human structure stick in the memory of the people and are handed on, while those things that are somehow influenced by the personal problems or complexes of individuals spread only in circles that have the same problem.

For instance, the fairy tales of Hans Christian Andersen, who was a neurotic personality, had a tremendous success in a society that had the same problem. He had mainly a terrific sex problem—absolutely, well, as big as a cathedral. And he never solved it. If you know how to read his fairy tales, you see that there is a tone of unredeemed neurotic sadness going right through his stories. And it spread in Scandinavian and European countries insofar as that problem was the problem of the whole society. But I would venture to assume that by now they are very seldom read, and I would predict that in about two or three hundred years nobody will know about them any more. One of his best stories, one he became most famous for—"The Traveling Companion"[4]—is based on a Scandinavian folk tale. He didn't invent the story himself; he only retold it. But those which express his problem are unsatisfactory for a more general public. There is still a lot of writing going on, and quite a bit of publishing of new fairy tales. Generally, they are so close to the classical pattern that they pass, but sometimes you see that they are influenced by a definitely neurotic trait of the inventor. Those, I think, will never have any success in the long run, when they are put through the process of collective selection.

Then there is also a collective process of rechecking. For instance, if a chap in a peasant country comes to an inn and the people there say, "Tell us a story," and he tells a story but perhaps he has drunk too much or is a bit in a sloppy mood so that he leaves something out, or tells something differently, then the

---

[4] *Fairy Tales* (Cleveland: World Publishing Co., Rainbow Classics, 1946), p. 21.

public says, "No!" They do just like children: "No, it isn't like that, it is like *that.*" And sometimes there are big quarrels in an inn. "No, my father always told it like *that,* and you must tell it *this* way." And they are indignant if the storyteller doesn't tell it in the right way. It is just the same when you try to tell fairy tales to children. They are furious if you vary them. They interrupt you at once and say, "No, it is like *that.*" They say you must tell it again; they want to hear it literally the same way. It is like a ritual.

So, in the folk tradition, there are two powers at work. There is one that tends to eliminate what is only personal and doesn't click or make sense to the general public. And there is another that tends to preserve the form: "No, you must not vary it, you must keep it the way it is."

In these two ways the constancy of the archetype manifests. You could call the archetype the "nature constant" of the human psyche. It is eminently conservative, and furthermore it always eliminates impurities that have been added by individual problems. On account of that, we have in the classical folk tales an end product which represents in the form of symbolic images certain typical collective unconscious processes. Since fairy tales have a form by which they naturally repeat themselves, they are one of the best kinds of source material for studying the "nature constants" of the collective psyche.

There is one strange thing, however. When I became acquainted with the symbolic material of alchemy, I was struck by the structures pointed out by Jung in *Psychology and Alchemy,*[5] namely, the mandala, the quaternary structure, and the whole basic structure of the process of individuation as a process of becoming conscious. In fairy tales, too, we find all the elements of the process of individuation, or sequences that are clearly parallel to what we can observe in the process of individuation of humans.

But somewhere in fairy tales there is very often an unsatisfactory note. In this Danish fairy tale it is not very clear, but it is much clearer in the German version; that's why I had a disagreeable feeling about it. There it is said that the princess with whom the twelve princesses dance in the Beyond are pulled back into the realm of the kingdom. They are forbidden to go on dancing. In contrast to the troll, the princes are not killed, but it is said that they have now to remain cursed for as many nights as they had danced with the princesses. So the partners of the dance are badly cursed. Now they are called princes, cursed princes, which means they are decent human beings who have been put under a spell or

---

5 CW 12. [CW refers throughout to *The Collected Works of C.G. Jung* (Bollingen Series XX). 20 vols. Trans. R.F.C. Hull. Ed. H. Read, M. Fordham, G. Adler, Wm. McGuire. Princeton: Princeton University Press, 1953-1979]

bewitched by black magic. They have danced with those girls many nights and now they are *punished* for it; that revolts one's feeling. An unsatisfactory end. Besides, the hero is an old soldier who marries the oldest princess, which is absolutely not the normal thing. The hero always gets the young, the innocent, the most beautiful one. At the end of the German story, the old soldier says, in a rather melancholy way, "As I am an older man, I'll marry the oldest princess. That is completely atypical. It's again slightly unsatisfactory, especially since the youngest behaves far the best in the story—so one would want her to marry the hero, from one's fairy tale expectations.

Very often fairy tales contain such a question mark: "Now what about those princes?" They aren't explained. They are cursed. They are cursed again at the end of the story. We don't know why.

In our Danish version too, there are two unsatisfactory aspects. We have that strange white girl, who is simply forgotten in the course of the story, and there is no mother figure. We have a king and a princess, but where's the mother? In a whole story, somewhere you always have the father, somewhere the mother, somewhere the son, somewhere the daughter. So in this Danish version there is a satisfactory solution in one way, and a lot of question marks in another.

However, this is not unusual. I would say that eighty-five to ninety per cent of the stories I have read have left me with such questions. When I tried to squeeze them into what we understand to be the process of individuation, they didn't fit. There was something disquieting about this until Jung, in a discussion in the Psychological Club, gave me the explanation.

Namely, in alchemy the alchemists experimented with the processes of the collective unconscious in themselves. That is, they experimented with the projected forms that they made with chemical substances by means of their active imagination. You could call alchemy a work of active imagination—made not by painting or writing but with chemical substances. But not only did the alchemists have a *laboratorium,* a laboratory where they worked with the substances; at the same time they tried to construct a *theoria,* a Weltanschauung or theoretical explanation. They nearly wrecked their heads to interpret or to understand what they were doing.

Naturally, looking back from our modern standpoint, their *theoria* is mythological and symbolic and not very clear to us. With the exception of, perhaps, Gerhard Dorn and a very few Arabic mystics, the alchemists did not realize that their work was really an experiment with their own inner psyches, a religious experiment they were making with their own personality. In most of the alchemists we miss that, but at least they had some kind of *theoria,* and they puzzled how that fitted with the Christian Weltanschauung—they tried!

In alchemy you have all the beginnings of natural science. They had the concepts of matter, of energy, of energic processes, and of particle. All the intuitive images or thought models that are still used in modern physics and chemistry already existed in alchemy. They were meant to explain what the alchemists were doing, to bring their experiences into consciousness as much as they could. And therefore, in alchemy, it's also individual. If you study two hundred alchemists, you find that each one has his different *theoria* in which he tries the best he can to explain to himself what he is doing.

This attempt to understand and integrate one's experiences into a conscious collective Weltanschauung, or into general scientific or religious concepts, is lacking in fairy tales. Fairy tales are like dreams—pure nature phenomena of the collective unconscious. Therefore, in a way, they are illuminating, but their light then peters out and disappears again in the unconscious. They are really as Jung explained when he quoted from Goethe's *Faust:* "Gestaltung, Umgestaltung des ewigen Sinnes ewige Unterhaltung"—"Change and change and transformation, the eternal meanings, eternal transformation."

Fairy tales are a play of nature. They are as meaningful or as meaningless as nature is when we look at it or when we don't. They are like the products of the unconscious of someone who is not analyzed.

Somebody who does not analyze and does not look at dreams can have the most marvelous dreams repeating themselves over a series of years, as though there is no beginning and no end. This is because such people do not try to bring them into a dialogue, to connect them with consciousness. And those storytellers, they function in folklore as representatives of the unconscious. They compensate the collective consciousness, and they have much the same healing function as a not-understood dream.

We do know that dreams have a healing function even when they are not understood. From experiments in dream laboratories we know that if we stop people from dreaming, we could even kill them. This has been seen in some animal studies as well. There are heavy physical and psychic symptoms if we wake sleepers each time they have a REM (Rapid Eye Movement) phase. So we know that dreams have a biologically and psychologically restorative function. They affect us positively, even when we don't understand them. What we do as dream interpreters is simply to reinforce the healing function of the dream by providing a kind of sounding board, so that it has a stronger restoring quality than if it happened by itself. It is just like when a mother hen wants her chick to eat: she pecks with her beak on the floor, and that stimulates the chick to eat; that's how it learns to eat when it comes out of the egg. A Prussian chicken breeder once got the idea of putting his young families onto sounding boards. When the hen pecked, the sound was much stronger, and those chickens fed much better. They became fat in a much faster time because they ate double the normal portion.

It seems to me that our dream interpretations are like that Prussian's sounding boards. We simply try to reinforce the healing effect of the dream by our interpretation. That also explains why it is that the interpretation must never be intellectual and must never really resolve the meaning of the dream, so that one feels one *has* it. A dream interpreter should never feel as though the dream is now completely understood, because that would kill its resonance. A dream interpretation should be a way of talking *around* it, so that its own message becomes better heard. Only then does it have a healing effect.

Obviously, the telling of stories in primitive societies was also felt to have a healing effect. There's a beautiful story that Laurens Van der Post tells about a Bushman who was punished with a sentence of twelve years in prison for stealing sheep. A German scholar redeemed him from prison, for otherwise he would have died there at once. One can't imprison Bushmen—they die.

So, the German rescued this Bushman and made him his servant and explored the Bushman's language, and he wrote the first Bushman grammar. And as far as the servant could be happy, the German made him happy. But he was never *really* happy, because he was homesick. In a very moving way, he once said to his master, "You know, I have only one longing, and that is to be back with my tribe and to hear the stories of my tribe." He didn't long for the people; he didn't long for his native kind of food; he didn't long for the kind of hut he had lived in with his tribe—oh, he longed for these too, I'm sure, but what he really longed for, and what he missed to the point of feeling he had lost his life, was to hear the stories of his tribe. He had said, "Stories are like the wind." Well, the wind is the healing power of the spirit. His one wish was that before his death he could once more hear the stories of his tribe.

Such stories are healing because they express life dreams and the compensatory processes in the collective unconscious that balance the one-sidedness, the sickness, the constant deviations of human consciousness. And these stories have this healing effect although there is no attempt to understand them. They are simply *told.*

Yet, you must not expect to find in them certain elements you can only find in religious systems or high cultures or in alchemical or gnostic symbolism, where those elements are consciously understood. With tribal stories like the stories of the Bushmen, or with folk tales and fairy tales, there is no wish for conscious understanding. These stories are told in order that the people can *feel* the refreshing, vivifying effect—not for them to *think* about it.

But if we put many stories together, we see that each one enlightens some typical archetypal process in the collective unconscious. If you put two or three hundred together, then you get a kind of intuitive mapping of the structure of the collective unconscious and the possible structures and processes in it. This knowledge is invaluable for an analyst. That's why Jung said that studying fairy tales is a good way to study the comparative anatomy of the collective unconscious, the deeper layers of the human psyche.

We return again to our fairy tale. We start with the fact that we have a prince or a young man. The young man in our story has no name, and so we see that we cannot identify him with an ego. I remarked earlier that if you consider the story from a feeling standpoint, the men will identify with the young man and the women will identify with the princess. But from the standpoint of interpretation this is not correct because the men and the women are individuals who have names and individual identities, but our young man hasn't. Therefore, from that simple fact, already we see that it's not right to identify him as the ego. It is said, "A young man . . ." And *"a* young man" therefore means something general, something typified. So you have to amplify and explain the young man motif as if you do not know what "a young man" is. You must not assume naively, "Oh, a young man—that's me, or any young man."

The best way to understand a hero figure is to look at what he does. Because, as Max Lüthi has explained, fairy tale figures are very abstract.[6] They have very few personal traits. For instance, nothing much is said about our young man's feelings. Was he afraid when he slept? Was he angry with the troll? Was he pleased when he got the princess?—not a word! All that is said is that a young man *does* this, he *does* that, . . . this, . . . that, . . . that—and becomes a king. That's terribly impersonal, really. So you can say of the young man motif, that it explains itself best in terms of what he *does.*

Now what does he do? He goes into the world to find his luck. He shares his bread with a poor old man. He has a desire for an adventure, to find out about the princess. We don't know if he wants the princess or not. He just has a desire to go for that adventure. And then he does the necessary things to have that adventure, and unintentionally he becomes the king of three-and-a-half kingdoms. So we must assume that he is an archetypal collective "something" which is seeking adventure, which has a kind of zest for life, a certain enterprise, a certain

---

6 *Das europäische Volksmärchen* (Berne: A. Franke, 1947).

male initiative, a spirit of adventure. Also, the young man has a certain charitability; he has a good heart, for he shares his bread with the old man.

So you can say of the young man that he wants to live; he is looking forward toward life and is a generous person. Then he goes on to do everything right and in the necessary way. He is intelligent too, and courageous. But that's about all we know about him. He is a typical anonymous hero, and the result of his activity is that from being an anonymous young man, he comes an enormously powerful king, a king who is more powerful than the ruling king of his country.

This rise in status is typical for most fairy tale heroes. But therefore, we cannot explain what it means before we look at what the king is. We cannot explain the young man separately from the king. Or we can first, as a kind of working hypothesis, suppose that he represents a masculine content which is moving toward building up the future, by the right means. And now let us go on to look for the meaning of the king—because that's the end result of all that the young man does in the story.

In general, in primitive societies the king represents *the* magic individual on whom the life of the tribe depends. He is the one who sticks out against the background of the many. The many are, so to speak, the "soulless" many, and the king is the One. For instance, in the ancient Egyptian kingdoms only the king was embalmed, and in their liturgy he became immortal, while the Millers and the Johnsons, the ordinary folk, also died but nobody knows what happened to *them* after death!

At first, an individual spiritual destiny was attributed only to the king. But already in the Middle Kingdom, the higher society shared in this fate, and in the latest kingdom of Egypt, every Egyptian (at least those who had the money) could be embalmed and have a whole tomb and liturgy of the dead and thus have their immortality guaranteed. So you see that in the beginning, to be an individual and to be more conscious than the masses was the prerogative only of someone "chosen," either by heritage, by election or by some other means. This call, however, was paid for very dearly in that, in most primitive societies (as you can read in James George Frazer's "The Dying God"),[7] a king was always killed after a certain period—five, ten, maximum fifteen years. They were killed ritually, or whenever they showed signs of impotence or illness, or when things went wrong, like a big drought or a cattle disease. The king was killed not only because he was the One, the only conscious individual of the tribe; he was killed also because he was the only human being who had connections to magical and

---

[7] *The Golden Bough,* part 3 (3rd edition; New York: St. Martin's Press, 1966).

divine powers. In the earliest societies he was archpriest and king—all in one.

And you know that our kings in Europe were "from *Gottesgnaden*," "by the grace of God," king of so-and-so. And even in the eighteenth century, they were still believed to have healing power: they could heal illness by touch. They were still king-priests to a certain extent, although the Pope had taken some of that power to himself. And therefore, we had the big battle in the Middle Ages between the sacerdocy and the worldly power of the imperium.

The king draws his power not only from his physical strength and from his armed support, but also from his connection with the powers of the Beyond. A most spiritualized interpretation was that of the Chinese emperors. Up to the time of Mao, it was believed that when the emperor was in harmony with the Tao, the spiritual world principle, then things in the Chinese empire went right. And if something went wrong, for example if the Yangtze flooded, it was the emperor who had to change his habits and do penitence in order to overcome that evil. He was, so to speak, the *axis mundi,* the axis around which the whole empire—the whole world, for the Chinese—revolved. Everything depended on his right or wrong attitude. He had divine power; he was an incarnation of the central divine principle. If we translate this into psychological language, we can say that the king represents that aspect of the God-image, or the Self, which has become a ruling concept in a society.

However, in myths and fairy tales, kings are always aging, and there is always something wrong in their kingdoms. If you count how many kings in myths and fairy tales have kingdoms where everything is right, you will find that such kings practically don't exist. They wouldn't be worth talking about.

When the story begins, it is always the king who is ill, or his daughter is making mischief, or he can't find a follower; he's become evil, or the devil has attacked him or stolen his son. Something is always wrong with the king. The story begins always with a state of imbalance, and balance has to be restored through a compensatory process.

Now, in our fairy tale, the story does not actually begin with the king in trouble; rather it begins with a hero who breaks off from the unconscious and looks for adventure. And that, I think, is a very interesting variation. Generally, the story will begin with an ailing kingdom. But occasionally it begins with a young man who, just for the sake of adventure, goes out and *stumbles into* an ailing kingdom. That brings up questions I have often asked myself: Is the unconscious only reactive? Is every dream action only compensatory or complementary to something wrong in consciousness? Or is the unconscious a creative, spontaneous matrix that also corrects various individual conscious premises?

From looking at myths and fairy tales, I know I would say both. Sometimes it works one way (compensatory) and sometimes the other way (creative). You can never understand unconscious processes *only* as a reaction to something found in consciousness. The unconscious is equally capable of just producing something on its own, out of a "spirit of life," so to speak. And here, in our fairy tale, this is very clear. The young man represents something that spontaneously breaks up in the unconscious psyche: an unknown male initiative—something powerful. It is then, luckily, and only after certain events, guided and maneuvered into having to compensate for some diseases of psychic consciousness. Our story stresses the fact that the action of this power from the unconscious is spontaneous, that it arises by itself.

If you read Arnold Toynbee, you see that he has a very convincing and spirited description of how a civilization looks when it's flourishing, when it is on its rise, so to speak, and then when it is in decline.[8] And one of the characteristics of a civilization on the rise is that, in general, all the different fields of life—law, religion, political order, social order, art, etc.—express the same symbol. They are all on the same wavelength.

Think, for instance, of early Christianity and early Christian art. Whether or not you like it, whether you think it's good or bad, you must admit it all expresses the basic religious and psychological concerns of the people of that time. Their religion and their social order were all one. In these early Christian communities, no one would say, about medicine, for example, "Oh, that doesn't concern us! That's a field in itself where you just go the old Roman doctors, the pagan doctors. Medicine is just a science, and that has nothing to do with the coming of Christ."

In fact, the early Christians ruined antique medicine because of this attitude. All of antique medicine, with all its knowledge and its high achievement, went out the window. Instead of using that ancient knowledge, they slept at the graves of martyrs and hoped to be cured that way. If you look at it negatively, their attitude was destructive. But if you look at it positively, you could say that with the rise of Christianity, once again all of humanity's cultural expressions were unified. It is as if a light fell upon the whole world from one center and gave it a wholeness. And oneness as pervasive as this imparts a sense of oneness to the individual also.

Now, in civilizations in decay, one can observe a compartmentalization. They are like a businessman who behaves like a shark from Monday to Friday, and on

---

[8] See, for instance, *A Study of History* (London: Oxford University Press, 1988).

Sunday goes to church. If you say to him, "Now how do you put that together?—your Sunday and your week days?" he will say, "Look here, they've nothing to do with each other. In business, everybody behaves like a shark. You *have* to. You have to, because otherwise you would succumb." Or they are like a medical doctor who says, "I am a surgeon, and being a surgeon has nothing to do with my Weltanschauung. When I remove an appendix, that's a purely technical job. What I feel or think as a human being doesn't come into it."

We know that's not true, but the surgeon claims it is so. In many American hospitals, and here in Europe too, often the great surgeons don't even know their patients any more. All the preparation is done by the assistants and the nurses. The surgeon just goes into the operating room with a mask and, disinfected from tip to toe, takes a knife, does the cutting and walks out again.

Once I knew a doctor who revolted against this way of doing things in a hospital in New York, so he decided that he would pay a visit to every one of his surgery patients on the evening before their operations and have a good, human talk with them. Later on he did a statistical survey and found that the mortality rate of these patients was infinitely lower than before. So what the compartmentalized people say, that these things have nothing to do with each other, is simply not true.

In a decaying civilization you find compartments, each with its own ruler, its own rules of behavior, its own team-work, its own basic Weltanschauung, and its own ultimate hierarchy of values. And each is neatly kept apart from the next compartment. For instance, sometimes you have military people who simply play with weapons. Naturally, they are deeply interested in how they function. So, even in Russia, where they pretend to have a one-kingdom affair, one Weltanschauung, all Marxist-Leninist and so on, they really have two kingdoms, the military and the political. In other words, here you have many kings. The people are compartmentalized. Such a situation in an individual, where one's relationship to the Self isn't alive, is typical of what leads to neurosis.

I have a friend whom I've known since I was eighteen. Though she likes me, she has never gone near Jungian psychology. Periodically I dream of that friend. And I have found that every time I dream of her, I had behaved the day before in a certain compartmentalized way, as if I had never heard of Jungian psychology. So now, when she comes in a dream, I know! I say, "Hah!" and then I ask myself, "Now yesterday, what did I do?" And I always find that in some situation the day before, I had thought to myself something like, "Well, that has to be decided by reason. That's not worth thinking of in terms of the unconscious or the Self, etc. That's just obviously so-and-so."

I have now been in Jungian psychology nearly thirty years, and it is still so: certain compartments in me still have never heard about it. You may laugh, but I bet you have them too. And it's just absolutely amazing how that is so. There are little "kingdoms" that just organize themselves and have their little rules; and you take them so much for granted that you don't even notice.

So we can say, the deeper or greater the impulse toward individuation or higher consciousness, the more kingdoms it will unite. We could take the hero in our story, for the moment, as representing an impulse toward reaching a higher state of consciousness, starting from the unconscious. Not only does that impulse redeem a kingdom, restore it and bring new life into it; also it might suddenly "pull in" certain other kingdoms which have until now just scraped by on their own—badly in this case.

Jung once said that in an analysis it is most important that the analysand is honest and listens to what one says and to the dream interpretations, but that it is also crucial—and the analyst should also listen for this—that his other *complexes* listen. Sometimes there are people who come into analysis quite benevolently and with good will, generally because they want to get rid of some nasty symptom from which they suffer. But their animus or anima or some other complex says, "Oh, pooh!" You can see this, sometimes, in the cold, mocking look that comes into the analysand's eyes. I've seen analysands listening to me as if the Holy Ghost Himself were speaking, and then suddenly there's a twinkle: "You talk! You talk! I know better!" And then sometimes I say, "Now, now, now . . ." I mean, I've temporarily stopped these things from interfering. So then I ask the person, "What have you thought now?"—and the analysand couldn't say anything. In such cases I don't think they lied or wanted to hide anything from me, but their complex did. *It* thought like that, but *they* (the analysands) didn't. *They* were listening, but *it* thought, "Oh, pooh!"

You must look, therefore, at the face. It is sometimes visibly trembling, and at such times it is very, very difficult to do something about this interference. Generally, if by the grace of God something very powerful comes up from the unconscious—for example a deep and moving dream—and if again by the grace of God you succeed in expressing it in a way that hits the emotions, then those walls or barriers fall down. There's a unification and the person is shaken into a new perspective.

I once talked to a man who had been in analysis many years, and he said, "I don't know what it is. Sometimes the penny drops, I do understand it. And then it goes away again. When I read my dream book through during the holidays, I found that certain insights I thought I had seen just recently for the first time, I had already had three years ago, but I just forgot them again." They didn't stick the first time. Only the deepest ones do.

Something can happen only when the Self is activated, when the deepest layers of the personality are activated. But sometimes we don't seem to have the power to hold on to these insights and to keep on making things happen.

This problem is very much like the old quarrel which, in theological language, is the issue of works versus grace: Is man redeemed by good works, or is man redeemed by God's grace? That issue has been debated endlessly. And in psychological language you would raise this question by asking, "Can a person be cured simply by working with the analyst honestly and with good will, or is one cured only when the Self and the unconscious want it?" We psychologists can't solve the problem, either. All we've done is to reformulate an old paradox in a new way.

As far as I can see, there is always an interplay of both, works and grace; you can't do without either one, they are both needed. Neither the analyst nor the analysand has the matter in hand completely. But when someone works on and on over years, with devotion and patience and in spite of great disappointments, seemingly with no results, I have never seen that all that work has not finally helped. But then, on the other hand, there are those lucky ones who make very little effort and yet have it all given to them by the unconscious. No one can understand it; at least I can't.

In our fairy tale, the stress is on spontaneity. The primary fact is that the young man feels the need for adventure, and it is only secondary that he stumbles into the situation of deficiency. He seems to be very unconscious because he doesn't know what he wants; all he wants is "to find his luck," the text says. He's just like a young man breaking away from home, looking at the world and wanting to experience life. But he isn't quite on his own, because an old man has an eye on our youth, coming to meet him and begging for food. He then gives the young man magical gifts, the stick and the ball.

I want to refer you to Jung's paper, "The Phenomenology of the Spirit in Fairy Tales."[9] There you will see that most frequently, what Jung calls the "spirit" appears mythologically as the Old Man. He could be the wise old man, or he could be the Wicked Old Man, because the phenomenon of spirit has a double aspect. Usually it's either a wicked old man or a wise old man, but most puzzling of all, it is sometimes both. For instance, Mercurius, the trickster of alchemy, is both good and bad; it depends on the human being he meets, which

---

[9] *The Archetypes and the Collective Unconscious,* CW 9i, chap. 5.

of these he is going to be. Also, Jung tells several stories from the Eskimos, where an old man comes to help the hero and then another old man comes and behaves destructively to the hero. But actually, from certain signs in these fairy tales you can quite clearly see that both of these old men are really one and the same. It is as if he would slap the hero with the left hand and help him with the right (or vice versa). So the spirit, in the form of the old man who is both good and bad, is a pure nature phenomenon.

Jung defines the spirit/Old Man as the active power of the unconscious which invents and arranges or orders images. You could therefore say that the spirit, for Jung, is that in the unconscious which makes dreams, because a dream is a series of symbolic images arranged in a definite sequence. And we know *we* don't make them. No one can make a dream. If, after the event, you analyze a dream, you find that it is a highly intelligent arrangement of symbolic pictures which you haven't made. That is how Jung defines or describes the spirit.

Therefore, you could also call it the active intelligence of the unconscious—that aspect of the unconscious which strikes us, when we experience it, as a kind of intelligent activity. It doesn't manifest only in dreams. It sometimes manifests in the most strange arrangements of fate, in synchronicities and in all those experiences where one has an uncanny feeling that one is being manipulated by a higher intelligence. Sometimes it appears in an evil trickster form to make you fall down, and sometimes in a helpful form, but always it comes most surprisingly. Generally when it appears in an evil form, it's because you are all wet, and then the trickster makes you stumble over your own feet; you feel there's quite an intelligence at work, a wicked intelligence in that case. In other cases, you feel it is a helpful intelligence. And that same thing is what arranges dreams. Because it is something active, it is represented by a masculine power, as in the archetype of the spirit god. And in fairy tales, it appears as the old wise man or as the little old dwarf who always comes in helpful moments. And he generally comes, as Jung points out in his essay, when the hero badly needs intelligence and doesn't have it.

Jung tells of one fairy tale where an orphan boy is ill-treated by his parents. He blindly runs away from home. Soon he is nearly starving in the forest. Suddenly an old man stands before him and gives him good advice about how to get on. As Jung says, that helpful old man is activated when consciousness badly needs advice but finds that it cannot produce it on its own. In other words, we get this spiritual help from the unconscious only when we have made our utmost effort ourselves. If, out of mental laziness, you simply sit back and hope that the spirit of the unconscious will maneuver you through all the difficulties of your life, then it will play you tricks. But if you make your utmost effort to face life on your own with great courage, but find that you can't, that you are up against a wall and it's beyond your capacities, then, generally, these helpful gifts emerge from the unconscious.

In our story, the young man obviously has not enough purpose or insight into the meaning of life. He's too much enterprise and not enough thought. And so thought comes to him because he's a "called" one, he's the hero. He's meant to do something great. What he's meant for comes in the form of the wise old man, as an independent unconscious figure who first asks that young man share his food. In so many fairy tales you find that same little old woodman, or that wise old man or old woman in the woods, or a dwarf, who comes to the hero (generally at the start of the story) and asks for food.

Sometimes you have three brothers: the two elder ones say, "Oh no, I haven't enough myself," and they eat up all their own bread and wine, but then they are cursed. The old man or the dwarf or the old woman says, "Well, you will run into disaster"—which they do. The youngest brother is the one who says, "All right, we'll share." And then he receives the magical gift.

The hero in our story had this same attitude of willingness to share his food with the powers of the unconscious, in the guise of the wise old man. This shows the basic law which the alchemical Mercurius expressed so beautifully in one of the old texts by saying, "Help me, and I will help thee." It is as though the unconscious were saying, "Give me my right, my share, and then I will give you your share"; if we do not give the unconscious its due, if we do not pay attention to it, then it can't do a thing.

Perhaps in your life you have already met people who have an awful neurosis, who come to howl to you about their symptoms and about the great fix they are in, and you know exactly how you could help them, if only they would turn to the unconscious. But they won't do it. And then, after a while, you can only shrug your shoulders and say, "Well, sorry! If you don't want to do that, if you don't want to do your share, and do something for your own psyche and make the effort, then I can't help you." With some people, it's hopeless; they prefer to wallow, maybe for twenty years, in their neurotic symptoms. You see, they are required to have a certain generosity, a certain willingness to risk something, to give away something. They must also have a spirit of adventure, in a way, so they can say, "Well, why not, let's try! Let's make an effort! What have I got to lose—only an effort; no more than an effort is at stake. So why not?" This kind of generous attitude is needed in order that these powers of the unconscious can come to help.

Now, you see what a dirty trick I have played! I've slipped into treating the young man is if he were a conscious human being who is sharing what he has with the spirit. But that's not true, because the young man is an archetypal image, and the old man who represents the spirit is an archetypal image too. That's where students, in interpreting fairy tales, always "slip off." And now I've slipped off myself—consciously, because I noticed it while I did it, but I thought, "I'll just carry on to show you how one slips off."

But how does one keep from slipping? I could have said, for instance, "Archetypal image A gives his bread to archetypal image B." Well, it's quite crazy if one begins to think like that! You see, that's why I said it's only half bad to identify the hero with the conscious ego—because one just can't understand what's going on, at first, without this naive identification.

But now, after we've done that, and know that we've been slipping, we have to correct ourselves and say, "In the collective unconscious rises an archetypal impulse, an *élan vital* toward higher consciousness. That *élan vital* isn't yet coupled with insight and wisdom. In the unconscious itself, it couples with insight and wisdom."

That's what the sharing really represented. And that's what happens all the time in the unconscious: certain contents couple themselves with (or repel themselves from) certain other contents. The collective unconscious or the inner human being—altogether, the unconscious—is like a field of particles in which certain particles attract each other and others repel each other. They form links and then fall apart again. That is the eternal play, and it seems to have a certain directedness toward the compensation or complementation of consciousness.

You see now that that happens in our story. The old man gives the hero a stick and a ball, and the ball leads the young man to the court where things are so wrong, to his task. So the old man, *via* the stick and ball, gives the young man a direction. He moves him toward the place where things are wrong, where he has to put things right. So, you can say that in the collective unconscious there is first just a creative *élan vital* toward new possibilities, but in itself it has as yet no direction. Then it couples itself with the higher wisdom of the unconscious. The wise old man here is a higher potential, that is, something greater than the young man. The wise old man is the wisdom of the unconscious, the archetype of the spirit, which gives that undirected *élan vital* of the young hero—the life drive in the unconscious—an opportunity to move in the right direction, toward where it could help to correct some wrong things in collective consciousness. The wisdom of the unconscious helps the young man because he is willing, in his exuberance, to share food, to impart some energy to the older figure.

This linking of archetypal figures is very strange. For instance, I recall a Russian fairy tale where the hero has to rescue a princess from the clutches of an evil dragon. In a way, that story is similar to ours, but the old dragon who has cursed the princess did so because *he* has fought with the ruling king. So, the enmity in the Russian fairy tale is between the Czar—the ruler—and the dragon. As for the hero, he just goes on a "straight way" and gets orders from the ruler to kill that dragon. Things happen in the way we would expect, but with a few detours: the dragon doesn't revenge himself on the king but rather on the princess, the king's daughter. The hero falls in love with her. He himself has no animosity toward the dragon at all, but he's forced to kill it.

So there's a funny kind of play of fate between the contents of the unconscious. Sometimes the healing process doesn't occur directly, but happens via certain detours. It is as if a disturbance at one place brings about a disturbance in another place. So, too, the healing process sometimes has to begin indirectly, in a more remote corner of the psyche, and then slowly find its way to the central area. It's as though the light doesn't go in through the shortest route, by a Euclidean straight line, but rather by the shortest route in the sense of the path with the least resistance—even if this means the path is more circuitous.

So, the healing process in the psyche always takes the shortest possible path, but that sometimes involves a detour. And often the detour is necessary because there are certain blockages that the "straight" healing process can't surmount.

For instance, a person will come to analysis and say in the first hour, "My marriage is impossible. I have to get a divorce. And that is my whole problem. Let's be honest. I'll just start with the real problem." And then they howl for an hour about their marriage and represent their spouse as being so impossible that, at the end of sixty minutes, you too are convinced they must get a divorce. Naturally you say nothing about this; you just say to the person, "Well, let's see what your dreams say." And you expect the person has been dreaming about that horrible partner or at least about a horrible animus or anima problem.

But instead you find that the dreams are concerned with a creative problem. So you tell the analysand, "Well, you have a creative problem. You should do some writing or painting." And then they look furious, because *they* want to decide: "But I have to decide if I divorce or don't divorce!" They have no libido to even listen to the other possibilities. But they have to take a risk and give the unconscious credit. It is like taking a completely new medicine and watching the result; then, most likely, the creative new process will begin.

Later, when you have watched such a development, you see that that was the only point where the unconscious could communicate with the ego. And from that point on, all the other parts of the whole problem become solved in their own way. In such cases, you discover that the solution actually began in a corner where you might have least expected anything important to happen or to be constellated. So you have to ask yourself, "Now why on earth does the dream not speak about the conscious problem?" Perhaps we become so accustomed to having things happen in one certain way that we lose sight of the fact that sometimes we have to just adventurously look forward.

Thus, if someone tells me of a big problem, I say, "Okay, that's the conscious problem. Now let's see what's underneath . . ." And then sometimes I try to guess just how the healing process will progress. But I have never guessed it right, never in my life. It's always so incredibly intelligent and so incredibly creative and unexpected that you *never* guess it. It's just a wonderful thing to say, "Now I wonder what the *dreams* will speak about," after I have been told the conscious problem.

By studying such processes afterward, you see that they move absolutely without loss of time or energy, in the straightest possible line in each specific situation. A detour is the straightest possible line. One can only try to formulate it that way. In fact, I often think that one's whole life unfolds circuitously as on a detour, but that it is nonetheless still following along one's straightest possible line. I often think that's really the pattern. It's a paradox.

To get back to our story: The unconscious, or this wise old man who is the wisdom in the unconscious, directs the young man's life impulse to where he is needed—to where a change is needed. And he does not simply tell the young man, "You must go and redeem this princess or kill this troll." He only gives him a stick which makes him invisible when he lifts it up, and a ball, and says, "If you push the ball with the stick, and then follow it, the ball will guide you rightly." So now we have to take a look at this stick and this ball.

The stick is probably the oldest instrument human beings have ever used. It is also used by chimpanzees. It's the oldest instrument the animal kingdom has invented. There are certain apes who live in the Congo forest who love to eat a certain type of big ant. These ants are very good food, but they sting diabolically. And so the apes break off a twig, make a long stick, and then, from a safe distance, they dig into the ant hill. The ants attack the stick and when the stick is full the apes gobble them up by licking them off the stick. In this way they avoid getting bitten by the ants. From the behavioral standpoint, this exemplifies a clear use of an instrument. So the characterization of man as having made a great leap out of the animal kingdom is a myth we now must discard. Even birds can use sticks as instruments. The stick is therefore certainly the simplest instrument, and also the very first. It's a kind of extension of one's hand, and thus an extension of one's will power or purposiveness beyond the body—a tremendous invention, really.

Now in the oldest civilizations, the stick is most frequently used for driving animals. From that evolved the use of the stick as the king's scepter: the king is the good shepherd of his people. Therefore, like a good cattle driver, he has a scepter-stick with which he rules. The scepter became the symbol of the ruling power. It is simply a shepherd's stick that has been formed into a greater thing.

Bishops in the Catholic Church, for instance, have a stick. The medieval interpretation of the bishop's stick in the Catholic Church is that it represents the authority of the Church doctrine. So you see, the bishop is also a spiritual shepherd—and with his stick, the authority of the doctrine, he gives spiritual direction so that people do not fall into error.

We discover another aspect of the stick, one I think is important, in an old Germanic ritual. In medieval times, the Germans had folk courts for trying cases of murder and serious theft. These were judged not by the ruler or the king but by a group of men of the tribe. Before they judged, another man went out and peeled hazel sticks and gave one to every man in the group who was going to judge. They were all made to swear an oath by taking the stick in hand and saying, "I will not judge according to subjective sympathy or antipathy. I will judge according to objective rule."

So here a stick signifies a kind of directing, objective rule which ensures that the judge won't take the wrong attitude: "Oh, I don't like the chap, so I'll condemn him." Again, the stick here gives the judging man a feeling of being in the presence of an authority which goes beyond his ego, beyond his fluctuating thoughts and sympathies, to something objective—just as the authority of the bishop's stick is meant to preserve objective truth against personal opinions, and just as the stick of the king represents his rule to which everyone must submit. So the stick has to do with an objective orientation, an objective direction. Thus it extends one's will power and one's purposiveness to a greater, more objective goal, beyond mere momentary impulses.

A stick that makes one invisible is unusual; most often it is a cap or a cloak. So one has to separate the functions of conferring invisibility and giving objective direction. Making oneself invisible must have to do with annihilating or wiping out, or putting into the background, the personal subjectivity, the individual concrete features. In French, if someone is very good, or very modest, or if he can "put himself behind his task," they say, "Il s'efface"—"he takes away his face." He becomes, so to speak, anonymous; he disappears. "S'effacer" in

French also means "to disappear," but only in a metaphoric way. For instance, if someone works at the big task, and does not constantly put his own ego into the foreground but puts the task in the foreground, he "disappears" in this sense.

If we're talking about an artist, it would mean he gives himself completely to the painting. He himself is only a vessel. Until the painting is finished, he isn't there. A friend of mine, a painter, always said to his wife, "First the painting, then the women." He gave himself completely to his creative task. He had that attitude where one says, "My own needs and reality do not matter now."

Of course, this attitude has been advocated by Christianity so much that now it is generally considered to be a very bad quality. Eighty per cent of the time, we have to teach people to be visible again, to be themselves, to be *there.* But in itself, for anyone who has a great task or a call to be a creative person, this attitude is still valid: sometimes one has to sacrifice one's momentary personal desires. If you talk to someone who is creative, be it a scientist or an artist or whatever, he or she will bear witness to this; you have to put yourself aside.

Even in hunting, if the animal is approaching and you want to sneeze, you have suppress your sneeze. You have to put your ego and physical needs aside. Otherwise your greater purpose, the hunt, is lost. So there are always moments where you have to suppress something the ego or the natural impulse wants, for the greater thing. At such times this "disappearing" attitude is meaningful.

So, one function of a stick is to represent an attitude that puts the ago aside. But, as we saw, a stick is also used to find one's direction. To lift the stick means that one spiritualizes that direction, puts aside any personal desires.

In other words, through the interference of the wise old man, the *élan vital* that breaks away from the collective unconscious attains a spiritual, not a visible or concrete, purposiveness. This is a decisive, creative moment. This kind of creative energy would not lead to, say, a political revolution; that would be an earthly purpose. Rather, it would lead to a psychic revolution, a change that takes place on a higher level.

Throughout the history of mankind, only psychological changes have brought about the great creative changes. The purely concrete changes, such as political or sociological reorganizations, have always brought about as much evil as good; generally the people land in just the same kind of soup as they wanted to avoid. I don't think I need to give you examples of this. If there is no psychic change going on together with such movements, nothing really changes. You can change the external, concrete aspects of life in a society; on that level, you can change everything. But if people are still the same inside, then nothing really changes. Therefore, the great innovator of consciousness and of culture in human life is always the one who can lift the stick and become invisible—put its purpose into the invisible realm of the psyche.

The stick is important because it points to something like an objective direct-edness, a transpersonal purpose, a means to a goal beyond mere temporary personal intent. Because of this, it also represents the scepter of the king, the symbol of sovereignty. The king must not take personal advantage of his position as top dog of his nation. What makes him a true king is rather that he espouses some transcendent purpose or rule of which he is the representative.

Now, the things which make one invisible have to do with a similar fact. That is, in order to get through certain situations, one has to eliminate all egocentricity. For instance, the *I Ching* says in one oracle that in order to achieve a great goal, one has to set aside any superficial or personal gratification and then, so to speak, disappear from the scene. On the personal level, if you have such a transcendent goal in your own life, that goal can make you, too, become invisible: people will be unable to make you out. They won't see you any more. Often they will say of such a person, "So-and-so is obviously seeking such-and-such a goal," or "So-and-so wants only this-and-that," or "So-and-so has such-and-such a plan"—and it's all off the point. They don't really see you, and because of that you can quietly go on to do what you have to do, for nobody is really aware of what you're doing. People would perhaps prevent you from doing it if they knew where you were. But they don't. They can't interpret you psychologically any more and therefore they can't manipulate you or stop you in your purpose.

That is true too for collective, archetypal processes. For instance, if you read the letter Pliny wrote in the year 119 to the Roman emperor Trajanus, you find that he was called upon to investigate a certain sect of so-called Christians which some people had accused of being revolutionary and dangerous to the state. Pliny writes the most naive letter to the emperor. He reports that he picked up some of those people, including some women slaves whom he had tortured (Roman citizens weren't allowed to be tortured). Yet, he says, "I couldn't find out anything except an odd superstition, a kind of distorted superstition, so I thought those people are completely harmless, and we can let them go."

So, you might say those early Christians became invisible to the Roman Empire. Nobody knew where they were, and yet they were the carriers of a new light and a new civilization to come. In a way they were the carriers of that new consciousness which is here represented by the hero of our story. But because of that, they became incomprehensible to the others. They weren't seen as what or who they really were; otherwise there would have been a great panic in the Roman Empire and they might have been squashed. As it happened, that panic only came later, when the Christian movement was already so powerful that it couldn't be squashed any longer. But in the beginning it profited from being invisible. What made it invisible is that the Christians were "lifting the stick": they had not an earthly but rather a transcendent purpose.

You see, to lift something away from the ground, to put it into the air, means you elevate it so it is not in contact with material reality. Now there were great temptations in the early Christian movement to pin it down to earth. St. Paul was asked, as you know, what his attitude toward slavery was.[10] That was a trick question: they tried to make him take a stand about slaves so he would be caught propounding a certain political idea. He would then become embroiled with earthly political issues. But as you know, he very wisely evaded the question. That is an example of how to lift one's stick, and by doing so become invisible. The key is to refuse to allow oneself to be pinned down. One must not be too hasty to ask, "Now what does that mean concretely, and what are the concrete consequences of this attitude?" For in certain situations, and before the time is right, one should not try to "pin down" the messages from the unconscious.

This applies too when you interpret a dream to certain rather concrete-minded people. They nod and say, "Yes, that makes sense, but what shall I *do?*" The animus of women especially loves to ask that question, and Jung therefore said that if a woman asks such a question she's already in the animus. There are certain dreams which in their symbolism clearly contain no concrete hint as to what to do. Their message should be taken in as a purely psychological message. It should sink into and change one. And then when one has become a different person, one quite naturally knows what to do and what not to do "outside." If you are a different person, all your outer problems look different. But if you always want to deduce from every dream, "Now what does that mean concretely?" then you are trying to use the dream like an oracle, which is an infantile attitude toward the dream or the unconscious. Therefore, if a dream does not clearly point to a concrete outer step, one should not interpret it in that direction. One should leave it in suspense, in mid-air so to speak.

I would say that in eighty per cent of the cases when I had spent an hour with Jung, I went home very pensive, wondering, "Well, that's very impressive, that's very moving, but where does it link up with reality?" But I did not force myself to link it up with reality. I focused on the emotional message of the dream. And then, generally, there came the next dream and the next, and then one day, finally, there came a dream that pointed to a step in reality. Before that, the stick

---

[10] 1 Corinthians, 7:20.

was guiding me: that would be the transcendent purpose which the dreams were driving at. That purpose was not yet standing on the ground; it was in mid-air.

So, lifting into the air always denotes spiritualization. You have the same, for instance, in the symbolism of the Mass. There you have the elevation of the chalice, which is officially interpreted as an ecstatic placing of the chalice into the spiritual realm, lifting it up into an elevated space.

You could say that the young man in our fairy tale, by lifting the stick, represents a transcendent purpose, a movement toward a renewal of collective consciousness. Because he's going to become king, he has a means of pursuing his goal in a nonconcrete form. Thus he can pass unnoticed by those around him who would otherwise pounce on him at once, just as, for instance, the Romans would have pounced on the early Christians if they had known what they stood for, and what that germ of new consciousness they were carrying would achieve in the end. If they had known that, they probably would have wiped them out.

At that time, there were already many concrete issues that could have ensnared them. One of the groups to accuse the Christians most adamantly were the dealers in sacrificial animals. They complained that their business was going bad, because with the rise of the Christians the demand for sacrificial goats and cows plummeted. They became upset and made a stink about it. If they had known that the Christians would win out and that in a few hundred years all those animal sacrifices would be completely stopped throughout the Roman Empire, you can imagine how they would have screamed. For the Christians it was essential that they always pointed out Christ's word, "My kingdom is not of this world." By that they remained literally invisible.

That's only one historical example, but it is always so. Whenever something new and creative comes up in a culture, it is generally not discovered right away. The public are concerned with everything else, but the savior is always born in a dilapidated stable at a time when nobody cares about what happens there. That seems to be a law of nature, that the saving new impulses come from the corner where nobody looks.

It is the same thing in an individual. Let's say, for instance, you have a tremendously intellectual analysand who is caught up in his head. Then all the healing or redeeming possibilities pop up in the area of feeling. Now if you make them too visible, then the person's intellect would grab that feeling thing and try to organize it intellectually—pull it, so to speak, into the intellectual realm—and thereby destroy it. Generally if you tell an intellectual, "You see, that has to do with feeling," he says, "Yes, yes," because he doesn't want to admit he doesn't understand. And because of that, the process for the moment can go unhampered. You have told the truth, but the real thing is still completely invisible, and one should not break through that. One should not want to say, "Now you've got to know what that means." He isn't yet ready. He would only destroy it with his intellect if he saw what it meant.

In many, many fairy tales, the hero has either a cap or a coat that he gets from animals, or from some magic powers, that permits him to pass unnoticed. If you read the context, you know why the young man in our story has to become invisible: it is because he could never find out what the princess was doing if he couldn't pass unnoticed through all the doors.

The other gift our hero receives is a ball, which is a symbol of the Self. But there is one point I want to stress. If you look at many fairy tales, you find there are countless symbols of the Self. The hidden treasure is a symbol of the Self. So is the unobtainable treasure. Many magic objects with which one can transform or redeem people (wands and so on) are symbols of the Self. The mandala formations, like castles and towns if they have a mandala shape, are symbols of the Self. The diamond, golden and silver forests in our story could be interpreted as symbols of the Self, as we will see later. You could, in a way, take the old wise man as a symbol of the Self. So I get absolutely furious if students who interpret fairy tales for me are satisfied merely by calling all these things symbols of the Self. It's just too boring! One cannot say only, "With the help of a symbol of the Self, he found a symbol of the Self." One has to say, "Yes, okay, that is true, but which specific aspect is stressed?"

For instance, in a ring, the specific aspect of a relationship and being bound, or being bound negatively or positively through an obligation, is stressed. In a ball, what fascinates children and even young animals so madly is that the thing by its shape is touching the ground only at a small point of its body; so it can overcome the laws of gravitation and friction. You give a ball a little push, and if you have a smooth surface, it runs God knows how far! If you play billiards, you know that's the whole fascination of the game: you give a pointed little push and the thing will roll on forever and even make certain mathematical angles if you know how to do it. And if you have never played it, even to watch is exciting. You feel as if those billiard balls have a life of their own, a secret life, which you have only to start in motion, and then they take over. It is amazing to see how a master player pushes the ball in one direction, and how it bumps off here and goes over there and pushes the other ball. That's the fascination of a ball. You throw it against the wall and it comes right back into your hands. No other object does that. So the ball stresses, within the idea of being a symbol of the Self, the possibility of autonomous movement. It can move on its own much further than any other concrete object. That gives it a spiritual or magical quality.

The ball is also a symbol of the cosmic structure. In most world models, the cosmos was conceived of as an enormous sphere composed of different layers. It is also historically a symbol of the soul, beginning with the atomist Democritus, who said that the soul consisted of round fiery atoms. Because those fire-ball soul atoms were small and because they had no angles, they could roll through all the other matter. That's why our souls are spread throughout our whole body, because the soul has this ball structure.

As well, the ball is a symbol of the godhead. "God is an infinite sphere whose center is everywhere and whose circumference is nowhere." That is a deep saying which since the age of Plotinus has been quoted by practically every great Western philosopher, as Jung often noted.[11] It's one of those fascinating images that have always been used to describe the godhead, and also sometimes the innermost center of the human soul.

In the context of our fairy tale, we have to limit ourselves mainly to the fact that the ball can roll on its own. Here, it obviously has a guiding function: it rolls right to the town where the hero meets his task. However, there is a subtle detail that I have never come across before. The rolling ball is a very widespread fairy tale motif, but generally the hero or heroine meets a wise old man or woman in the woods, like we have here, who then gives them a ball or more frequently a rolled-up ball of yarn. In such cases the ball will roll ahead and they follow the thread; they have only to hold the end of the thread and follow. In European fairy tales there are over a hundred examples of this, but in all of them the ball begins rolling by itself as soon as the hero has it in hand.

In our story we have an additional nuance, namely that the ball does not begin rolling on its own. The young man first has to give it a little push, although from then on he doesn't have to push it again—once it starts rolling, it doesn't stop. So there is a very different picture here, because the autonomous activity of the Self, the process of individuation, does not start without an initial push.

Now, you know that is what people often have to do. One of the main ways in which the process of individuation becomes a continuous activity, something more visible than if one merely writes down one's dreams, is active imagination. But you have to get it going. You have to start, and the starting effort has to be exerted by *you*. If you don't make the first try at active imagination, you don't start the process rolling. Once it gets going, it goes so much on its own that you

---

[11] See, for instance, "A Psychological Approach to the Dogma of the Trinity," *Psychology and Religion,* CW 11, par. 229, n. 6; also *Mysterium Coniunctionis,* CW 14, par. 41.

cannot even stop it. Then you know: "Now I am in for it!"

That may be why so many people never get started, or have such strong resistance—they have an unconscious hunch that this is the kind of thing where once you are in it, you can't get out. You can leave it alone for a while—if it leaves *you* alone—but you can never really stop it. And if you do, if you drop an active imagination and leave it alone because you have too much to do for a few weeks, you find that when you resume there has been a complete standstill. You have not really lived during those times. You have to start all over.

I've seen people who for various reasons had abandoned an active imagination for three or more years. For instance, I had an analysand who married and in the first years of marital adaptation and having two children, just dropped working with her active imagination. Then she became severely depressed, and the same image came back which she had left several years before. So it seemed that on an unconscious level nothing had happened during all that time. Active imagination is a continuous process that goes on according to its own laws, but it is essential that consciousness initiate the contact.

Returning to our hero, we can't interpret him as an ego, so you must just imagine that what he represents is a process that, because it is portrayed in a fairy tale, happens entirely in the collective unconscious. Think of the collective unconscious as an electromagnetic field. Then you could say that there are certain excited points, points in which the energy of the field is bundled, so to speak. These points are the archetypes. And now, in some corner of that field, a vital impulse springs up: that is our young man. He is an indistinct force in the unconscious, which is an overflow of vital impulses. That force then connects with some traditional wisdom in the unconscious, which begins to give it a direction. Through that link it acquires a certain directedness—the stick—and a certain capacity to start the ball rolling. The hero has started a continuous and autonomous movement, a flow of life which he is now following. It is as if first, in the unconscious, energy swings up and slowly makes contact with other contents of the unconscious and literally snowballs on toward consciousness.

Jung thought that the origin of greater consciousness in human beings—compared to those higher warm-blooded animals that exhibit some flickering traces of consciousness—is due to an overflow of instinctual energy which was not used up in survival occupations.

You see something like this even in zoo animals. Because they have not so much worry about fighting enemies and getting their food, they are relieved of certain biological instinctual occupations. And therefore they play much longer and much, much more frequently than do animals in the wild, who rarely play except when they are very young. Adult animals practically never play. They are much too harassed by the worries of survival. Zoo animals, for whom man takes away the worries of survival, play.

Play is certainly the beginning of all spiritual and civilizing conscious occupations. This is not Jung's idea but my own guess: that the prehistoric geometrical lines and scratchings we have found—which are even older than the cave paintings—were put there by a rhythmical movement or banging which probably was some kind of playful amusement. This would mean the people dwelling in those caves felt relatively safe from attack by other animals. Since they had fire, they could light their cave and if they weren't too tired after hunting all day, perhaps on winter nights, they sat together. They had no instinctual occupations to perform at those times. What did they do? They began to bump against the cave walls and to make lines or rhythmically scratch patterns. Then slowly, they began fantasizing into these etchings, and there finally emerged those famous Paleolithic cave paintings. So you could say those marks represent a more consistent or continuous form of awareness, the beginnings of consciousness.

You can see this evolution also in children. The first thing a child does is to make rhythmical movements. That's why you generally give it a bell or something similar, which the child swings to and fro, up and down, for hours. If you give the child a pencil at the age of about one or two years, it will first only move it up and down on the paper, with the greatest pleasure—just scratching in rhythmical movements up and down, up and down, with a great feeling of gratification and delight.

The rhythmical games you play with very small children generally have to be repeated twenty or thirty times. They won't let you go until they're exhausted. It is as though the child repeats on an individual level the same developmental route mankind has followed as a species. And if you observe the play of zoo animals, you see that a lot of it too is a rhythmical kind of movement.

Now, the hero in our story represents that same overflow of vitality which is not meant to be invested in any concrete purpose of life. Then it snowballs by assimilating all these other things: the old man's wisdom, the stick and the ball. It grows or it amplifies itself in the unconscious until finally it becomes a figure with a purpose in life who is led to the center of the problem.

So you see that the new healing process in the collective unconscious is guided by certain regulatory processes, of the collective unconscious, toward the place of conflict. It is just as if in a single individual who has one huge conflict, a new impulse of life springs up in the unconscious, which seems to have no connection with the conflict itself. I've amplified that in discussing how the dreams speak, as when someone comes and says he has an enormous marital problem, but his dreams speak about something completely different. Yet eventually the process slowly enriches itself, and comes to land where the conflict really is in consciousness. And then you begin to see that this whole preparatory process in the unconscious where the dreams spoke about different things finally builds up a foundation from which the conscious conflict can be solved.

Our hero is in such a position. He can enter the realm of collective consciousness (that is, the kingdom), and undertake the task of putting right what is wrong there, which is that the king has an only daughter, the heiress of the kingdom, on whose marriage its prosperity depends. She disappears every night and tears up twelve pairs of golden shoes, and no one knows what's behind that. It upsets the old king so much that he promises his daughter to whoever finds out what she is doing in the night; but if a man should try and fail, he must be executed.

In most fairy tales where similar situations arise, the king is evil. He has an ambiguous attitude. Secretly, he doesn't want to marry his daughter to anybody because he doesn't want to give up his throne. Therefore, he surreptitiously plots to prevent his daughter from marrying, and he really enjoys executing all her suitors because that way he himself can remain king.

In our fairy tale we have an exception to this rule; namely, the old king is frightfully unhappy that this vicious game of his daughter's has not been stopped. He seems to be altogether a good-hearted fellow, because when he supposes he will have to condemn the hero to death he is very, very unhappy about it. So he doesn't like what he's doing. He's doing it, but he doesn't like it at all. He has a heart, and he would very much prefer not to execute those suitors.

The princess, on the contrary, is evil. As we soon see, she is not evil in and of herself, but she's bewitched. She wants all those men to be killed, and she does not want to be found out. Her evil comes from the troll. But the king seems to have no part in it. It is just that in his despair, he becomes cruel. What I mean is that he creates a situation where spying on his daughter becomes a matter of life and death: "Either you find out what's wrong, or I'll kill you!"

On a primitive level, you can say that the king does this simply to reinforce the eagerness of those suitors to succeed. The old king probably feels he needs to put such pressure on them because otherwise they would not find out what is the matter. Underneath, obviously, he himself is in mounting despair. He is desperate, and desperate people, as we know, will do anything. They are dangerous.

Now, if we look at it psychologically, we see that in general theories of neurosis, one speaks of the "pressure of suffering." In German the technical expression is *Leidensdruck,* the "suffering pressure." You usually find that if a person goes into analysis without having such a suffering pressure, not much comes of it. Someone can come and say, "I'm just bored at home and I've read a bit of Jung and I think I'd like to get a bit deeper into it, so could you take me in analysis?"—and then in the third hour, they confess that that wasn't the truth at all; they were in an awful fix, suffering like hell, only they didn't want to admit it.

But then there are those who are not under that suffering pressure, and in my experience I have found that nothing comes out of analysis for such people. Generally, after a few weeks they telephone: "I've too much to do! Do you mind if I don't come?"—and then they come sporadically, and then they go traveling, and then they say, "I'll phone again in the autumn," and so it goes over the years. Maybe they have not much wrong, but nothing happens either. Either they discontinue analysis completely, or one day God blesses them by hurling a brick on their head and *then* they come running back; then they pull up their socks and work seriously—but not before.

It seems to be that we are innately lethargic. Our tendency to be satisfied with getting on in the way one gets on anyhow is very strong. In fact, this sort of lethargy is probably found in all of nature; it is a strong, conservative force that tends to preserve the status quo, so that one needs a terrific bout of suffering to bring about any progress. Perhaps the fishes would never learned to walk on land if they hadn't been under such a pressure. Loren Eiseley, in his book on evolution,[12] states that probably all the great mutations and jumps in evolution have been caused by absolutely crucial situations where it was a matter of, "Now change, or disappear from the face of the earth!" And this is so in the life of nations and of collective groups as well as in the lives of individuals.

Jung once said that the strongest passion in humans is not hunger, sex or power, although these are quite strong; the very strongest passion is laziness. The longer I study human beings, including myself, the more I am inclined to agree. Laziness is the strongest passion. Therefore, the king acts perhaps not quite as cruelly as we initially thought. He makes up his mind to say, "Now it's either-or. It's a matter of life and death, and we can no longer be friendly about it. We *must* find a man who will really get to the bottom of this damned secret."

This reminds me of how Jung, at a certain stage of his active imagination, in the beginning, felt one evening before going to bed that if he could not find the solution to a certain problem in that active imagination, he would have to kill himself. He felt that the problem became a matter of life and death, as though he was saying, "I can't go on living like this, there's no more meaning." Through

---

[12] *The Immense Journey* (New York: Random House, 1957).

giving himself the spurs this way, so to speak, he finally realized how to go on.

One of the greatest problems in analysis is that you often see people dawdling along with their problem, and you have the feeling something awful is going to happen to them if they don't wake up. They are in for some shock treatment. And then the question is, should *you* give the shock treatment, or should you leave it to fate?

I often discussed that with Jung. He said that sometimes it's a good thing to try to give the shock treatment oneself because one can control how much or how little of a shock to give, while God seems to be not quite aware of the human side. He (or you can call it Nature or the unconscious) sometimes bangs a bit too much, and then the catastrophes are sometimes too big for our human feelings. So one sometimes tries to apply the shock by throwing the person out, or shouting, or giving awful threats: "You will be dead if you don't . . ." and so on. But very often it doesn't help. One just makes an enemy, and then fate has to take its course, something awful has to happen. You get a letter: "I have cancer of the breast and I'm in hospital; please help!" or some such thing. You had seen it coming five or six years before, but you could not get through.

So you can say that in our fairy tale, what the king faces is a situation that must be taken as a crucial one. He also stands in a certain relationship to a special primitivity, the brute primitivity of the troll.

Whenever such a brute, barbaric primitivity threatens to emerge from the unconscious, whether in a nation or in a single human being, then an accordingly strict discipline of consciousness is needed. You see, therefore, in history that whenever a population rises out of a state of natural primitivity to what the historians call the beginnings of high civilization, their rules of behavior and their military discipline are extremely severe. A good example of this is the medieval Japanese Samurai civilization, with its extremely strict, formalistic rules of conduct. Japanese films often portray conflicts between explosive forces of brute primitivity and this absolutely chivalrous formality of the Samurai. To a certain extent, the European chivalry of the Middle Ages is another example. The behavior of the knights was very formalistic. Even the armor they wore represented their inner attitude of absolute loyalty, absolute obedience, absolute this, absolute that, and breaking any of these rules meant expulsion.

Such strictness is always necessary where there is much primitivity. Modern ethnologists are often terribly shocked by the legislations of primitive tribes; they cut off the hand of a thief and such things. But one must understand these acts in context. They are a symbolic representation of the fact that against brute forces in the unconscious, only absolute brute firmness helps.

That is true for us as well. Whenever someone is confronted with, let's say, letting oneself go into drinking, or into fits of rage or promiscuity, such a person can become a slave of primitive impulses. He or she will come into analysis wanting to be understood and treated as sick, pitiable. But the moment always comes one day in such a person's life when they must face a brute either-or; they have to say to themselves, "Now you understand why you drink, why you enjoy your fits of rage and don't want to pull up your socks or whatever, now you see the whole context, it's all understood. But now you still have to take the last step, namely to say *no!*" And that must be an absolutely firm decision. Naturally, when people are facing such a firm decision, they always say, "But I *can't*. I want to but I can't. I want like hell to do it, but you see, when I get into such-and-such a situation, I *can't*. It's stronger than me. It overruns me."

One has to weigh such feelings very carefully, because it is often true that people cannot deal with certain cravings or desires. They are bewitched by trolls, so to speak, and the trolls *are* stronger. They possess and dominate one. In order to make a firm decision against primitive impulses, one has to know for sure that it is possible. And that is very difficult to know. One can partly know it from dreams, for the dreams sometimes tell you it *is* now possible.

Sometimes it's only ill will or laziness that is causing the bewitchment to continue. Then, when the person tells you that he or she can't do it, you notice a strong flicker of bad conscience in their eyes. You can often see this and then you know: "Bah! I don't buy *that!* Even you don't believe it. You say you can't but you don't believe it yourself!" That is the moment where the building-up processes of the unconscious have reached the point where now consciousness *could* change.

That's why individuation must be seen as an ethical problem. To understand is not enough. Again and again, in certain situations, everything depends on the ethical attitude of consciousness.

In the kingdom of our story, to compensate or to keep on top of the troll, the king has to make several severe rules, against his will. When our young man comes to the king, the king is sorry for him and says, "Don't try," because he likes the young man. This shows clearly the nuance I mentioned before, that the king really is in a fix. He doesn't want to kill his daughter's suitors. He tells the young man what he has to do: he may sleep three nights in the bedroom of the princess, and if he can't find out what she's doing, he must be killed. The young man goes there, puts down his clothes and his knapsack and decides not to sleep, but twice he falls asleep anyway. Only on the third night does he stay awake.

This is an exceptional story in that it is not explained why he can't stay awake. In most other versions, and also in the German parallel, the princess secretly gives the hero a sleeping potion, but on the third night he notices her game. Then he pours the sleeping potion down his shirt and only pretends to sleep; that way he is able to find out her secret.

Here, this motif is skipped. It's just a fact that our hero can't stay awake. Perhaps, although the princess has not given him a sleeping potion, he nonetheless meets some bewitchment. Maybe because she's bewitched, he got pixilated too, so that he's now under that influence.

You see that again and again, and it's something to really watch out for if ever you become an analyst. The unconscious problems of people can have such a suggestive influence that they can blind you or put you to sleep. Sometimes in an analysand there is a strong resistance to bringing up a certain problem. Then this attitude infects you. You become absolutely stupid. There is a certain something that prevents you from getting at the problem. And only after the event, if you do wake up, do you discover that you too have been bewitched. You say, "But why didn't I see that before?" And then you realize that a kind of drowsiness in which the patient lives had spread like a cloud over you. It is as if you couldn't see what was right before your nose, because there was somehow a resistance in the atmosphere against its being seen.

That is the witch work of unconscious complexes. The patient is bewitched. He can't help it. He's not lying or hiding anything; he's just bewitched. It's terribly infectious. I have noticed that sometimes, even hours after being with such a person, I'm still in a bit of a daze; not really tired, but not quite there. And if it happens frequently that I am in such a funny state after the hour, then I sit down and really try to figure it out: "Now why am I affected like that? What do I feel during that state?"

I once had an analysand who have a very strong effect on me that way. She was a very sympathetic, friendly person. We got on very well, which perhaps explains in part why this happened. She had an inexplicable problem: several times, more or less against her better judgment and will, she had slept with men and become pregnant and had aborted the child. That had happened outside the rest of her life, so to speak, like an autonomous left-hand action. And when she came to me, she had few but rather pleasant dreams, all quite clear. Some shadow things and so on—the usual; nothing pointing to those tragedies. The dreams didn't touch them, but what struck me was that after the hour I was always in a daze. I always had that feeling, but I didn't understand it, I didn't see it clearly. She got much better. She had a severe physical symptom which completely cleared up, so that she already thought of herself as cured. She thought she'd had a wonderful, successful analysis. But I still hadn't understood what had happened. And I thought, "That really makes me mad!"

On the day of our next meeting I was driving home from having lunch with friends. Just as I approached my garage, I said to myself, "Damn it all, what's the matter with her!" Distracted, I got out to open the garage door, then back into the car. A few seconds later—*bang!*—I had not shut my car door and it was ruined. That cost me a hundred francs at the time, which I couldn't afford. At that point, I really felt I had *had* it!

Later I asked Jung, "Now how are these things connected?" I was sure there must be some connection. He laughed and said, "Don't you see? The unconscious gave you the diagnosis. She became pregnant and ruined her body by sheer stupidity. And that's what you did with your car! That was sheer stupidity. And the unconscious made you do it to tell you that's how it happened with her, just in a moment of sheer stupidity. There's nothing more behind it. That's why the unconscious doesn't comment on it." Later on, I found out that her father's brother was an imbecile. She wasn't an imbecile at all, but somewhere she must have had a little touch of that. So there Jung taught me that you must always watch what your body does when you don't understand an analysand. Your body often tells you what's the matter.

When such drowsiness is present a shock treatment is needed, but again there is that problem of whether Nature or the analyst should supply the shock. It's a very ticklish problem because in deliberately causing a shock, one is wielding power. I would say you should do it only if you have an urgent feeling of real danger. Sometimes in such a situation I get upset and say, "Damn it all, you *must* wake up!" Sometimes I nearly say too much because I desperately want to wake the person up. I share in the feeling of panic because I feel concerned. I feel, "My God, this is going wrong!" It is just like when you see a child about to run into the street in the way of an oncoming car. You don't pull it back gently and say, "Look here, you shouldn't do that." You say, *"Damn!* You'll be *dead* if you do that!"—because you want the child to learn and to remember.

So much about drowsiness, which often calls for a shock. In our story the hero wakes up by himself. On the third night he makes a real effort to stay awake, and he does. In the room he sees a girl wearing white clothes. She comes to his bed and says to the princess, "I'll find out whether or not he really sleeps." She takes a golden needle and puts it in his heel and, although it hurts, the young man doesn't give himself away by reacting. Then the girl and the princess go off to visit the troll.

This girl in white does not exist in the other versions. In the German version, for instance, although the princess doesn't go alone, she goes with eleven other princesses. But here the princess has only one companion—this very hazy figure of a girl in white. She simply appears and tests the young man with a golden needle, with which he later kills the troll. She's also the one who, on the way to the troll, always calms the princess by saying no one is following them and that what she hears is only the wind. Otherwise, the white girl has no function at all. She is a specter that appears and disappears.

Let us amplify this motif as well as we can. We can't make much out of the figure of the white girl, because the context doesn't reveal what she is, except that she belongs to the troll, spreads unconsciousness, and carries the weapon with which the troll will finally be killed: the needle. So we have to look around in related mythology to see if we can find something similar to this girl.

There is a Norwegian fairy tale called "The Princesses in White Land."[13] In it, a young man has to redeem three princesses who have been bewitched by a troll. He is washed away from the seashore to the far, far North, and he lands in a completely snow white country. There he finds three princesses stuck in the earth right up to their heads. They are in the clutches of a troll, whom the young man fights and kills. He thus redeems them and marries the youngest.

So there you have the same combination: The troll has to do with a country of pure whiteness. Again, he has imprisoned the feminine principle in a land of whiteness. Whiteness there is obviously something negative, associated with curses and bewitchment, just like the whiteness of the girl in our Danish story. The color white in itself is like black, a "no-color." In German the word *blank* means "shining" and is the root for the French word *blanc,* "white." It is the same root that produced the English word "black." So you see, even in semantics, black and white are interchangeable. Also, throughout the world, the color of mourning is mostly either white or black. The ancient Greeks, mainly the Spartans, wore white mourning clothes, and there are still many countries where people wear white clothes when mourning. We have the habit of wearing black. So the colors of death—white and black—are again interchangeable.

J.J. Bachofen pointed out that black and white are colors of the Beyond, of the ghost world.[14] Even in sketches that make fun of ghosts, we generally represent them as a kind of skeleton in a white sheet. Spooks walk about in white. There is a legend of the Prussian imperial family according to which a white woman lived in the castle. Whenever a member of the family died, she would

---

13 MDW, *Nordische Volksmärchen,* vol. 2, Norwegen, no. 24 (Jena: Diederichs, 1922).
14 *Versuch über die Gräbersymbolik der Alten Bahmeier* (Basel: C. Detloff, 1859).

appear as a harbinger of death.

In psychological language, white and black have to do with the remotest depths of the unconscious, where it becomes an almost abstract, pure structure with no human feeling.

Sometimes, in dreams that go very deep, you find representations of the Self, for instance, where it is a stone of some kind. Or people dream of cold, cosmic space filled with strange abstract structures of a secret order. Sometimes people have strange mathematical dreams which point to mysterious paradigms representing the deepest level of the psyche, the collective unconscious. But these are all characterized by having no connection with life; you can have no empathy with these things. You can't feel what they mean. They may be very interesting and fascinating, but they're far away from human experience.

Sometimes these dreams come before death or close to death. People who are dying have already begun to leave this earth and its human concerns. So if the context of the story evaluates black or white negatively, we have to remember this association with death. Naturally, in Norway the far north is the land of the Arctic, a white land. There the animal life thins out until there is almost none left. You can't live there. It's the land of eternal ice and snow, a land we can scarcely penetrate. The color white is also associated with snow, with the negative aspect of coldness, with the weird inhuman coldness of the unconscious psyche. I would therefore assume that the troll is a secret power that has frozen up, so to speak, estranged from all human warmth.

The white girl is perhaps one of his first victims, and now she is his messenger. She might even be the troll's wife—we don't know. But there must be some vital connection between them, because she has the weapon that can kill him. She knows his secret; she has that thing on which his life depends. So this is the one who fetches the princess down into the troll's kingdom.

Now we must reflect on the fact that in the beginning of the story there is no mother figure. The young man has no father or mother. In the forest he finds the old man, a spiritual father, but there is no mother figure. Where is the archetype of the mother?

Generally, when the archetype of the mother is not represented in the realm of collective consciousness, you find its equivalent somewhere in what is characterized as the compensatory unconscious realm, but I can't find it in this story. There is one symbol that points to archetypal mother symbolism, and I'll come to that later. But for the most part this whole story is characterized by a tremendous weakness of the feminine principle. I think, in a way, the white girl is the very symbol of that. The feminine is practically nonexistent. The troll has taken all its vitality. What we would call the mother figure, the archetype of the maternal, has not taken a shape of its own. It could be mixed up with the troll, however, because trolls are sexually neutral figures. They can be male or female. We don't even know what this troll really is, but likely he is male because he flirts with the princess.

This tremendous weakness of the feminine principle is a specific Germanic inheritance. Those German tribes that have not been Romanized by being for a time under Roman rule tend to show a lack of formed femininity. Of course, you might say there is just as much femininity in them as in any other human group or society, but it's not formed. That would mean the men have no anima culture. You notice this more if you are a woman.

If you live for awhile in the German part of Switzerland or in Germany, you slowly develop a vague feeling that you have to apologize for being a woman. The men in Germany treat you much more politely than they do in Switzerland: they hold the doors, help you into your coat and so on. It isn't that you aren't treated correctly. But there's a certain vague feeling that something is missing.

Then you go to Paris, and after three days you feel absolutely the cat's meow!—because the way the French treat you plays partly on a very low level. The taxi chauffeur and the porter at the station look at you as though they are thinking, "Hmmm . . . ?" It is not always pleasant, but at least they notice you are a woman! It might be on a low level or on a better level; that depends on the person. But they always let you know they are thinking, "Ah, that is a woman!" And if you are old and have gray hair, still you are a female; you are not a male, and you are not a neuter. There is a kind of anima atmosphere. That's why one enjoys so much to be in Italy or in France or in the Latin countries. There is a certain anima culture where men are aware of women.

In the Germanic countries you have the feeling that the men, like in the traditional English clubs, are much happier when they are among themselves: "Yes, let's retire from the ladies and have some nice serious relationships with each other. And the ladies can gossip in their own corner." This is due to certain cultural developments and perhaps to a backwardness of the Germanic tribes that immigrated into Europe. They have kept their primitive patriarchal warriors' social order, while other tribes that settled earlier have, by becoming agricultural and settling on the land, developed the feminine and the anima qualities.

You might say that there is a bleeding wound represented in this story, this strange "not-thereness" of the feminine principle. There are also certain Nordic women who are a bit like trolls or pixies; they are very nice and good-looking and polite, but you don't feel a human contact with them. They seem to be living in a dream. I'm sorry, I'm probably hurting some people's feelings here by saying such things, but I assure you I could say just as many negative things about other countries too! It's just that each country has its own weak spot. After this we will have a Spanish fairy tale, and there you'll see the weak spot is something quite different—so don't be hurt! Also, like all generalizations, of course there are a lot of personal exceptions. But the feminine is a problem in the Germanic countries. I think that is why the feminists are especially fierce now. It is because the women feel uncertain in their own femininity. They don't feel recognized and this is just as true for the anima in men.

So, this white girl is a cool, deadly feminine shape, ghostlike, that lures the princess to the troll. But she also has that gold needle which can kill it. And that is always so: the healing factor is generally hidden in the very factor that is making one neurotic. A neurosis is always a package with an unpleasant outer shell, and when you open the package you find the elixir that cures the neurosis. The neurosis itself contains the healing thing. You need not look elsewhere, for neurosis, according to Jung, represents a failed attempt of nature to cure a psychic imbalance.

Nature works in a double way. You see how Nature means well and does healing things, but sometimes it goes too far and kills you. For instance, fever is in itself a symptom that the healing process is going on. It's the fight of the leukocytes against intruding bacteria. So the fever is in itself something very healthy. But if you have too much of it you can die. Thus the healing process in Nature sometimes goes astray. All internal medicine is really based on the idea of supporting and regulating the already existing healing processes in nature, helping them along so they don't go astray. And that, in a way, is true also in psychotherapy. Therefore, that very same cold white cruel girl, who pricks the hero, also has the healing needle. The image of the golden needle itself will be amplified a little later.

Thus, we come again to the fact that when something cold in the unconscious is overpowering, it sometimes needs an equally cold attitude to overcome it. That is something people have often misunderstood in Jung. Both inside and outside analysis, he could be very sarcastic; he made a lot of enemies that way and often shocked onlookers who might have overheard him make a caustic remark. But if you knew what was really going on, you realized that he always said those things in situations that needed a cold determinedness in order to wipe out a wrong attitude.

Naturally, it's better to refrain from doing this unless one knows how. It is better not to play around with those golden needles, at least not until you have tried them out on yourself.

Many people simply cannot be cynically sarcastic with themselves. They can't face themselves or sit down and really reduce everything to brass tacks. But that is sometimes needed. Naturally, a woman mustn't do this with the animus, for that would mean pulling down one's true values and destroying them. That's what the animus adores to do—to pull a woman's true values down, telling her everything she hasn't and isn't and so on when it is not so. That's the troll. The troll destroys the real values. To prevent the troll from destroying some real values, one sometimes needs an absolutely reductive sarcasm toward one's own shadow and one's own animus. One must then have no sentimental self-pity about really putting it down in one's dream book and looking at it. Otherwise one can't finish cleaning up certain dirty corners. There are always certain things no one else can tell one; one has to tell them oneself. They are so negative that one couldn't stand to hear them from somebody else, so one must have the honesty to say them to oneself.

Now we come to the needle. We can begin on the surface, with language association. You have all heard the phrase, "to needle someone." Now what is it to needle someone? Needling, or picking on someone, generally has to do with stinging that person's complexes; one needles people, for instance, by making specific personal remarks. And if needling remarks are to work, you have to make them about something you know the person has a complex for. Whee!— they hit the ceiling! That is the colloquial meaning of the term "needling."

There are witchlike women who love to do that (and some men too!)—they spy around on people's complexes and then turn up to make personal remarks about them, thinking that if they aim right the person will become helpless. And this does happen when a complex is hit. Then you can't answer, you are confused and the needle witch goes on. She aims a stream of directed psychic energy onto your complex.

Ninety per cent of the essence of archaic witch work and curses that made people ill was made up of the same kind of activity. In my book on projection,[15] I talk at length about projectiles that make one ill. In the oldest and most universal form of witch work, the illnesses were produced by either needlelike thorns or pointed stones or anything shaped so that it could be used for pricking. Through these needlelike objects illnesses were sent by evil demons or evil people to other people. And most archaic medical cures amount to finding out the

---

[15] *Projection and Re-Collection in Jungian Psychology,* trans. William H. Kennedy (La Salle, IL: Open Court, 1980).

place where the person was pricked or needled, and then having the medicine man suck it out. Certain medicine men or shamans would then even produce an object to represent the illness, and they would say to the audience, "Look here, this is it. Now the patient is cured." (They had put it in their sleeve beforehand.) Always, we find the idea that a projectile has made the person ill. It can come, as I say, from a god or from a human being, and it is closely linked with negative projections. You can project negative things onto other people, and such projections can hit them and make them ill.

Needles are used in witch work, and it is often mentioned in fairy tales that a witch has used a so-called sleeping needle. They means they put a thorn or a needle into a person's head (generally behind the ear). You can find recipes for doing this in works on black magic. The person then falls asleep and can't wake up for a hundred years or whatever.

So there are needles that make one ill, needles that make one sleep, and there are needles which prick one into confusion. When you make personal remarks aimed at a person's complex, you can completely knock them out. In a way, that is also giving them a sleeping needle, for they are no longer composed mentally. They can't answer your questions. They are confused. They are pushed, for the moment, into the unconscious and made helpless. The art of needling is still used today in diplomatic and political discussions. Some use it unconsciously and some use it consciously, but always this bringing out of a needling remark at a certain moment is the thing that throws the other off balance. Some people are real wizards in that way. But they are only putting to work the same forces that spring up by themselves in the unconscious.

In our story the white girl uses a needle in an evil way. But one must not overlook the fact that though the needle here is negative, it is also one of the most useful instruments ever invented. Even in primitive societies, the sewing of fur to make shoes or clothes made the needle an object of vital importance.

A needle makes it possible to join pieces of cloth together, therefore it also signifies connection, eros—joining things that would not hold together otherwise. In a psychological context, even if one needles another person in a negative way, one is at least showing directed interest. Often the first love play between young people begins by teasing, and by that indirectly shows a certain interest. If a girl always needles a particular young man, then he may conclude that she is interested in him. She wants to find out how he is; she wants to provoke his reactions, and she wants *him* to be preoccupied with *her.*

Certain hysterical women do that all the time. Whenever they want to arouse another person's interest, they start by making negative personal remarks. As

Jung once said to me, they don't care if the other person thinks about them positively or negatively; the main thing is to make that person think about them. When one does this, it is the beginning of a transitional state where the needle also begins to show its positive aspects of making a connection—linking one's life thread with that of the other.

In our fairy tale the needle is golden. Gold always signifies the highest value, and sure enough, later we find that it is the ultimate weapon, the one thing that can kill the troll. So we are justified in interpreting the needle as a positive object. In spite of being a negative figure herself, the white girl carries the instrument of redemption.

I also amplified the needle motif in terms of the psychology of Scandinavian women, since we are studying a Danish fairy tale. Though many Scandinavian women have an underdeveloped, cool femininity due to a lack of goddesses in their religion, they also have a certain genuineness; there is a truthfulness about them that supplies a potential from which their femininity could develop. They may have a less developed eros than women in Latin countries, but they also have less of the Latin "cattiness" and a more straightforward character. The needle also points to this quality, this capacity to really get to the bottom of the evil within oneself. On a personal level, it means that Scandinavian women are able to see their own negative animus and recognize their own shadow.

The white girl sticks the needle into the heel of the hero. We know from the famous story of Achilles that the heel is a particularly sensitive spot; it has thus become the proverbial weak spot of the hero. First, the heel is on one's back side; it therefore signifies a place where one doesn't see oneself very well—where one is unconscious of oneself. Such places are unguarded and vulnerable to evil forces. Secondly, the heel has to do with the foot and therefore is associated with one's standpoint. Where the hero is blind in his standpoint is precisely where the white girl strikes. But she does not get him because he stays awake and pulls the needle out. By doing so, he gets possession of the needle for future use. In other words, he is aware of his own weakness since he knows he must struggle to stay awake.

After he takes the needle, he sees the princess and the white girl push aside the bed to reveal a door in the wall. Through this they go down some stairs and come out into those woods of silver, gold and diamonds. Next, they cross a lake in a little boat. This is obviously a descent into deeper layers of the unconscious.

Again and again we find it is helpful to imagine the unconscious as having several layers. The higher up, the closer to consciousness; the deeper down, the further away. Those layers also correspond, more or less, to the historical evolution of civilization. Each layer blends into a yet deeper, more primitive and earlier stage of humankind.

Very often in fairy tales, one gets into that deeper layer by falling down a well or into a chasm or a hole in the ground. But sometimes this motif is characterized by a hidden door beyond there is a stairway leading downward. When there is such a human construction, it points to the fact that the deeper layers of the unconscious were once connected with consciousness, though they have long since been forgotten or repressed. But the structure, the possibility of going deeper, is still there. You don't need to fall; you can go step by step. In our fairy tale, the journey made by the princess, the girl and the young man clearly signifies a descent into the deeper layers of the unconscious, because they come to the nature kingdom, the woods and the kingdom of the troll. In the pre-Christian religion of Scandinavia, the unknown powers of the collective unconscious had already taken shape.

Jung points out in one of his letters that the situation of the Germanic people is very different from, for instance, that of the Indian people, where you have a continuous development from a nature demon cult to an elaborate polytheism, and from there to a philosophical monotheism.[16] In the Germanic countries, however, and especially north of the borders of the Roman Empire, the people had never quite had the opportunity to develop an elaborate polytheism. The lower layers of the population were still of the level of worshipping a vague diversity of nature spirits such as the trolls. No sooner had they begun to develop a more structures polytheistic religion with cult, priests and an organization, than that structure was brutally cut down by the much more developed Christian religion which was superimposed upon it; the Oaks of Wotan were felled, so to speak, and over them was implanted a religion of highly spiritual quality that had already matured within the Roman Empire as the end result of a long period of development.

Because of this, the Germanic people lack a full, harmonious connection back into the lower layer of the unconscious represented by the pre-Christian religion. As a result, these people suffer from repeated outbursts of primitivity from this lower layer of the unconscious, which is not organically connected with the uppers layers of the psyche. This is just what has happened here, where the troll in our story has taken over three of the four kingdoms, plus a bit of the fourth.

Still, the Scandinavians have preserved some connection to the lower layers

---

[16] *C.G. Jung Letters,* vol. 1 (trans. R.F.C. Hull, Bollingen Series XCV:1; Princeton: Princeton University Press, 1973), p. 39.

of the unconscious, for there are many folk tales and traditions about trolls and nature spirits still very much alive in the culture These tales and traditions are like the stairs going down: by them the people have preserved a means of reconnecting to the unconscious, though the stairs have become hidden or invisible.

Now the trio comes to these strange forests of silver, gold and diamonds. They are completely unnatural, inorganic kinds of forests, and, as we hear later in the story, the troll has bewitched the people and the animals and every living thing in these three kingdoms, transforming them into lifeless matter.

This is a very strange motif because mythologically silver, gold and diamonds generally have tremendously positive implications. Think, for instance, of the alchemical symbolism specifying the stages of development and purification of the *prima materia.* There, diamond or gold is the highest achievement, the goal to be reached. Here, on the contrary, this motif has a completely negative connotation. It is a cursed state that is represented by those forests.

There is a Norwegian fairy tale with the same motif, called "Kari Wooden Frock."[17] It is the story of a princess who is ill-treated by her stepmother. She runs away with the help of a blue bull from home, and they have to pass through a silver, gold and diamond forest. The bull tells the girl never to touch a leaf because if she does there would be a catastrophe. But in each forest she can't avoid touching a leaf, and each time a three-headed, six-headed, and finally a nine-headed troll appears. So here we have again this connection between silver, gold and diamond forests and a troll. The blue bull has to fight with the troll and can only overcome him with the greatest difficulty. All ends well—in fact this is a later version of the Cinderella story—but we should be careful to note this motif of negative silver, gold and diamond forests.

The only other parallel I can think of (and there may be some historical connection here) is that in the so-called novels of Alexander the Great, Alexander comes to different places of paradise, each made from silver or from gold or diamonds. Then he is summoned by a voice from heaven or by some ghost voices to go back and return to earth. These stories were very popular in the Middle Ages and they sank deep, even into the layer of folklore, for you can find many of their motifs there.

I would guess that our three forests therefore originate from them. That would give us an indication that these silver, gold and diamond forests have to do with the paradisical state, with perhaps a state of completeness after death, but in our

---

17 MDW, *Nordische Volksmärchen,* vol. 2, Norwegen, no. 27 (Jena: Diederichs, 1922); also in English entitled "Katie Wooden Cloak," in Stith Thompson, *100 Favorite Folk Tales* (Bloomington, IN: Indiana University Press, 1974).

story they have a negative connotation. We could say *cum grano salis* that the troll bewitched the inhabitants of these three kingdoms into the land of death, which is also paradise. But he dehumanized them too early, before their span of life had been fulfilled.

We can also look at it from another angle. Somewhere in the make-up of every human being and in every culture you will find a "paradise dream." Sometimes, on the one hand, this is projected backward in history onto some Golden Age where everything was perfect and since then human reality has slowly degenerated. On the other hand, the fantasy of paradise might be conceived as an eschatological goal. For instance, the Heavenly Jerusalem in the Apocalypse occurs at the end of time. It comes down from heaven to earth, as a future goal. It is as if we come from a dream of paradise and are walking toward a dreamland of paradise, but it makes a great difference whether this paradise lies behind us or ahead of us.

Paradise in itself, with its fourfold structure as a mandala or as a zoological garden, or later in the Apocalypse where it is identified with the Heavenly City, is a feminine symbol. Now, you remember I pointed out that nowhere in our whole story is there a mother figure. The maternal element is completely lacking. The princess has only a father. The hero has no mother. He has a spiritual father, the old man who advises him, but where is the mother? I would guess, therefore, that this paradise or these three forests contain the maternal element, but in a completely negative and regressive form. That means we have to give this dream or ideal of paradise a negative connotation and suppose that it is a childish dream of happiness, of nonsuffering, or becoming happy on earth—a neurotic utopia as Jung so aptly described in *Symbols of Transformation*.[18] The paradise ideal—the three forests—in our story thus represents a regressive longing to return to the mother's womb, which prevents one from living with purpose, from looking forward to the future.

An interesting detail in the history of the paradise motif is that in medieval sources and patristic literature, we often find it pointed out (for instance, in Hippolytus) that the paradise in which Adam and Eve lived and picked the apple was in the West. But after the Fall, paradise was secretly transferred to the East. The West is the part of the horizon onto which is projected the sunset, death, going down into the underworld, the end of life, the end of a culture. East, the place of the dawn, is always the place where the new illumination comes from, where the light is born or where mystical enlightenment takes place, for example

---

[18] CW 5, esp. chap. 6, "The Battle for Deliverance from the Mother."

in the Persian, Arabic and Christian mystic traditions. The famous title, "Aurora Consurgens," which plays a great role in alchemy, in Arabic mysticism and in Jacob Boehme's books, points to the fact that the East is the place of the dawning, the new form of consciousness, where cultural consciousness will be reborn after a time of decay and darkness. You have that same symbolism in the Egyptian religion, where the old sun-god goes down in the West as a decaying old man and is reborn as Horus, the young sun-child, in the East.

Paradise, therefore, has two distinct connotations. When it is in the East, it is the locus of the rebirth of a new form of consciousness. But when it is in the West, it is regressive, the past that lures us into childish and utopian fantasies.

One is tempted to make a little poisonous excursion into more modern times and remark on how interesting it is that the dialectic materialism of communism is basically devoted to this utopian dream of a paradise of earthly happiness, of bringing back a heaven on earth, but on a primitive, material level. That would be an illustration of such diamond, gold and silver forests in the hands of the troll. That would be a tremendous unredeemed primitive spirit linked up with a kind of childish dream of luck and happiness, materialistic because it is in the realm of mater, materia, matter. But not only in dialectical materialism do we find this fantasy. You could write a whole history about the utopia fantasy in European politics. Each one contains this doubleness: the regressive, childish dream of bringing heaven back to earth in an unreal way, connected with the most primitive drives, which here are personified by the troll.

Trolls in Scandinavian mythology are very strange creatures and there is little agreement on what they look like. From time to time I have bought or been given modern illustrated children's books from Scandinavian countries. I always search passionately through them to find out how those damn trolls look! But they are always depicted according to the completely subjective fantasy of those who did the illustrations. Some draw them like big bags, more or less giantlike. Others draw them like funny little dwarfs. There is no standard viewpoint, no consensus on how a troll looks. In *Peer Gynt*, for instance, the troll is a kind of cloud; it has no shape at all. It is something that comes from the sea or the fjords and envelops you in a confusing fog from which shapes arise. So the troll is, so to speak, the tricky side of nature.

Then there are genuine folk tales in Finland, Lapland and Norway where the trolls are represented more like mountain giants. In an Icelandic story called "Trunt, Trunt and the Trolls of the Mountains," it is told that a man went once with two comrades to look for berries. But then he went a bit further away, and when he came back he had a strange look and just disappeared. After a year he reappeared in his village, still with that strange look on his face. The people were quite frightened, and someone asked him, "Do you believe in God?" He shook his head and once again disappeared. In the third year, he appeared again for a day, and was asked again, "Do you believe in God?" He said, "No, I believe in Trunt, Trunt and the Trolls of the Mountains." Then he disappeared again.[19] So the troll is something that makes people dissolve in a strange way into nature. They leave their human community and dissolve into the stones, the glaciers and the forests.

This still happens in a similar way in some of our desolate Swiss mountain valleys. Edward Renner, a doctor in the Canton Uri, who was a very good man and in contrast to modern general practitioners still took the trouble to walk for hours and hours up the Alps to visit all his poor patients in heir huts, collected such stories in a book called *Goldener Ring über Uri* (Golden Ring over Uri).[20] In this book he says that although Uri peasants officially are all Catholics and pretend to be Catholic, if you scratch a bit below that layer you find that they believe much more strongly in something which he calls the "id." This "id" has nothing to do with the Freudian id. It simply is "it." When they say, "It rains," or "It snows," this has the implication that the "it" rains, or the "it" sends snow. Or, the "it" sends avalanches or the "it" sends a mountain crashing down on your hut. We too say "It rains," "It snows," but for us there is no such implication.

You can sometimes talk to the Uri's "it." The "it" is not benevolent, nor is it malevolent. It's just indifferent. For instance, one cattle herder was with the cows on high land by the mountains. He had his boy to help him. One evening, after having driven the cows into the stables, he went out again and looked around, and suddenly he heard a voice high up on the mountain slopes saying, "Shall I let it down?" The herder replied, "No, you can keep it, you can hold it." The boy heard it and was very frightened. The next evening the same thing happened. The voice said, "Shall I let it down?" and the man said, without respect— and that is the horrible part; you should be very respectful if you experience such a thing—"Oh, you can hold it." The next evening, the boy was so frightened that he decided to run away. Just as he finished packing up, he heard the cattle herder go out again, and the voice said, "I can't hold it any longer!" And the boy ran off. At that very moment, the whole mountain slid down and buried the cattle, the herder, everything. The boy escaped just in time to be able to tell of it.

You see what a great role "it" plays in that story. It's shaped, it's not shaped,

---

[19] MDW, *Isländische Volksmärchen*, no. 37 (Jena: Diederichs, 1923).
[20] Zürich: M.S. Metz, 1941.

it's personified, it's not personified; it isn't evil, because after all it had been challenged. It actually half warned the cattle herder! If he had been as wise as the boy he could have escaped. You have to be very careful with "it" powers.

There's another story, in Seelisberg, that when you go around a certain turn of the mountain with your cattle, they regularly disappear. Now the "it" wants to play you a trick, and if you lose your head and begin to shout and become confused, you might fall down the mountain or something else awful might happen to you. Therefore the rule is, you have to just pretend the cows are still there; you have to just quietly walk on, pretending you notice nothing, and say, "Huh, huh, huh!" to your cows, and then suddenly they'll turn up again. In that case, the "it" hasn't gotten you.

I once went around that corner of the mountain because I wanted to find out if I would experience something like being without cattle. And I must say it *is* quite amazing! At first, one has no view of the higher Alps and the upper part of the Vierwaldstattersee at all. But when you come round that corner, you are suddenly in front of an overwhelming panorama of the entire range of higher mountains, with the lake spreading below and glittering in the sun. It's an absolutely awe-inspiring sight, so I can well understand that one could become ecstatic and forget all about oneself. If I had had cattle, I might not have seen them in front of me for ten minutes. I would have lost any awareness of my earthly situation. You get a glimpse of paradise when you come round that corner. And although our peasants never look at the view consciously—they don't care in the least about the beauty of the country they live in, because they are stuck in the earth right up to their necks—they are probably still gripped by the numinosity of this place on a deeper level. One cannot help being gripped when one turns round that corner; you are suddenly in a completely different world. And that is bewildering. It can put one completely out of oneself.

So you see, the "it" in our mountains is similar to the trolls in Scandinavian nature. They both show the mysterious way in which the genius of *place* affects us, through which we change for good or bad. It's an unexplained phenomenon; we have no rational idea, really, how much we are part of the geographical surface of the earth, and how much our psyche still completely lives in it. Trolls are personifications of these local powers that live in the mountains and forests and streams, especially where human civilization hasn't yet spread, where we haven't chased away the gods, so speak. When you feel that strangeness, that uncanny numinosity of nature, you suddenly feel completely lost and small. You cannot cry out for help. You're alone and small, either happy or shivering from cold in an overwhelming greatness of nature. It is a religious experience, perhaps one of the earliest forms of religious experience humans had.

This is the way one sometimes experiences the spirit of the troll, but in our fairy tale he is evil; he has dehumanized three kingdoms. Now, you see from that parallel, "Trunt, Trunt and the Trolls in the Mountains" that the trolls have the effect of estranging one from human society. The man became queer and said he didn't believe in God any more. He doesn't talk to the villagers; he completely fades away into nature. That is the effect of the trolls. If we translate that on a psychological level, the troll would represent a spiritual primitiveness so great that it kills all relatedness.

We need not go far to find that. We see again and again in our history, right up to the present, that if an individual or a group or even a whole nation is filled with the primitive spiritual possession of some ideological ideal, a paradise dream, for instance, they feel absolutely and unashamedly justified in killing other people for it. They are dehumanized. If you try to argue with such people, they say it is right to kill everyone who is against that ideal or tries to prevent its realization. They lose their human feeling and their conscience, their relatedness to others. It is a state of possession by an ideal, one that is not transcendent but generally on a very concrete, earthly level. So our story has something to tell not only to the Danes but to many others as well.

Our hero breaks off a twig in each forest, and these twigs he takes with him in order to be able to prove afterward that he was there. This is a motif you may know from Aeneas' descent into the underworld in Virgil's *Aeneid.* To have access to the world of the dead, Aeneas has to pick a golden bough. (That's where Frazer got the title for his twelve-volume book, *The Golden Bough.*) This motif shows also that we have to interpret these forests of silver, gold and diamond as the land of the dead. The people of those forests are, so to speak, in Hades. They have been bewitched and taken out of life. They are like people who are possessed by a paradise ideal: as human beings they are dead.

In order to reach the troll's castle, the hero, the princess and the white girl take a boat. The hero is still in his invisible form because he holds his stick up, as you remember. He gets into the boat, and each time the boat wobbles, and also when breaks off those twigs, the princess has a moment of nervousness and says, "I have the feeling somebody's behind us." But the white girl always says, "Oh no, that's only the wind." You see here the difference between the two. The white girl, who belongs to the realm of the troll, has no awareness of human presence. But the princess, who is more human and only the unfortunate victim of the troll, has a kind of hunch that something is following her.

It's an amusing reversal. If we are here on earth and a ghost follows us, then we have this feeling, "Something is behind me!" You may remember having had in childhood those uncanny feelings of being followed by a "something" in the dark. But here it's the other way around: the living are to the ghosts as the ghosts are, usually, to the living. I could bring in a lot of amplification of that from spiritualistic and parapsychological literature. It's a widespread archetypal motif that the country of the living and the sphere of the dead interpenetrate. They are, so to speak, simultaneously present all the time, but we, the living, are not aware of the dead except in those situations where an uncanny shudder creeps up our back. And for the dead, it seems to be vice-versa.

Psychologically, we can say that the princess is a bit more human and therefore more capable of sensing the human being, which the white girl just calls "the wind." We could perhaps interpret that best by saying the princess has a kind of conscience left, because when one is doing something one oughtn't do and then has this kind of feeling—"Somebody is following me, someone is watching"—this is typically a symptom of a bad conscience. One feels seen. It is our higher conscience that watches us and whose presence we feel in this way. So, since the princess keeps having these feelings, we know she is not completely in thrall to the troll, and her bad conscience is reinforced by the invisible presence of the hero.

The ugly troll receives the princess and asks why she is so late, and she says she was afraid someone had followed them. But he doesn't believe it, and so the troll and the princess have dinner together from golden plates. And when they finish, the hero steals the princess's golden plate, her knife and her fork, and puts them too in his bag in order to prove later that he had been there. The troll and the princess can't explain how that stuff could have disappeared, but they don't bother about it and begin to dance.

Here the princess has communion, so to speak, with the troll in an unholy way, and then they dance. The golden plate again shows that there is a kind of divine or royal quality around her relationship with the troll, as if he were a secret king or even a godhead of the underworld with whom she communes.

If we switch for a moment to a more personal level, it is interesting to note that this same situation presents one of the greatest difficulties in dealing with women who are completely possessed by a negative animus. At the bottom of a negative animus possession, one very often finds a secret religious element. It is like serving or communing with a god, an underworldly god, with all the ecstasies and absoluteness of so doing. That is why such women cannot easily pull out of it. They cannot simply wake up and say, "Well, that's the negative animus, and that's that! I'll finish with it now." It is a question of disentangling the positive spiritual and religious values in this figure from their negative connotation. The negative connotation generally comes from the fact that the animus tends to have opinions about outer and human affairs. That's where a woman's animus becomes so completely destructive. And then all the judgments about what other people think or feel, or how one ought to behave in this or that way— all these judgments are just off the point.

You can really diagnose animus possession by the fact that from morning until night such women tell absolute truths, but they are applied at the wrong moment. You can never argue, therefore, with an animus, because he's always right. Generally the animus produces such general bits of wisdom that you can't even argue against them. You can only say, "Yes, yes, *in general* you are quite right, but look here! In this specific situation it is not so!" If you want to argue at all (which is always unwise!), you have to keep your eyes and ears, your whole attention, concentrated—not to determine whether what the woman says is true or not, because it's *always* true, but whether it's true or not concerning *this specific point* she's arguing about. That's where it goes off the track.

So, we can say that the animus contains the general truths or collective wisdom of the unconscious. But these truths cannot be simply, inhumanely applied to outer reality, especially not to human relationships. In itself the negative animus is not wholly wrong. There is sometimes deep wisdom in what the negative animus says—deep, ruthless "nature truths" that one cannot reject out of hand. But one has to sort them out.

When I illustrated how the troll affects people possessed by an ideology, we had an example of the same thing. In most political utopian ideals, there is a tremendous amount of general truth. That's why they sound so emotionally convincing to so many people. But when we come to the way they are put into practice, that's where the devil appears, where the troll shows his hand. The most primitive impulses, criminal impulses—lust for power and so on—get loose and destroy all chances of realizing the ideal on earth. That's why in revolutions you always have forerunners who are more the intellectual/ideological type. They are idealists. But shortly after the revolution has begun to spread, it is overrun by power-possessed criminals. That's the troll in action.

Returning to our three forests, note that they are made from inorganic matter. Jung says the forest symbolizes the layer in the unconscious that is very close to the somatic processes.[21] One could call this the psychosomatic layer or area of the unconscious. That is because, just as the forest draws its nourishment from

---

[21] "The Spirit Mercurius," *Alchemical Studies,* CW 13, par. 241.

inorganic matter, so this layer of the unconscious is in immediate living contact with the physiological processes of the body—matter itself, so to speak. This has to do with the individual. We generally project onto our body the "just so" reality of our existence and personality. That is why symbols of inorganic matter, like the diamond body or a golden sphere, are so often symbols of the Self, of achieved individuation.

In our story, again, the inorganic state of these forests has a negative connotation. This points to what Jung describes so well in the symbolism of the transference, where he shows that if one who is called to individuate does not take up the problem of individuation consciously (and that always goes with the problem of the transference), then that process fulfills itself negatively.[22] If I am called to it, the process of individuation cannot be avoided; I can either do it consciously or it will happen to me unconsciously.

Jung says that the unconscious process of individuation results in an incredible hardening of the individual against others, while consciously working on the problem of individuation and the problem of transference leads to humanization, to greater consciousness, wisdom and relatedness. Some stupid people reproach Jungian psychology, saying we are making people into solipsistic individuals. In fact, it is just the other way around. The further the process of individuation goes, the more socially adept and positively related a person becomes. On the contrary, however, if one does not take up the process of individuation consciously, one becomes a diamond body all right, but only in its hard aspect. Then we have this incredible hardening of the heart against others. Such people can shoot you down for no reason other than for fun, or execute millions in gas chambers without the slightest remorse in order to fulfill some utopian ideal.

One can hardly understand it because, as Konrad Lorenz says so clearly, most animals don't go beyond a certain degree of aggression against members of their own species.[23] Only humans can do that to such an incredible pathological extent. The reason for this lies in part in the pseudo-religious convictions with which people arm themselves. Charles Manson, for instance, was absolutely convinced that he represented Satan and the Antichrist and that was that! He is an example of a religiosity turned negative. You see, the religious instinct is one of the most basic instincts in a human being. If it is warped, if it is not taken up consciously—and that has to do with the process of individuation—then it leads to that inhuman hardening, to the incredible, incomprehensible cruelty we see

---

22 *Aion,* CW 9ii, par. 125.
23 *On Aggression,* trans. Marjorie Kerr Wilson (New York: Harcourt Brace, 1966).

spreading everywhere.

And now we come to the dance. There again, we have a religious element. As we know from ethnology, the dance is one of the most essential elements of all ancient cultures and religions. The dances of primitive tribes are almost never just for fun, although they are also for fun, admittedly. They always have a deeper, transcendent meaning. They are danced for the purpose of helping the sun rise, or helping deities of fertility, or for some other specific purpose. Even in the apocryphal Gospel of St. John, Jesus dances a mystical dance with his apostles while his body is crucified on Golgatha.[24]

Dance represents or reproduces a cosmic rhythm. Throughout the Middle Ages and until the rise of modern astronomy, the turning of all the heavenly spheres and of the planets around the sun were considered to be parts of a great cosmic dance. Very often it was believed that those bodies did not move on their own accord, but were moved by some angel or by a planetary or cosmic soul. Together with the music of the spheres, they were all performing a huge dance around the center of the cosmos or the deity. Therefore, most ritual dances, with their circular movement, expressed the image of the deity or of the Self in its eternal rhythmical manifestation.

The Self is not static. Although it is sometimes represented by a crystal or a diamond, which stresses its eternal nature and its indestructibility, it is more often represented by some moving or dancing body. The Self is in constant movement. Continuous change in Chinese Taoist philosophy expressed the very meaning of existence. According to the *I Ching,* you cannot relate always to the Tao in the same way; you must relate to it differently at every minute. And so it is with the Self. You cannot have an experience of the Self and then stick to it for once and forever. It is well know that if you have an experience of the Self, after one or two days, or even after only a few hours, it has already disappeared. The goal, therefore, is to be able to hold on to it when it transforms itself—to follow it in its dance. If you stand still and say, "Now I *have* it!" while the Self moves on, then you lose it. The secret is to be able to follow it, to dance with it, because the Self is constantly performing a dance, a circular movement of internal renewal. It constantly changes and yet always remains the same.

Another aspect of the dance is human communion. Nothing brings people closer together, into a kind of communicating spirit. Practically nothing expresses as close a psychic relationship as people dancing together. That's why

---

24 Acts of John, 94-96, *Apocryphal New Testament,* trans. M.R. James (Oxford: Oxford University Press, 1966).

dance can be so restorative. For instance, if a tribe performs a holy dance, it restores its social coherence. It unifies the people in their feeling and in their spirit.

So dance expresses the movement of life, and to dance in a right way would be to go along with this movement, with the psychic movement of life.

The dancing princess fulfills all these things with the ugly troll. But here something that could be of redeeming religious significance has turned negative. Her dance with the troll reminds one of the witch dances on the Blocksberg, where witches dance with the devil himself in riotous nocturnal parties. Margaret Mead and others think that the negative connotations of such dancing represent merely the bedeviled remnants of an older fertility-mother cult that has been given a negative accent through Christianization.[25] I think there is some truth in that theory, but I don't believe it is the whole story. For beyond that, as for all great religious archetypes, there is always both a positive and a negative aspect, and the negative aspect forms just as integral a part of the archetype as the positive.

To dance with the devil is an archetypal motif we find all over the world. You can say this expresses negative possession. In practical psychology, you sometimes see the extremes of such a phenomenon in acute schizophrenics who lie in bed completely catatonic. But after they come out of such an episode, you can communicate with them about what happened, and you often find that they had the most ecstatic meetings and dances with demonic figures. Far from being immobile and half dead, as they seem to be, their soul is far away, dancing a devil's dance with some semidemonic, semidivine figure, having the most ecstatic experiences. There you see how a religious archetype that is positive in itself can negatively affect those who aren't up to meeting it in the right way. One must never forget that it is the very same archetype which in other connections, if understood and assimilated without losing one's humanness, is of the highest positive value. That is what makes these things so terribly paradoxical.

The princess and the troll dance twelve dances during the twelve hours of the night, and the princess wears out twelve pairs of shoes. It is the hero's task to find out how that happened. In the German parallel, as I mentioned, one princess does not dance for twelve hours with one troll, but twelve princesses dance with twelve cursed princes; so the number twelve is distributed onto the figures of the dance themselves. In both cases, the number twelve plays an essential role.

If you know a little bit about Egyptian religion, you know that the sun god Ra

---

25 See, for instance, Margaret Mead, *Coming of Age in Samoa* (New York: William Morrow and Co., Inc., 1928).

runs through the upper hemisphere of the earth and the sky in twelve hours, and transforms himself through twelve hours into twelve different shapes. Then he goes down in the West and runs under the world where again he takes on different shapes for twelve hours. During the twelve hours when he runs through the underworld he has to fight the battle with evil—the Apophis snake—and he is then reborn as the new sun, Horus, in the East. We can therefore associate the number twelve as it occurs in our fairy tale with the twelve nocturnal hours spent with the dark sun.

In *Mysterium Coniunctionis,* in the chapter on the sun, Jung goes to a great extent into the strange mythology of the shadow of the sun, the "black sun" or *sol niger.*[26] Contrary to all astronomical facts, the alchemists spoke of a black shadow of the sun, or even of a "pitch black sun," with very negative and destructive qualities. This stands in contrast to the moon, which is always a bit light and always a bit dark; it is full, then it is half, then it is new, and then it is a full moon again. And Jung, in commenting on the principles of sun and moon, shows that the sun principle is the archetype of consistent or continuous consciousness. It is more typical of the Logos principle, for a masculine rather than a feminine consciousness. But because it is so extremely bright, it builds up an extremely black shadow. So now we begin to realize what the shadow of the principle of consciousness is.

Think of it: after more than two hundred years of the Age of Enlightenment, we have practically destroyed the surface of the earth. We have practically annihilated most of its animal and plant life, and we are on the way toward annihilating ourselves. To what or whom do we owe *that?*—why, to our enlightened consciousness! It's like this: If a plant doesn't grow, you dump fertilizer into the ground and, enlightened, the plants grow well. But after a few years you realize what you have destroyed. You see, to the extent that we carry on with our light of consciousness, to that same extent we refuse to tolerate ambiguity or inconsistency or discontinuity.

For instance, nowadays whenever something goes slightly wrong with us, we immediately set out to "do something" about it, not realizing that the more we do to correct it, the more we pile up the blackness and the evil on the other side. Instead, we should always ask, "Is that an evil we can tolerate, one that probably, if we tolerate it, will balance itself out after awhile?" For in that case, one ought not do anything about it. There are still plenty of situations where one clearly has to do something to fight against evil. But one should note that to do

---

[26] CW 14, pars. 110ff.

something rational against anything that is evil is a half-devilish measure, and more liable to disturb the balance of the whole than to improve the situation. If we would realize that, our sun would not be so bright, but its black shadow would not be so dark either.

The moon, on the other hand, with its ever dim and changing light, is identified with the conscious attitude or principle of feminine consciousness. It tends to be not so overly bright and clear but more vague and more poetically dim, so to speak. Yet because of this, it does not carry with it such a black shadow. We could therefore say that the troll in a way represents the midnight sun, the shadow of consciousness, the dark principle. That would explain his role very well in relation to the old king, for the king is the ruling, dominant symbolic idea that carries collective consciousness, while the troll is then its shadow side which has not been realized and which has attracted to it everything that has been rejected by the ruling conscious attitude. And now the princess has fallen for it and dances with it through the twelve hours of the night.

The number twelve is also interesting in that it is the product of three times four. Therefore it contains the famous relationship, *proportio sesquitertia*, between three and four which, as one knows from the study of Jung, is central to the problem of individuation. Twelve also points to the time factor. It is interesting that in China as well as with us, there is a twelve-unit counting system for time, while in the West we use a decimal system for almost all other measures. In number symbolism, twelve is always connected with time.

Dance too is intimately linked with time, for when one dances one must continually "keep time"—maintain a rhythmical movement. In the same way, as discussed before, one has to keep time from moment to moment with the movement of the Self in the process of individuation. When it becomes conscious, the Self establishes a whole new attitude toward time. It changes one's conscious attitude from a static one to a more flexible attitude: one knows that one has to live from minute to minute in the right way and at the right time.

Now, one of the main characteristics of traditional Christian consciousness is that its dogma is generally taught as a completely static body of eternal truths, principles that are in themselves absolutely true. But if you read a theological book on moral casuistry, you see how the poor theologians get into trouble when they try to apply these eternal and absolute principles to special single cases. Then it all becomes ridiculous!

For instance, when the Host is transubstantiated you have to treat it with great reverence. That is obviously quite justifiable from the Catholic point of view. But then, I once found in a book a long discussion about what happens if a priest gives the transubstantiated Host to a woman and lets it drop into her bra!—a very tricky problem: how does one go about retrieving it? You see, when it comes to the moment, the actual detailed fact of the matter, how strange and antithetical such things become—just impossible! The book I read devoted two pages to describing what has to be done in such a case.

What Westerners have not bothered enough about—the old Chinese civilization is infinitely further ahead in this respect—is to work out an attitude according to which ethical and religious principles are not considered to be absolutes. We ought to realize that moral decisions are not independent of their context, the situation at the moment. In Zen Buddhism, for example, one distinguishes between enlightenment as an inner experience and what is called "functioning." A Zen pupil is enlightened when he experiences satori, and becomes a master. But after he has been enlightened, he must be capable of doing the right thing from moment to moment in every situation. He does not go around teaching his enlightenment as a static principle to which others must adhere; if he did this, he would be getting off the track.

We can therefore say that the dance of the troll and the princess contains in a compensatory form what the ruling consciousness, which seems to be the Christian Weltanschauung, is lacking.

Northern countries seem to lack an ability to adapt to the specific moment. As we saw in the stories of the "it" in the Swiss mountains and in the stories of the trolls, the people involved all had momentary religious encounters in everyday life, but they were pagan, non-Christian experiences. In repressing paganism, the Christian missionaries destroyed that exceedingly alive and positive element of the former nature-cults. If you read any representation of a pagan religion, for instance of some African tribe, you see that the religion is completely built into the way they live. It's built into the moments of their life, what they do every morning or every day, what they do in every situation. There is a complete interpenetration of one's religious functions and actual life, minute by minute. Such a religion is not some abstract metaphysical belief-system that the tribe has to believe in on a theoretical level while being allowed to behave completely differently in day-to-day life.

Of course, there have been repeated attempts in Christianity to correct its overly abstract, absolutist attitude. This has succeeded more in Catholic countries than in Protestant ones. In Catholic countries, generally, the lower layers of the population live in a half-Catholic spirit but also in a half-pagan folklore spirit where everything one does is still somehow connected with the right moment and the right religious attitude. For instance, you wash your vinegar bottle and start a new "mother" on Good Friday because Jesus was given vinegar on the cross, and so on. You must do many specific things on certain days, and these things have a religious connotation.

But such practices are rapidly dying out, even in Catholic countries, under the pressure of so-called enlightenment. And because of this we have a split between abstract religious belief on the one hand, and on the other a completely profane and meaningless everyday life that therefore quickly falls into the grip of some unconscious archetype or regresses, in other words, into the grip of the troll.

Now, after each dance the princess's shoes are torn up. Well, perhaps just because she dances so long, the shoes become worn out. But since this motif is also in the German version and others, it must have a more special meaning.

Shoes generally have to do with one's standpoint in life. For instance, in German we say that when a boy or girl grows up, they should put off their childhood shoes. Or if a son follows exactly the life pattern of his father, we say he steps into his father's shoes. And if a woman has her husband completely under her thumb, we say, "He's under the slipper." Traditionally the victor, as you know, puts his shoe on the neck of the vanquished enemy, as if to say, "It's my standpoint to which you now have to bow. *I* say how it should be and you must bow to it." That's what is expressed by this gesture.

So, if the princess ruins all those shoes, it means she progressively loses more and more of her standpoint on earth. She becomes estranged from reality by those nocturnal escapades. She's really dancing in the realm of the dead. You might say she has become completely fascinated by the ambiguous, if not dark, side of the unconscious, and so more and more she loses her grip on reality.

Losing one's grip on reality can happen not only to individual, but collectively as well. For instance, regressive ideological possession demonstrates how whole groups of people with some childish fantasy of bringing heaven to earth can also lose their grip on reality and kill off their surroundings in the process. You see this quite clearly in the development of the Nazi movement. The "blessed" Führer, and with him the whole circle of Nazi leaders, became more and more unreal. They lost their grip on reality and that, naturally, led to their downfall. That is what happens in the long run to all such movements: they slowly lose their grip on reality and have to defend their ideal by more and more criminal means, until finally they go completely off the rails.

The princess brings back her torn shoes in the morning. That is what makes the king suspicious. He begins to think, "My daughter must do something strange at night," and that's why he gives the order to find out what's going on. On the morning after the third night, the old king asks the hero if he has seen anything. The young man pretends he hasn't, and so is led away to his execution. The old king feels miserable, but the princess is triumphant. You see how inhuman she is. So the young man is led to the gallows, but before he is to be killed he asks the king if he might tell the dream he had in the night.

Then he relates everything he experienced, but as if he had dreamt it all. He brings out the twigs to prove the dream was real; then he brings the golden plate out of his bag and all the other objects he brought back. He wants to show that although he tells his experience in the form of a dream, it was still real.

This is a mythological motif you often find in fairy tales: a dream is shown to be not merely a dream but something real, by the hero's collecting some object of proof. For instance, there is a Nordic fairy tale in which a shepherd sleeps under a bush. As he falls asleep, he sees a rat hole. Then he dreams that a rat comes out as a beautiful princess and gives him a golden girdle and says he should go by a certain route to a castle and redeem her. He wakes up under the bush and everything has disappeared, but he still holds that golden girdle. From that he knows the dream was more than just a dream, and so he goes and redeems the princess. These kinds of motifs are widespread and always stress that the dream is more than a dream, it is reality.

I think I can save myself a lot of work in finishing this fairy tale, for we could say, briefly, that the hero knows about the reality of the psyche. And he can give proof for the reality of the psyche, which the ordinary person thinks is nothing but a dream. So the young man shows the proof and the princess is horrified, but the king is happy and says he should now marry the princess. If that had actually happened, the catastrophe would have been complete, because we can be pretty sure the princess would have killed him on the wedding night or soon thereafter.

But the hero knows what he has yet to do—you see, the troll is still around. So he refuses to marry the princess right away. He asks her for her golden thimble. Then he goes down and kills the troll with the golden needle, catches three drops of blood in the thimble, and with that he exorcises and redeems the three kingdoms and also the princess. Only then can he safely marry her.

It is interesting that in the medieval Grail legend one of the main motifs is the lance. According to certain versions it is the holy lance used by Longinus to open the side of Christ. And the Grail contains the blood of Christ. These are the central holy symbols of all the different versions of the Grail legend.

In our story we have a similar combination. We have the lance, only here it is very small, a needle, and the vessel is a thimble, but their function is essentially the same. These two symbols also represent the masculine and the feminine. The one is piercing and aiming, the active masculine principle; the other is receptive, the feminine principle. Because the thimble as vessel is a feminine thing, the hero asks it from the princess. He has to get it from her because she has to give something toward that process of redemption. Also, a thimble protects one from the pricks of the needle; that's why we wear thimbles when we sew. As well, the thimble protects against witch influences.

In those two symbols are the basic essence of the Self: its uniting, penetrating, directed activities and its receptive, containing qualities. The hero needs them both to get the blood of the troll, with which he brings back to life everything the troll had dehumanized.

Trolls very often have no blood, but this one has, and on account of this I tend to think it is blood he has sucked out of his victims; he has the blood his victims are lacking. I make that guess because by sprinkling the blood over them they come alive again. So we could say the troll has stolen or attracted all life and emotion away from the human realm where it belongs, and thus brought the people into a state of possession.

People who are possessed, be it by some religious or political fanaticism or something else, are often physically pale. It is as though they literally have no blood. And they certainly have no blood in the sense of having no warm feelings, no normal human affects. You cannot make such people laugh, you can't even make friendly contact with them. Their vitality is drained by their fanaticism. Therefore, they can't enjoy life. They have no private life, no moments of joy, and because of that they lack the enjoyment of life.

When their blood is returned, the kingdoms are redeemed. With the troll gone, the hero becomes ruler of the three kingdoms and it is implied that later on he will also rule the fourth. You will remember he was promised half of it, and although it is not actually said that he receives it, we can guess that at least after the death of the old king he will get the fourth kingdom as well.

So the hero first becomes the ruler of those kingdoms that had been neglected and which therefore had fallen into the grip of the troll. This means that within the total cultural situation, the accent shifts into previously neglected areas that now become important, and only perhaps later will there be a renewal of the dominant cultural center. For now, other centers are vivified, but life will slowly emanate into the main center, the last kingdom. You find that moments of renewal and new life generally do not come up where one expects them to, but rather in other previously neglected areas.

2
The Three Carnations
(Spanish)

The next story is a Spanish tale, "The Three Carnations."[27]

A peasant was out in the fields one day when he saw three marvelous carnations. He broke them off and brought them to his daughter. The young girl was very happy, but one day, when she stood in the kitchen and looked at them, one fell into the coals and burned. A beautiful young man appeared then and asked her, "What's the matter with you? What are you doing?" Since she didn't answer, he said, "You don't talk to me? All right, then you can find me near the stones of the whole world." And he disappeared. She took the second carnation and threw it in the fire. Again a young man appeared before her and said, "What's the matter with you? What are you doing?" But she didn't answer. So he said, "You are not talking to me? Well, near the stones of the whole world you can find me." And he disappeared. Maria—that was the name of the young girl—took the last carnation and threw it in the fire. And again such a young man appeared, again he asked the same questions, and again he disappeared.

But now Maria was sad because she had fallen in love with the last young man, and she decided after some days to go on a journey and find the stones of the whole world. She went away quite alone, and walked further and further until by chance she came to a place where there were three high stones. She was tired, so she sat down and began to cry. When she cried, one of the three stones opened and the young man she loved came out and said, "Maria, why are you crying?" And as she continued to cry, he said, "Don't be sorry, just go up there where you see a farmer's house. Go into it and ask the mistress if she will take you as a maid."

The girl did so and was taken as a maid by the mistress. Because she worked very hard and had a good heart, she was soon the favorite of her mistress. That made the other maids jealous. They went to the mistress and said, "Do you know what Maria said?" "What did she say?" "She doesn't understand why you have so many maids, because she can clean all the dirty linen herself in one day." "Come, Maria," said the mistress, "you said that you can clean all the dirty linen in one day?" "No," said Maria, "I did not say that." "But the other maids said so and now you have to do it," said the mistress, "otherwise you have to go." Then she ordered all the washing to be carried to the river.

Poor Maria didn't know what to do. She went to the stones and cried. The same

---

[27] MDW, *Spanische und Portugiesische Märchen,* no. 5 (Jena: Diederichs, 1940).

73

young man appeared and said, "What's the matter with you? Why do you cry?" And since she didn't answer, he said, "Well, don't worry about my mother's laundry. Go to the river and say to the birds, 'Birds of the whole world, come and help me.' " She did so, and when she said that, an enormous swarm of birds came and began to wash the linen, and in one minute everything was finished. By afternoon it was all dry. The mistress was very glad, and again was very pleased with Maria. But that only infuriated the other maids more, so they thought up another trick.

The mistress had an illness in her eyes. It was caused by her crying so much the day after her three sons went hunting, because they were bewitched and never returned. And the mother didn't know where they were. She called Maria and said the maids had told her that Maria could find the water that could cure her eyes. Maria denied it, but again the mistress said, "You have to do it or you must leave." So Maria went to the stones and the young man came out again and said, "Don't worry. Take a glass, go to the shore of the river and call out, 'Birds of the whole world, come and cry with me.' When they have all appeared, the last one will drop a little feather. Put it into the glass and touch the eyes of your mistress with it. Then she will be cured." Maria did so, and all the birds came and cried into the glass, and the last one dropped a feather, and with the tears of the birds and the feather she cured the eyes of her mistress.

But this wasn't enough. Again the maids slandered Maria and said she boasted that she could redeem the three sons of the mistress. So the mistress ordered her to do so. But the young man came out of the stones again and said, "I know our mother has ordered you to redeem us, but don't worry. Go to her and tell her to assemble all the girls from the surrounding countryside. Tell her they should come in a procession, each with a burning candle, and walk three times around the stones. But they must be very careful that none of their candles are blown out."

So Maria told the mistress, and all the girls of the surrounding neighborhood came, each with a burning candle, and made a circular procession around the stones three times. But when they went around the last time, a gust of wind came and blew out Maria's candle. She cried out in despair, "Alas! my candle went out!" At that moment the stones opened and the three brothers came out, and the youngest said to Maria, "Thank God you spoke. Now we are redeemed." Then the stones disappeared, and the young man told them that a wizard had bewitched them when they passed this place. He had turned them into carnations and said they could be redeemed only if the person who had burned the carnations would talk near the stones.

The mother and her sons were overjoyed and the youngest asked Maria if she would marry him. Since she loved him, she said yes. They married and were quite happy. And the maids no longer plotted against Maria but asked to be pardoned, and she pardoned them.

We have here a mistress and three sons. Also, we have a lot of maids and a black magician who like the troll in the Danish story has bewitched the three sons. We also have a peasant and his daughter.

On the one hand, then, we have a mother and three sons, but no father; and on the other hand we have a father and a daughter, but there the mother is missing. These two deficient groups unite later; then you have the young group consisting of the three sons and the daughter, and the old couple. It is not said whether or not the mistress and the girl's father marry, but certainly the young group comes together, and the maids remain with them in the house as a kind of benevolent power.

The whole story centers on the interplay between the family of the peasant and his daughter, and that of the mother and her three sons. The mother and sons are apparently rich for she has all those maids. The peasant isn't explicitly described as being poor, but he is obviously not as wealthy as the mother.

Note that the daughter, the heroine, doesn't set out to perform heroic deeds. She is made to do them under pressure of the slandering housemaids. That is a motif more usual in a king's court. There are innumerable stories where the hero becomes a servant at the king's court, and then some jealous ministers or courtiers slander him, which makes the king order the hero to do his heroic deeds. So from the fact that it is generally a king's court where this happens, we can be fairly certain that this mistress-farmer and her three bewitched sons are socially above the peasant and his daughter.

Nevertheless, the setting of our story is entirely pastoral. Generally the farmer represents the milieu in which fairy tales were told and retold more than in any other part of the population. Farmers are, so to speak, the keepers of tradition; in agricultural communities there is a tendency to keep to old habits. Even our word "pagan" comes from the Latin *paganus,* which means simply "peasant," because the peasantry did not at first accept Christianity. It was in the towns that Christianity spread initially, while the peasant communities kept their previous forms of worship much longer. That is so throughout history. The peasant is the keeper of folk tradition.

In his everyday life, the peasant often represents simple common sense. You cannot be a peasant without having a lot of common sense. A peasant has both feet on the ground; he is usually not sentimental. He can't be because, for instance, he has to kill and butcher his own animals to survive. He has a kind of realistic attitude to his surroundings, and therefore we have many fairy tales where it is a peasant boy who comes to court and becomes the king through his deeds. And this peasant boy is generally characterized as being naive, forthright and realistic. He therefore compensates the refined cultural differentiation of the people at the king's court who have lost touch with their instincts.

The fact that peasants live with their families and their animals in a "community of fate" makes it important for them to be in the right contact with their instincts. A neurotic peasant is very quickly bankrupt.

In the peasant family here, what is lacking is the mother. The peasant has an only daughter and it is stressed that he loves her very much. But he is a very unusual peasant. He brings three carnations home and gives them to his daughter. That is a gesture which probably no peasant would ever do. You bring flowers once in a while your beloved, but not to your daughter, especially if you are a peasant. So it seems there is a very close, rather incestuous bond between this father and daughter. If it were a personal story, we could say that the daughter is destined to develop a father complex.

We cannot look at this beginning set-up without taking into account the other family, the mistress with her three sons, for there it is the father who is absent and the boys are obviously "mother's boys" from all we hear about them later. So we have a split. There are two compensatory realms in the collective. Both are deficient, and only when they unite is the balance restored. To put it in general terms, the basic story line is to bring together two separate realms within the collective area of feeling and thinking.

The more dominant attitude is represented by the mistress and her three sons. She has the higher position and she dominates the proceedings in the second part of the story. Obviously, we have here a matriarchal order, with a mother who dominates her bewitched sons and all those maids, and who also takes the young girl into her clutches, half benevolently and half malevolently. She is good to the girl, but she listens to the mischievous maids and as a result gives her impossible tasks.

If we look at the social situation in Spain, as well as in Greece and Italy and the rest of the Mediterranean area, we find a strange set-up. In political life there is a conservative patriarchy. For instance, in Italy there was strong resistance against women behaving too independently or even studying at the university. The men reserve to themselves the area of the mind and of politics. But at home sits the great mother, and there she, or the grandmother, the *nona,* rules completely. *Mama mia!* This is true to an even greater extent in Spain where the women do not even take the name of their husbands. They are still Señora So-and-so, using their maiden name first and then only do they add the husband's name. And they completely dominate home life. So this is a split situation. You have a patriarchal spirit in the public world but a matriarchal spirit in everything that refers to the home, the bringing-up of children, and generally material things and money. Matter and money are really in the pocket of the Señora and not of the husband, who is just allowed to work and bring it home.

The peasant gives his daughter those three carnations, one of which turns out to be her future bridegroom. We know that if those carnations are burned, the girl will have the difficult task of redeeming those three young men. Thus the father imposes on the girl, in a hidden form, an enormous challenge. Giving her those carnations looks like a gesture of love, but really it throws a difficult task at her feet. On the personal level we could say that the peasant is a man who has an inadequate relationship with the feminine. His wife is never mentioned; perhaps she is dead. So now the peasant has a claim, a projection, on his daughter, which takes the form of throwing carnations at her feet. In doing so he challenges her to make a relationship to the problems of the masculine.

We know from experience that when a daughter has a close positive tie to her father, this gives her an active spirituality and an aliveness of the mind, with mental and spiritual interests. As Jung pointed out, such women are not like others who do things only to please men. They really do these things on their own.

Here the heroine is faced with the problem of the weak father, and that is the usual problem in such a set-up. When the mother is dominant in a culture, then the fathers become weak, at least at home. They are "under the slipper" and generally develop incestuous fantasies toward their daughters because their wives won't allow them to look out the window. The only erotic fantasy they can spin is onto the daughters in their own home. And that conditions the daughter to pick up the father's problem, to have a question in her mind about the problem of the true man—what a real man should be like—and with that comes a desire to find some spiritual and mental interests.

At the very beginning of the story we are confronted with the fact of the three carnations. Carnations have been imported into Europe from the Near East for some two thousand years. And because the original varieties of carnations were all flesh colored—rosy colored—they are called carnations. That word comes from the Latin *carnis,* flesh. So, the carnation was the fleshlike or flesh-colored flower. There is a medieval legend that carnations appeared on earth when the Virgin Mary cried on the way to Calvary. At every place her tears fell, a carnation grew. Therefore, carnations are a symbol of mother's love, which is why in the United States carnations are given on Mother's Day.

In this fairy tale we also have the motif of a woman bereft at the loss of her sons. The mistress who has lost her sons is like the Virgin Mary on her way to Calvary. She is in tears; she has cried so much she has even ruined her eyes.

It is also interesting to note that our girl is called Maria. Not very often do the heroines in fairy tales have a name, but this one has, and naturally in a country like Spain the name Maria is collectively associated with the Virgin Mary. So, our heroine is like a human incarnation of the Virgin in her archetypal role, and therefore she is the one who has to restore the right ideas about femininity and love. In some dictionaries of flower symbolism, white carnations are said to be the symbol of pure and ardent love, and also a good luck gift to a woman. You know there are such rules, for you find them sometimes even in flower shops: different flowers have different meanings, and therefore if you want to buy flowers for someone, you may pick them according to what they mean. And white carnations especially mean pure and ardent love. Now, ardent means "burning"; the girl drops these carnations into the kitchen fire and they burn up, and with that action the whole story begins.

The fire, especially the fire in the kitchen, is akin to the alchemical fire. It is the fire of affect and emotion, but it is contained and used for the transformation of food. In alchemical symbolism, fire and cooking denote a continuous warm participation or interest, an emotional concentration on the process. But the alchemists say one should never make the fire too hot, because then one would burn up the lovers in the retort. One has to bring the lovers together with a moderate but constant fire. So, when the girl drops the carnations into the fire, it means that what was meant to be pure and ardent love now becomes passionate. Maria, therefore, must have an earthly passionate nature which is awakened by her father's attention. And, since she is alone, she is burned, so to speak, by love-passion. That is why she burns those flowers.

That's the first time the three young men appear and ask the strange questions, "What's the matter with you? What are you doing?" They don't say, "Please redeem me," or "Please do something for me." They say, "What's the matter with *you?* What are *you* doing?"

There are some reverse parallels where a hero comes into a paradise garden and picks some oranges or lemons (there are different variations). When he breaks them open, a girl comes out and says, "Give me bread and water!" And because has hasn't any bread and water ready, she says, "Okay, I'll return to my tree," and disappears. But the third time he breaks open those oranges or lemons, he has bread and water ready for the beautiful girl who comes out, and this time she remains human. Then he can marry her.

In these there's a question of having to provide the feminine with some bread. This would mean giving the feminine incarnation and some psychological concern. But in our fairy tale it is the other way around. The boys say, "What's the matter with you? What are you doing?" But we find out why they ask this question in the end—it is because the girl has to speak. We don't know what would have happened if she had spoken earlier; a dialogue might have developed and the young men could have told her how to redeem them. But, because she never answers, the young men just disappear. Maria is not yet able to redeem them. She has to go on that long trip first.

We know that the more "burning" a problem becomes, the more we become inarticulate and silent. The more emotional we are, the more difficult it is to express what is the matter. You see this in word association experiments when a word touches off an emotionally-laden complex. People cannot answer, sometimes for two or three seconds or even longer. In extreme cases, behind the complete mutism of a catatonic schizophrenic you will often find an absolute *burning* fire of emotion which is so strong that that person can only lie rigidly in bed, unable to utter a single word. That is the extreme, but it is something we all experience to a lesser degree. The more we are hit, the less we are able to react.

So, the girl has a passionate, fiery nature, but she has no articulate mental capacities. Now, this is just the same problem that arises in a civilization where women are not allowed to study or develop their minds. It becomes most acute if they have a gift, if they are talented in a certain way, because they are prohibited from expressing their potential. So it remains bottled up in them as a huge emotion, which then surfaces in irritability, hysteria or silent, grudging ill temper. It is as though they have a fiery ball in their chest for which they have no use; and yet they cannot dispose of it.

This extreme irritability in a woman is in Jungian jargon generally interpreted as a symptom of animus possession. There is the verbalizer animus, who talks too much and talks a lot of nonsense, and then there are silent, ill-tempered animuses, a hard attitude behind which there is generally a very passionate nature which the woman cannot express.

Now, our girl cannot answer. She can't take up the dialogue, and therefore each young man says, "All right, you can find me near the stones of the whole world." We see later that far, far away, after she has gone on a long journey, the girl finds the stones "of the whole world." They are simply three high stones and "by chance" she lies down by them and comes into contact with the bewitched young men again. The same expression, "of the whole world," is also mentioned in connection with the birds who help her in her task, so this expression, "of the whole world," must have some meaning.

It is a natural feature of the feminine, be it a woman or be it the anima in a man, to be personal. Eros is personal; it means relatedness, and one cannot relate into mid-air. Relatedness always means being related to something, to this or that. By "personal" I don't mean only from person to person; one can also have a personal relationship to one's cooking pot or to one's house or one's garden, etc. But it is the essence of femininity to give one's attention not to generalities but to concrete or personal things. And if a man has a developed anima, then he can do it too.

On the other hand, for the woman it belongs to the realm of the logos, or in her case, of the animus, to acquire some general, *impersonal* truths. In its beginning, raw form, you find that the animus says "always." Women in their animus rarely say, "This and this is so and so." They say "This and this is *always* so and so." In other words, the animus loves to generalize. That's where even he goes wrong—when he talks about personal things in generalizations. But if we look at it positively, we can say this tendency to generalize signifies that the woman has begun to take an interest in broad spiritual values and truths. She has begun struggling to free herself from that totally feminine life where she has been confined to live in a small circle with her husband, children, cats, dogs, curtains and furniture, never looking further. We see, therefore, how much those two principles, eros and logos, need each other.

Maria had been cut off from such completeness, but through her father complex she is destined to find those things that belong to "the whole world," those things which would give her a wider horizon and an expansion of her personality beyond the merely personal. If one looks in on some homes in the Mediterranean area where the *nona* or the Señora dominates the family, one finds that the ability to expand one's personality is just what is lacking. There is often a very warm, personal atmosphere among the members of the family, but one has the feeling one cannot breathe. Time stands still. There is a kind of conservative mental atmosphere that consists in the mother's or the grandmother's animus opinions, and that is that. In such cases and here in Maria's case, therefore, it is especially needed that the spirit of "the whole world"—fantasy, creativity— should be let in.

The young men always say, "You don't talk to me? All right, you can find me near the stones of the whole world." So Maria walks and walks. She seems to walk instinctively in the right direction because suddenly she finds a place where she sits down on the ground and begins to cry from fatigue and desperation. And that place where she sits down is just the very place where the three stones of the bewitched young men happen to be. And later, if you remember, it is mentioned that the young men passed here, and in this very same magic place they were bewitched by the wizard.

This is a strange circumstance: everything happens at a single specific spot.

When the three young men hunted quite by chance at that spot, they became bewitched. The girl now sits down in despair quite "by chance" in that same place and they come into contact with each other. We must therefore assume that this spot belongs in a special way to the wizard because it is there he waited for the young men in order to bewitch them.

The wizard is mentioned only once in the whole story. Like the girl in white in the Danish tale, he just whisks through and you never find out much about him. You don't know why this wizard bewitched the three sons; you don't know his reasons or anything else about him. He's just there; he functions to bewitch the young men and then he disappears. But in spite of his elusiveness, we have to go into this fact, just as we did with the white girl.

It is specifically said that the one who did the bewitching was a wizard, and therefore a masculine figure. We could assume he is like a negative father figure toward the young men. He certainly acts like one. In that case he would also be an "evil husband" of our mistress. Or, we can connect him with the peasant, the father of our heroine; then he would be the shadow of that loving father—because, although he is a loving father, in a strange way he also imposes a difficult, deadly task on his daughter, so he can't be quite as loving as he seems. We could say the wizard is in a shadow relationship; he would be the dark father compared to the too naive peasant. And he is also the dark father of those sons.

Now it is not a matter of chance that we have a wizard and not a troll. In general, the evil figures in the Mediterranean cultures are either man-eating ogres or, much more frequently, black magicians and witches. The troll is more brutish, a nature figure without much refinement, while the wizard represents all that is meant by black magic. If you have read Apuleius' story of Amor and Psyche, you know how extensive a role black magic has played in the Mediterranean culture, probably since the Stone Ages. Even today, it still occupies the minds of simple people in those countries. The few Italians I have analyzed, to my great surprise have almost always dreamt of black magicians and occultist shadow figures. That seems to be a favorite form of the shadow in those countries. In other words, aggression and power do not manifest directly or brutally so much as through intrigue and witch work. I've seen many dreams where such figures are summoned by a black pope who turns out to be an occult black magician, like a shadow figure of the white pope.

During the Nazi era, Mussolini was pressed by Hitler to persecute the Jews in his country as much as they were persecuted in Germany, but this was simply not done. It was carried out to a certain extent due to pressure from above, but the people never quite joined in. So, one could say that this absolutely cold brutality of the shadow as it manifested in Germany didn't break through in Italy. On the other hand, the shadow in the Mediterranean countries plays its tricks mostly in the form of political intrigue and corruption—not so much open aggression as sly, corrupting intrigue. I mean that not as a value judgment; it's simply that different nations have different types or styles of the shadow. Whether one prefers the one or the other is a question of personal taste. They're both black. But you see from the dreams of black magicians as black popes that they represent a shadow of the ruling collective attitude.

The twentieth-century ruling Weltanschauung in Mediterranean countries is still Catholicism. And the black occultist wizard would be its shadow, which naturally also contains all the suppressed pagan religious elements, just as the troll represents the suppressed form of pagan elements in Scandinavia.

We can therefore say that if the masculine principle is repressed at home and tires itself out mentally with political intrigue, and if it repeats old cultural patterns in a rigid way, then all creative fantasy drops into the realm of the shadow and takes on these features of destructive black magic. What is mostly lacking and what has been suppressed by the organized religions of these countries is individual fantasy. As Jung put it, individual symbol formation has been suppressed by the Church and replaced by officially recognized symbolism. So any need of the psyche for individual symbol formation has fallen into the realm of the shadow and flourishes there, in the form of black magic.

And that has now stopped the sons. It has cut them off from life and petrified them. What this means is that the whole future of the masculine principle literally has been petrified.

Jung said that the unconscious psyche of people in the Catholic Church was contained in its rich symbolism, and therefore the people were protected against certain evil influences from the unconscious. This is true, but you must remember that in our tales we have the compensatory dreams of the community. In other words, we rarely find pointed out what is positive, but only what is problematic. Our fairy tale therefore brings up the problem of the danger of suppressing the creative building of individual symbolism. If an individual happens to have a rich capacity for symbolic creativity which remains unexpressed, then it can fall into the unconscious, and in that case arises this situation of the black magician, who then hampers any further development.

Ogres are a more international family of evil beings. They are not localized in the Mediterranean, but they do appear there, and they generally illustrate or symbolize the devouring quality any archetypal unconscious complex has. You see, one can be eaten by a passion, an idea or a fantasy. All powerful but unrecognized contents of the unconscious have a tendency to eat us, in the sense of possessing us. Ogres express this general quality of all contents of the unconscious. They aren't as localized as the black magicians who seem to frequent the Mediterranean countries. Although black magicians usually come to replace all other nature demons, the eating ogres remain.

The youngest son tells Maria that now she should go to a certain farmhouse, which turns out to be the home of his mother, and to apply to work there as a maid. She does this, and becomes a servant.

The motif of the hero or heroine serving for a while is common in folk tales. Even Hercules, who was not at all the servant type, was a servant of Eurystheus for some time. This motif has to do with the fact that the heroes or heroines must prove themselves. One can be pretty sure that, when some new psychological or spiritual movement turns up, claiming to improve the world and put everything right, that it is just nonsense. All cultural renewals that have been valuable in history claimed to be able to change the world, but they did not get started by overthrowing the outer order. Buddhism did not overthrow any of the former religions or political systems. Christianity did not, at least at first, concentrate on overthrowing the system of the Roman Empire. They all kept their values hidden, for they had something more important to do than to fight with the established order. It is more important to build up the spirit of the future than to destroy what has value in the ruling order. And therefore it is typical for heroes and heroines to prove their value for a while by serving the existing principle.

In our story this is the matriarchal order, as represented by the mistress. Maria has grown up without a mother, so she must be quite unconscious of the positive and negative values of the maternal archetype. So now she has to become involved with it. She has to fall under its dominance and have it out, so to speak, with the mother principle before she can proceed. This also seems to confirm my suspicion that the wizard who destroyed the sons is not entirely unconnected to this mistress-mother. They must be connected somehow, for Maria is not told directly to destroy the wizard and redeem the sons that way. Instead, she is told to go to the mother and suffer all sorts of difficulties with her in order to redeem the sons. I think the wizard had not a little to do with the mistress's hidden spirit or animus, in the background.

Now we must look at the motif of the maids slandering Maria by telling the mistress she can do things—supernatural things—which actually she can't do at all. These maids induced the mistress to order Maria to do them. It is as if Maria hadn't enough incentive or wouldn't know enough to engage her own spirit in the task. She has to be forced into it.

We see this motif just as frequently in stories of male heroes, as noted earlier, where the jealous men in the court, for instance, make the king order the hero to do impossible tasks. It also occurs repeatedly in mythology, where the hero becomes a hero only against his own will. He wouldn't have become a hero if he hadn't been forced to by dire necessity. Think of Heracles: he would never have become Hercules if Hera hadn't pursued him all his life. That's why his name means "the glory of Hera." It was by the pressure of his unrelenting enemy, the mother goddess Hera, that Hercules performed all his heroic acts.

That is perhaps the decisive essence of the true hero: that he doesn't have the ambition to achieve anything great by himself, that he has only the wish to be true to himself and to his feelings, and that then, through a clash with the world or with other antagonizing forces, the goal is brought out. It is always useful to look at how people behave in an impossible situation, because that is where their true nature comes out. That is where one sees if the person has substance or has none. And therefore, the true hero is most frequently a person forced into great achievements by fate.

This doesn't contradict the fact that one might have a feeling of vocation or a specific goal, but it's the circumstances that bring out one's capacities. For instance, Winston Churchill knew all during his youth that one day he would have to do some heroic task for his country. That's why he exposed himself to danger in the Battle of Omduram and other places; it was not because he felt so courageous, but because he knew he wouldn't die yet. And that gave him the confidence to risk his life. But when they offered him the position of prime minister in the midst of the most desperate days of the war, apparently he knew at that moment: "This is it, this is why my life has been spared until now. Now I have to prove myself." It was the circumstances that induced him to bring forth his best capacities. He did not try to do this work on his own initiative—he didn't even like it, except, perhaps, in a deeper way because he finally had the feeling, "Now I am in the place where I have to show who I am and achieve what my life was meant for."

Now the slandering maids tell the mistress first that Maria can wash a tremendous amount of dirty linen in the river, but naturally she can't do it. It is the birds "of the whole world" who help her.

Dirty linen is a kind of shadowy dirt, the dirt we produce every day. Part of the dirt in our linen we produce ourselves by sweating and other excretions. And part of the dirt in our linen is what we pick up from our surroundings. So the dirt in our linen represents our animal side and also the shadow we pick up through social contact with other people. We are constantly becoming impure, so to speak, through interaction with our surroundings.

In German, we say we have to "wash dirty linen" if we have quarreled and now have to have it out with the other person. We say, "I said . . ." "No, you said . . ." "Yes, but I meant it differently; you misunderstood, I meant it *that* way! And it's *not* true that I said . . ." and so on. That's what we call "washing dirty linen," and generally we never really get to the end of it.

It is often the hero's task to wash away all this petty, mischievous shadow-dirt that estranges people from one another: little egoisms, the silly projections and so on that infect all communities and all relationships all the time. People think they can actually clear these matters up by the "I said . . ." "You said . . ." kinds of confrontation. People want passionately to wash their dirty linen that way. But it doesn't work. Our story shows a better way, namely that you have to call the birds of the whole world to help. And birds, of all things! The idea of birds washing linen with their claws or beaks is really a strange picture! But the birds do it, and they not only get it clean but they even manage to get it dried in a single afternoon.

In hexagram 16 of the *I Ching,* called "Enthusiasm," it says that there can be no great achievements in a community unless a great uniting feeling or idea brings the people together.[28] Because it is a Chinese paradigm, it goes on to say that in musical or theatrical performances, the Chinese meet in their ancestral cult and that cleans away all pettiness. It activates their feeling on a higher level. It gives them a new, enthusiastic sense of the meaning of life, and that washes away all the petty negative projections human beings have on each other.

I have seen that myself again and again—that it is useful to show someone the animus or the shadow or some other complex, to have it out in "washing dirty linen," but it is very often best just to help people to find the essential meaning of their lives, what they are there for. When they become interested in that, they completely lose interest in petty nonsense. When the main water of life in a human being is flowing again, when there is, for instance, some meaningful creative interest, then one no longer has time to spend hours on the phone to one's sister or brother or a friend to complain that she or he has been wrong. One just hasn't the time, and therefore one is much more inclined to think, "Oh well, let it be. Never mind. It may be my fault, so let's make peace." Because life is flowing again. When one finds the essential meaning of one's life, this has a purifying effect upon one's "dirty linen" affairs.

---

[28] *The I Ching or Book of Changes,* trans. Richard Wilhelm, rendered into English by Cary F. Baynes (Bollingen Series XIX; Princeton: Princeton University Press, 1967), pp. 67ff.

So now we can understand why it is birds that help Maria: birds represent fantasies, and obviously here they represent creative fantasies. In our story, Maria's creative symbol-forming fantasies are precisely what have been blocked. So, with the help of those birds, Maria can finish off all the nonsense that has accumulated through the stagnation of her life.

But the maids are not satisfied, so they next induce the mistress to order Maria to obtain healing water for her eyes. She has cried so much, remember, that she has ruined her eyts. Again Maria has to go to the river—to the essential flow of life—and there she has to call out, "Birds of the whole world, cry with me." She collects those tears in a glass and with the tears and the feather which she puts into the water of the tears, she heals the eyes of her mistress.

In mythology, tears are often supposed to have a redeeming and healing effect. If you have ever dealt with people who have become petrified by suffering, you know how redeeming it is if they can cry. Once a person reaches a certain climax of suffering, very often he or she cannot cry or break down anymore. They simply harden in horror. And then there is danger ahead.

I once read of an American psychiatrist who investigated the reactions of people who had been hospitalized in England after being taken out of bombed houses. Often those people themselves were not badly hurt, but as soon as they came back to consciousness, one had to tell them that their husband or their children or their whole family had been killed or crippled and so on. And this heartless psychiatrist—I still can't understand how that man could do such a thing—simply watched the reactions of these unfortunate people and found that most of them broke down within three days. They either broke down crying at once, or they reacted by turning white and horrified, but sooner or later, within three days, they broke down and cried.

The psychiatrist visited these people again after ten years, and though they were still often very depressed or grieving, none of them had any serious neurotic problems. But there were a few individuals who did not break down and cry, who petrified in horror and stayed that way. They simply said, "Yes, thank you for telling me." The others did this sometimes too at first, but some never came out of their first petrified reaction. They never cried. And when the psychiatrist visited those people after ten years, he found what you could call a serious war psychosis, a serious trauma.

From that you see how tears and crying are a healing reaction. Tears are necessary for the realization of one's pain, and they seem to have this natural function of melting the petrifying shock effects. They melt them and bring us back into the human realm.

Tears also have an induction effect on our surroundings. When we cry, this is an appeal for help and those around us react with feeling. Perhaps the origin of this characteristic response to crying comes from those many appeals for help that you find in the animal realm. There are certain cries among wild dogs and apes and so on that function purely to make the surrounding tribe turn toward the animal in distress. They are a call for help. And tears in humans probably have that function too, so they both heal us and bring us into touch with others. One is more or less accustomed to young children howling at the top of their lungs for all sorts of things that we don't think so terribly bad. But if an adult breaks down in front of us and cries, it is always terribly moving, and one feels very upset. I always feel *awful*. I think, "Oh my God, I should now show my feeling, but *how?*" One feels at such times that no words, no reasonable talk, will help. Only a human gesture from one human being to another will help. Crying has this immediate appeal.

Now we know that the sons in our story are petrified—*literally* petrified, not just bewitched into animals or other things. And the mother, like the Greek Niobe, is bereft at the loss of her children and has cried her eyes out. To "cry one's eyes out" means that one has cried so much that one cannot cry any more. One is then in a state of resigned deadness. The mistress therefore needs the compassion of the birds, the compassionate, understanding fantasy only Maria can call up. If we have no imagination, we have no empathy, because generally our suffering is not the same as another's. But, generally, we do understand the suffering of others even when we have not had the same experience. We have an imaginative fantasy which enables us to empathize, and it is essential that this be called forth, for it can heal the eyes.

In alchemy, the magical water from which the Philosophers' Stone is made— called the mercurius, the permanent immortal water, and by many other names—refers to the *prima materia*. In psychological language, the *prima materia* would be the vitality of the unconscious psyche. One of its names is *collyrium philosophorum*, the "eye water" of the philosophers. Mercurius is the eye water of the philosophers. If your put it on your eyes, your eyes will open to a new sight. There are many texts praising this alchemical substance.

Now, Maria can also constellate the right type of understanding. She can call forth certain fantasies that enable her to understand her mistress and thus heal her. There are many alchemical stories where the alchemist is searching for the phoenix; the famous Michael Maier, for example, only catches a feather, but even with this one feather he can work miracles and heal people.

In fact, the feather of the miraculous bird that lives at the end of the world is a motif in alchemy that spread quite far into European folklore. You even find German fairy tales where the feather of the phoenix has to be found. These are borrowed directly from alchemical symbolism.[29]

Maria is instructed to use a single feather instead of the whole bird. This means the feather is *pars pro toto,* a part in place of the whole thing, but it also means she only has a hunch or an intuition—not the whole idea. If you have only a feather of the phoenix, it means you haven't grasped the psychological mystery that is expressed by the symbol of the whole bird. You have only *one* aspect, one hunch about it. But even that is infinitely healing, and so here Maria has at least a partial understanding of her mistress. She worked as a servant to the mother, a position she had not held previously, and has now forged a relationship to her.

Now, the last task becomes the redemption of the mistress's three sons. This time, all the girls of the surrounding villages have to come with burning candles, to form a procession and walk three times around the stones. No candle can be allowed to blow out before this has been achieved.

Here again we have a large group of females, like the evil maids. We don't know how many there are in either group, but obviously they function in a compensatory way. Maria not only gathers the birds of the whole world, she also gathers all the feminine forces available in the collective. They have to come together and concentrate for this big, final action: not only the birds, which are the creative fantasy in the unconscious, but the whole feminine in its human reality in the unconscious or the collective has to be assembled in a procession. The procession has to go three times around the stones. That is the famous *circulatio;* in all religions of the world this action has a magical effect by concentrating all the forces of the psyche onto one point.

The burning candles in this context are obviously related to a Catholic viewpoint. They represent the little light everyone has to carry in order to contribute to the solution of the problem. Processions are not an invention of the Catholic Church. There were already processions in the antique mystery cults, in the Egyptian religion and in many other religions all over the world. Generally they are connected with the idea of renewal and the aim of including all the people in the religious act. In Egypt, at the great Sed festival, the king left the palace and the people carried behind him his fourteen *kas* in the form of flags. He moved to the temple, and there he went through a kind of ritual death and renewal. That procession was meant to renew the spiritual life of the whole country. Also, the

---

29 See *Mysterium Coniunctionis,* CW 14, chap. 3d, "The Fourth of the Three."

Egyptians carried their statues in procession to the Nile and washed them there, and by that renewed them.

In all religions, the gods live in sacred groves or temples, and there they tend to become a bit segregated, just as the king in his palace becomes segregated. The gods are in those temples, and one goes to visit them from to time with a sacrifice. Otherwise one tends to fall apart, and that's why these great powers are brought out among the people from time to time. That is an archetypal motif. Even kings must move from time to time; by that they become *moving*—moving in the psychological sense of the word. Otherwise the people are no longer moved by their king and what he symbolizes.

Processions in Catholicism also have to do with redistributing a blessing to all the sacred stations where the procession stops. At these places the people say certain prayers and decorate their statues, for example crucifixes or statues of the Virgin Mary. Even the sacred Host is carried in the tabernacle through the streets at such times, while normally it is kept most carefully hidden in the church.

Being in procession means to move. It also symbolizes the idea that the archetypes of the collective unconscious are not static. They are in constant movement from one place to another. That is symbolically expressed in the idea of the procession. So, since petrification is what has to be healed in this case, procession would be essentially the countermagic, the way needed to bring the movement of life back.

Now, as the procession goes round the three stones, with all the girls carrying their candles, a gust of wind comes and blows out Maria's candle. "Alas!" she cries, "my candle went out!" And immediately the stones open. The three young men come out and say, "Thank God you spoke. Now we are redeemed"—because that was the condition: the person who had burned the three carnations had to talk near the stones.

This is a strange and puzzling motif. Ordinarily one would suppose that the ritual of circumambulation with holy or blessed candles would be sufficient in itself to bring the cursed sons back to life. Here, on the contrary, it is the fact that the ritual has gone wrong that is the redeeming factor. We must therefore look for parallels.

I have not found any other tales where a mistake in the prescribed ritual is the redeeming factor, but I did find one where holy candles have a negative aspect. There is a northern German fairy tale which in English is called "The Three Black Princesses."[30] In this story, a young man is sold to the devil by his father.

---

[30] *The Complete Grimm's Fairy Tales,* p. 620.

The devil takes him away to Hell, but on the way he escapes and goes into a deep dark forest. In it he finds a castle that is entirely hung over with black curtains. When he enters, he finds three completely pitch-black princesses sitting there. They tell him they have been cursed, and the only way he can redeem them is to stay with them for three years without talking. He swears to do that, but after awhile he misses his mother and decides to go home for a short time. The princesses are greatly distressed because they fear it will be dangerous for the young man to visit his mother. In fact, when he tells his mother what he has been doing she says it is an uncanny business, that he ought to take holy water and candles, sprinkle holy water on them and put some candle light on them.

He returns to the princesses and follows his mother's advice, but the moment he drops the water on them, the upper part of their bodies turns white while the lower part remains black, and they cry out, "You accursed dog, our blood shall cry for vengeance on you! . . . We have still three brothers who are bound by seven chains—they shall tear you to pieces!" Then the young man hears a thundering noise. He manages to jump out the window just before the whole castle collapses, but he breaks his leg and becomes a cripple.

There you see that the use of holy candles to chase away demons in an exorcising ritual has a negative effect. We can guess why: it is because the hero's mother advised it. The mother wanted to prevent her son from redeeming the feminine principle, and to do so she misused a sacred object of the Church. We could say her animus misused the means of the Church for her own egocentric purpose. The young man acts out of his mother complex, and on account of that the exorcism goes wrong.

It happens quite frequently that when one misuses a religious ritual it has a destructive effect, working as a kind of black magic. I remember, for instance, a young girl who had a very negative mother complex. Her mother was a real dragon, very destructive. The girl's early childhood dream was that she was lying in bed when suddenly she heard her mother moving about in the next room, so she went and peeped through the door. She saw a black man approaching her mother. But the mother, who was terribly pious, had a Bible nearby which she read every evening. It was black with a golden cross. The mother took this Bible and held it up against the black man, and the black man fled. The girl woke up sweating with terror, but not because she was afraid of the black man; rather, she was terrified at having seen her mother do that magical action.

According to this dream, the mother had an absolutely hellish animus and a suicidal tendency. She told her children repeatedly, "Oh, I wish I hadn't married and that you didn't exist." So you can imagine what a mother she was!

You could say that the mother was in a close connection with the devil. She was constantly threatened by the greatest destructiveness, and she used her so-called piousness to ward off her evil animus. But in fact, she really served the evil animus with piousness. She even used the Bible and her pious side in order to have commerce with the devil. And the dream of that young girl, who was only about three years old at the time, tried to show her what was going on in the unconscious background of her mother.

What is important for us to note is that here too we have a magical gesture that makes use of a positive religious symbol, but which is used for the wrong purpose. Therefore it has a terrifying and destructive effect. There is a Chinese saying that captures this point: "The right means in the hands of the wrong man work in the wrong way, just as the wrong means in the hands of the right man work in the right way." It also shows us that the Christian teaching and the Christian Weltanschauung, and in our case the Christian ritual, can be misused for egocentric ends, or in order to avoid an inner conflict. Then it is exactly the same thing as using black magic. We can therefore assume that in our fairy tale the religious ritual of the procession and the circumambulation of the stones with the candles, which is a purely Christian ritual, is negative. Hence the gust of wind that puts out the candle is the redeeming thing.

Now, the wind is a form of manifestation of the Holy Ghost. If you remember, the Holy Ghost came down at Whitsun in the form of a wind filling the whole room, and then there were flames on the heads of the Apostles. This is a continuation of the concept of the *Ruach-Yahweh,* the spirit of God, and was identified also with the spirit of God hovering over the waters in Genesis 1.[31] We must therefore ask ourselves, "What is the difference between the candle-light and the wind?"

Obviously, candlelight has to do with consciousness. In general, when candles are carried by people, or when you put a candle on the grave of a dead person as one still does in many Catholic countries, it represents the light of individual consciousness of that person, as though one were saying, "May that person keep his or her light in the darkness of death." That is what this gesture expresses. And when you carry a candle in the church, you offer to God your effort toward personal individual consciousness, the small light you carry through the darkness of the world.

The wind, on the contrary, has more to do with inspiration, with being emo-

---

[31] [See Rivkah Schärf Kluger, *Psyche in Scripture: The Idea of the Chosen People and Other Essays* (Toronto: Inner City Books, 1995), pp. 36ff.—Ed.]

tionally gripped by the spirit. The word "inspiration" comes from the Latin *spirare*, "to breathe." It is not so much a phenomenon of concentrated consciousness as of being moved by the spirit, swept up by some content from the unconscious, gripped by a religious experience. The wind comes from the unconscious and in certain situations can even temporarily put out the light of consciousness.

Now, finally, we come closer to an explanation of the petrification of the three young men. In the collective conscious situation that is compensated by this fairy tale, the Christian Church ritual had become a spiritless affair, a kind of mechanical magic. That is the danger of all rituals carried out with concrete gestures and prescribed prayers: they become lifeless and repetitive affairs to which one attributes a magical effect. And then one begins to use them thoughtlessly to protect oneself against the unconscious.

Jung often pointed out that the ritual of the Church serves to protect one against the immediate impact of meeting the collective unconscious and its potential dangers. But though this is often positive, it can also be negative. Whenever the ritual becomes an autonomous, habitual action that is thoughtlessly applied, contact with the unconscious is broken off too much; then it becomes a purely formal, mechanical affair. It becomes antireligious, in a sense. It prevents one from being immediately gripped by a religious experience. It literally cuts the Holy Ghost out of the Church.

We saw earlier that the wizard, who bewitched and cursed the three young men into stones, was a black magic occult master, a counter-pope, a shadow figure of the ruling conscious attitude. We can now see how that works. It is the dark, shadow side of the Christian attitude that has led to this petrification: ritualization that no longer has any spiritual meaning and which cuts one off from the experience of the unconscious instead of making a bridge to it. That is why, when the wind *puts out* the candle, we find the redeeming factor. There is a moment of darkness, so to speak—a hole in the ritual—through which a manifestation of the divine can break in. Generally, when one circumambulates in a religious ritual, one is very careful to prevent the formation of such holes, for the assumption is that through them the devil may break in. But here it is God or the Holy Ghost who wants to break in and who has been excluded by the ritual. This is what makes Maria speak, to cry out in despair.

There is a great temptation, when one is "contained" in the framework of an institutionalized religion, to become thoughtless, to accept "truths" from religious leaders, while contenting oneself in everyday life to simply making the appropriate gestures. One no longer searches and suffers personally from religious problems, for these have been settled long ago by other people; one has only to believe what one is told. In this way one can suppress an enormous amount of suffering, because when asking searching questions about God or the meaning of life, one inevitably gets into deep waters and profound suffering. That's why people repress these questions and, as the German proverb says, "Gott einen guten Mann sein lassen"—leave God to be a good man. They leave him alone and they do not ask the burning questions of who He is and how we, the single individuals of the human race, might connect with Him.

Maria's candle went out, and its going out was for her a call, indicating that she was meant to suffer, to go through agony and despair. And through this suffering she would come to a new light, a new conscious attitude. Her psychological suffering redeems the three cursed sons.

Now the mother and her sons are happy. Maria marries the youngest son because she loves him, and she pardons the maids who slandered her because they ask her to. This is the union of opposites, a common solution in fairy tales: the coming together of conscious and unconscious. The dark side of the psyche and the light side are united, and even the dark side is to a certain extent integrated, since the evil maids are not punished.

As in all fairy tales, there *is* a solution, but it is not quite perfect. And as in many others, one feels at first that it is a wonderful solution. But then one begins to be puzzled by it. We were puzzled about the solution in the last fairy tale, and now here, because nothing has happened with the evil wizard! In fact, the end of this fairy tale is even a bit more superficial than the ending of our Danish troll story, because there, at least, the troll is killed and the people he had cursed were redeemed with his blood. But here the wizard, who never appears but is only mentioned, stays discreetly in the background; we can expect, therefore, that he will show his hand again on the next propitious occasion.

In other words, there is a reconnection of the ritual religious attitude with certain aspects of personal emotion and individual inspiration, but the problem of evil is in no way solved or even addressed. It is only skimmed on the surface. This deep problem is never really resolved, as is shown by the pardoning of the evil maids. I would not be surprised if they got into mischief again.

This situation corresponds historically to the Franciscan reformation of the Catholic Church. The Church at the time of St. Francis of Assisi had been in great danger of completely degenerating into pure formalism, secretly overwhelmed by black magic and power drives. It was reformed and purified in the Franciscan Orders: the connection with Holy Ghost inspiration and immediate religious experience was revived. But here, too, the problem of evil was not really touched. The Franciscans put the soul back into the Church, so to speak, but they still ignored the problem of evil. They only skimmed over the surface.

Movements such as this take place again and again, and I do not mean to disparage them. "The Three Carnations" does show a tremendously positive compensatory development to the existing collective consciousness. Yet there is always that "But . . ." which we must never overlook.

3
The Rejected Princess
(Chinese)

Now we will make a tremendous jump and go to China. This tale, in a volume collected and edited by Richard Wilhelm, is called "The Rejected Princess."[32]

In the time of the Tung Dynasty there was a man called Liu I, who failed his doctoral exams. So he went home. He rode for six or seven miles when suddenly a bird rose out of a field. His horse shied and ran ten miles before he was able to stop it. And there before him he saw a woman herding sheep on the slope of a mountain. She was absolutely beautiful, but her face showed great sorrow.

He asked her what was the matter. She began to cry and said, "Luck has left me. As you are so kind to ask me, I'll tell you. I'm the youngest daughter of the Dragon King of the Dungting Lake, and I was married to the second son of the Dragon King of Ging Chou. My husband was very frivolous and had an affair with an evil maid, and so he pushed me out of the house. I complained to my parents-in-law, but they had such a blind love for their son that they did nothing for me, and they even sent me out now to herd the sheep."

The woman began to cry again, and continued, "The Dungting Lake is very far from here, but I've heard that on your way back home, you will be passing there. Could you give a letter to my father? Or can you not do it?" Liu I said, "Your words have touched me deeply, and if I had wings I would fly away with you. I'll certainly take your letter to your father, but the Dungting Lake is very big. How can I find him there?"

She said, "On the south shore of the sea is an orange tree. The people call it the sacrificial tree. When you get there, you must take off your girdle and swing it three times toward the orange tree, and then someone will appear who will guide you. Tell my father in what great despair I am." She took out a letter from her clothes and gave it to Liu I. Then she bowed before him and looked toward the East, and Liu I began to cry. He took the letter, and as he was leaving he asked her, "I don't know why you should herd sheep. Do the gods also kill sheep?" "These are not ordinary sheep," the woman said. "They are rain servants." "What are rain servants?" "They are thunder rams," said the woman.

And when he looked at them more closely, Liu I saw that the animals were indeed very proud and beautiful, quite different from ordinary sheep. He then left, but added, "If ever you come back happily to the Dungting Lake, you must then

---

[32] MDW, *Chinesische Volksmärchen*, no. 55 (Jena: Diederichs, 1919).

not treat me as a stranger." The woman said, "How could I treat you as a stranger? You shall be my best friend." And so they parted.

After a month, Liu I came to the Dungting Lake, and he found the orange tree and did everything he was instructed to do. As soon as he had, a warrior came out of the sea and asked, "Where do you come from?" Liu I said, "I have an important message for the king." The warrior gave him a sign, and also made a sign over the water, and a firm road came out of the sea, and he led Liu I in. There he found the dragon castle with its thousand entrances. Marvelous flowers and strange herbs were growing around it.

The warrior asked Liu I to wait on one side of the great hall. Liu I asked, "What is this place?" "This is the ghost hall," the warrior answered. Liu I looked around and saw all the most precious gems and treasures of the human world. There were columns of jasper and seats of coral and curtains of crystal. And there was a strange smell in the room that seemed to blend into the darkness.

Liu I had to wait a long time for the king. The warrior told him that his majesty was standing on the coral tower with the sun priest discussing the Holy Book of the Fire, but that he would soon be back. Liu I asked, "What is this Holy Book of the Fire?" The warrior answered, "Our majesty is a dragon. The dragons are great through the power of water. With one wave they can cover mountains and valley. The priest is a human being. The priests are great through the power of fire. With one candle they can burn down the greatest palaces. Fire and water fight each other because they have a different essence. Therefore our majesty is now talking with the priest to find a way for fire and water to complement each other."

Before they had finished, a man appeared in a purple robe. At that moment the warrior said, "This is my lord." Liu I bowed before him, and the Dragon King said, "Aren't you a living human being? Why do you come here?" Liu I gave his name and said, "I was in the capital and I failed my exams. And when I passed the Ging Chou River, I saw your beloved daughter herding sheep in the wilderness. The wind blew through her hair and the rain made her wet. I could see her sorrow. She told me her husband had rejected her, and she cried. She gave me a letter for you. That's why I've come."

He gave the letter to the king, who read it and sighed, "This is all my fault. I gave her a bad husband. I wanted to marry my daughter early, and now I have brought her into distress. I am very grateful to you." He began to cry, and everyone in the vicinity also cried. And after awhile, even inside the palace one could hear a loud crying.

The king became frightened and said to one of his servants, "Go in and tell them they shouldn't cry so loudly, because Tsian Tang might hear." "Who is Tsian Tang?" asked Liu I. "That's my beloved brother," said the Dragon King. "He was once the ruler of the Tsian Tang River, but now he's deposed." "Why shouldn't he hear the crying?" "He's so wild that I'm afraid there could be a great catastrophe if he did, just like the flood he caused many years ago. At that time, my brother was annoyed with the Emperor of Heaven, so he sent a flood that covered the five big mountains and lasted nine years. The master became angry with him, and since then he has been chained to a pillar in my palace."

But even as the king was telling this tale, they heard a terrifying noise that tore the heavens apart. The earth quaked, the whole palace shook and a red dragon appeared. The dragon was a thousand feet long, with burning eyes and a blood-red tongue, blood-red skin and a fiery beard. He was dragging behind him the column to which he was chained. Lightning and thunder surrounded his body. Snow, rain and hail whirled around him. Then, with a clap of thunder, he went up to heaven.

Liu I fell on the floor from fright, but the king helped him up and said, "Don't be afraid. My brother in his rage has gone to Ging Chou, and we will soon have good news." And so he arranged a dinner party, and it was good weather again, and they had a marvelous time.

Suddenly, a young man with a purple robe and a high hat came in. He had a sword in his hand. He looked very male and heroic, and behind him was a girl of great beauty. As soon as Liu I saw her, he knew it was the dragon princess he had met on his way. She was very well received and presented the young man with her, saying, "This is Tsian Tang, my uncle." [In other words, the wild dragon that had ascended to heaven had turned into this young man who now had brought his niece back to the Dragon King's palace.]

The king asked him, "Have you destroyed the horrible dragon?" [He was referring to the husband of the dragon princess.] "Oh, yes!" "How many have you killed?" "Six hundred thousand." "Have you destroyed any fields?" "Eight hundred miles far!" "And where is the evil husband?" "I've eaten him up."

The king said, "No one should be made to bear what my daughter's frivolous husband has done, but you have been a bit too brutal with him. You must not do such a thing again." And Tsian Tang promised.

That evening in the castle they had a marvelous dinner party together, with much wonderful entertainment and a grand menu. They gave Liu I many beautiful presents of pearls and coral and jade, and they also gave him a lot to drink. Liu I was the center of attention at the party, and he accepted the gifts graciously and was very happy and grateful to all. When the meal was finished, he slept in the castle of the frozen splendor.

The next day they had another meal, but Tsian Tang was still a bit drunk and so he was rather careless about his manners. He said to Liu I, "The princess of the Dungting Lake is very beautiful. She has been rejected by her husband, so her marriage is now dissolved. She should have another husband. If you wish it, it would be to your advantage to marry her. If you don't want her, then you may go, but if we meet each other again, I will not speak to you and I will pretend I don't even know you."

Liu I was furious about the arrogant way in which Tsian Tang spoke to him. The blood went to his head and he said, "I brought the princess's letter here because I was sorry for her, not to get any advantage for myself! To kill the husband and then take the woman away is something no decent man would do. Besides, I'm an ordinary man, so I'd rather die than act according to your remarks."

Tsian Tang got up and apologized humbly, and even the Dragon King begged Liu to pardon this tactlessness, but they didn't speak any more about marriage. On the next day, when Liu I was to depart, the queen of the Dungting Lake gave him another meal. And the queen said to him, "My daughter is deeply grateful to you, but now we will have no chance to pay you back. We are very sorry you are leaving." Then she ordered the princess to thank Liu I. She said, "Will we never see each other again?" And she began to cry. Liu I had been angry and had resisted Tsian Tang, but when he saw the beautiful princess crying before him, he became terribly sorry. Nonetheless, he pulled himself together and went away.

When he arrived in his home land, the treasures he had received at the castle made him far richer than any of his neighbors, even though he had already sold or spent most of them. Twice he married, and twice his wife died after a short time. So now he lived alone in the capital. He was still looking for a third wife, so a marriage broker told him that in the North there lived a widow with a beautiful daughter. "Her father was a Taoist." [The father had by that time disappeared into the clouds without returning.] They were living in great poverty, but the girl was very beautiful. Liu I was happy. The marriage was arranged. But on the evening of the wedding, when the bride took away her veil, he discovered that she looked a lot like the dragon princess. He asked her if she *was* the dragon princess, but she only smiled and said nothing.

After a year she had a son. On the day after the birth, she said to her husband, "Now I will tell you how it is. I *am* the princess of the Dungting Lake. When you refused my uncle's offer and went away, I became sick from longing for you and nearly died. My parents wanted to call you, but they were afraid you would be shocked about having children, since I am a dragon princess. So my parents clothed me as a human girl and arranged for me to be married to you. Until now, I didn't dare to tell you, but now that I have given you a son, I hope you will transfer the love you have for him also to his mother."

Liu I came back as from a deep trance, and was deeply happy, and they loved each other from then on. But one day his wife said, "If you want to live with me always, we cannot continue to live in the human world. We dragons live to be ten thousand years old, and it is fitting that you should become as old as I. So please come back with me to the Dungting Lake."

Ten years passed, and no one knew where Liu I had disappeared. But by chance, one of his cousins went to the Dungting Lake, and suddenly a blue mountain came out of the water. The fishermen in their boats said, "But in this place there are no mountains. That must be a water demon." While they were discussing this and looking around, a ship came to them from the mountain, and from its bow the crew lowered a little boat into the water. On both sides of the boat stood fairies. In the middle of the boat was a man. It was Liu I. He waved to his cousin to come into the boat. As soon as the cousin stepped into the boat it changed back into a mountain, and on the mountain was a beautiful castle, and in the castle was Liu I, surrounded by musicians and beautiful colors. They greeted each other, and Liu I said to his cousin, "We are only a minute apart in age, but already you have gray hair." The cousin said, "You are a blessed god, but I have a mortal body. That's my fate."

Liu I then gave his cousin fifty pills and said, "Each pill will prolong your life for a year. When those years are over, come and stay no longer in the dust of earthly life which is only despair and sorrow." And he sent him back across the lake and disappeared. The cousin retired into the world, but after fifty years, when he had eaten all the pills, he too disappeared and was never seen again.

You see, it's very elaborate, all this polite talk, so typically Chinese. We can simply let ourselves be charmed by them. We needn't interpret anything at all, for the details speak for themselves, so I will only concentrate on the basic structure of the story.

Here the hero is a man who failed his exams. I haven't seen this in any other fairy tale, but in China, for all higher posts in the state service, one had to achieve an advanced education in a very demanding system. One had to study for many, many years, learn all the classic books by heart, and so on. When a student had done this and passed the very difficult examinations, he could then qualify for the senior posts at the emperor's court, or in the military.

When Liu I failed the exams, he was finished socially. He could only retire and live as a private person (if he had money), or else become a lowly employee of some kind. We can find parallels from other countries where the hero of the story is also a social failure. For example, it could be the youngest son whom everyone considers stupid. Or there are many European fairy tales where the hero is a soldier who deserts: he was in military service but then he tires of it and runs away. He becomes an outlaw who doesn't know where to go or where to turn. Or you might have a wounded soldier who has been sent away from the army because he is of no more use; he wanders around as a cripple without money and then comes into the fairy world, there to become the great hero.

You can see immediately the difference between the archetype itself and an archetypal image. It belongs to the archetype of the hero to be some kind of social failure, but in each country the specific image differs slightly. Only the basic structure behind it is common to them all.

In this case, a man has arrived at a cul de sac that he doesn't know how to get out of. And that, as Jung pointed out, is typically the beginning of the individuation process. It is as if the unconscious arranges a complete failure for those it has called to become heroes and achieve higher consciousness or some specific inner task. So Liu I's failure in his exams marks that call from the unconscious that he is meant to go some inner way.

Still, you can imagine his utter despair, no longer having a secure future. When he rides home, a bird flies up; that frightens his horse, which runs ten miles away—not in the direction he wants to go, naturally.

The appearance of the bird is an augury. You know that birds appearing and doing the unexpected represents a sign from the gods. For instance, the Roman legions preferred to camp where they saw an eagle circling overhead, especially in the vicinity of an eagle's nest. And in the science of bird watching, it was important to note if they came from the right or the left, where they circled or settled, etc. These things were part of a whole science among the Etruscans, and bird watching continued to be a science among the ancient Romans. Also, in the Germanic civilization, the ravens of Wotan had something to say, the appearance of the eagle was interpreted, and so on. In China it is the same way; for instance, to see the flight of wild geese in the sky is a lucky sign.

In our story we don't know what type of bird it is, but we know this appearance is a typical sign from the unconscious. The bird represents an intuitive, autonomous thought jumping up, so to speak. It is the unexpected spiritual content that spooks Liu I's horse.

This is so frequently the case: the first intimation people get that the unconscious is *really real* simply terrifies them. Jung often quotes the dream of a professor of theology who had started analysis with him. One of his first dreams was that he was going through the woods to a dark lake, and the lake was lying quite undisturbed in the darkness, when suddenly a gust of wind came and rippled the surface of the lake in little waves. He woke with a cry of terror, and then left analysis. He had had enough. The panic was too great.

Jung comments that this is like the miracle of the pond of Bethesda, a manifestation of the Holy Ghost, just the kind of thing one might think a theologian would be deeply moved and delighted about. But obviously, this man was one of those who like to talk about such things and yet panic when faced with them in reality.

Another case Jung tells about is of a man who couldn't get his active imagination to work. He couldn't get himself close to the unconscious at all, and then finally, after about three weeks of attempting to do so in vain, he had a vision of a *Steinbock*, a capricorn, a kind of wild mountain goat. It's a specific thing here in Switzerland. So the man saw a capricorn, and Jung said, "All right, that's very good. Now you look at the capricorn. Look at what it's doing." But the capricorn didn't move. Each time the man came to analysis, he said he had stared at the capricorn but it still didn't move. Then one night at midnight, the telephone rang in Jung's house, and when he went to the phone the terrified voice came through, "The capricorn has moved its head!"

The man was in a complete panic. He stopped his active imagination and nothing could make him go on. That was the end of it. You see, it was too outrageous that something he thought he had only imagined could act autonomously. Don't laugh! There are many people like that. When the unconscious becomes real in a spooky way, they become frightened.

Anyway, Liu I's bird is an arrangement by the unconscious to bring him together with the dragon princess, whom he finds herding sheep.

In the *I Ching* there is a hexagram that says, "The flying bird brings a message," so in China as well as everywhere else in the world a flying bird symbolizes a message. Liu I's bird brings the first message. Because he has failed the exams, he's in a depressed mental level, and now his real fate is approaching from the unconscious. There he meets the dragon princess herding sheep. He finds out that those sheep aren't ordinary sheep but "rain servants" and "thunder rams." Strangely enough, Liu I asks, "What are rain servants?" The princess explains that they are thunder rams, but that's all she answers. That is beautiful because it's so dreamlike. That's how it happens in dreams: you ask a person a question about a riddle and you get an even more mysterious answer. In the dream you feel this is quite satisfactory, but when you wake up in the morning you can't find the explanation again. So this shows how Liu I is already gliding into the dream world.

It is interesting that in the same volume there is another story of a dragon princess who asks for a man's help. There is a big nature catastrophe, and a man from a town has to judge a lot of people who have stolen things in connection with this catastrophe. Suddenly, while sitting in the judge's chair, he falls asleep. And then a dragon princess comes to help him. She had been insulted by someone, so then the judge assembles a great army and overcomes the dragon princess's enemies. The story continues for a few more pages but then it ends abruptly: suddenly the man woke up! So we find at the end that the whole story is actually told as a dream. Liu I's story is not told as a dream, but it is as if he were gliding into that dreamlike world.

I must go into the symbolism of the dragon which is of such decisive important throughout the story. The dragon in China, in contrast to European mythology, is mainly a positive figure. It represents yang, the male principle in the cosmic order. It stands for creativity, dynamism, the force to move or to realize things. It is therefore present in all Chinese symbols of energy, especially of electric charge. One explained thunder storms as the dragon going over the sky. The dragons make all the violent weather phenomena, as in our story the brother of the Dragon King, Tsian Tang, makes hail, snow, rain, thunder and lightning. He is a symbol of all the creative but sometimes dangerous powers in nature.

In the *I Ching* the dragon belongs to the trigram Ch'ien, heaven. In the first hexagram, "The Creative," every line speaks about the dragon: there is the hidden dragon in the first, the dragon appearing on the field in the second, the dragon swinging up to the sky in the fourth, and so on. And the uppermost line carries the comment, "Arrogant dragon will have cause to repent."[33] It is the only line in the first hexagram where the dragon has a negative aspect, where he symbolizes a titanic power that has gone too far, an exaggeration of the male dynamic principle. (The dragon does not yet repent because the feminine principle does not come in until the second hexagram.)

The arrogance of the dragon shows up in our story, too. You remember how the uncle of the princess and the brother of the Dragon King behaves after the dinner party when he's drunk, treating our hero so haughtily and scornfully, and how that behavior calls forth Liu I's resistance. But otherwise, dragons are completely benevolent divinities of rivers and lakes, and of meteorological phenomena in the sky such as rain, snow and thunder.

In China as in other countries, sheep are also associated with clouds. We even have the expression "fleecy clouds"; in German we call them *Lammen Wölkchen,* "lamb clouds." The idea is that the clouds are like a flock of sheep traveling across the sky. And too, the idea of thunder clouds being rams is another international mythological image. The dragon princess thus shows that even in her more or less diminished state of shepherding, she has still kept her function as a nature goddess. She tells our hero, Liu I, that she had been married to the second son of the Dragon King of Ging Chou, and that an evil maid took precedence over her in the eyes of her husband. She has been rejected, and her parents-in-law have even made her into a shepherdess. We find out later that she had married this prince of Ging Chou on the advice of her father, who for the wrong reasons pushed her into an unsuitable marriage.

This sounds at first quite unlike the basic structure of European and Oriental

---

[33] *I Ching*, p. 9.

fairy tales, but we will see that that basic structure can be found if we look more closely at the story.

In our country there are many fairy tales where a father secretly doesn't want to give away his daughter, and therefore he imposes difficult and unusual conditions on her would-be suitors. For instance, in a Turkestan story, "The Magic Horse,"[34] the father feeds a louse until it becomes the size of an elephant. He kills it and makes shoes from its skin. Then he says, "Only the one who can guess what kind of leather these shoes are made from can marry my daughter." No human being can guess it, but an evil man-eating ghost turns up at court and guesses it is louse leather, so he gets the princess. There are also kings who imprison their daughters in an ivory or brass tower, or a brass coffin, etc. They make a riddle which their daughters' suitors have to answer. But they always do this with the secret intention of preventing the daughter from ever marrying.

Now, our Dragon King doesn't do that. He only says that he wanted to marry her off especially early, but that's what caused her difficulties. Traditionally in China, marriage was a purely social arrangement between families. Arranging an acceptable marriage always involved power plays, money and intrigue, but here the father destroyed his daughter's life presumably by also engaging in some political intrigue—he probably wanted a connection with the Ging Chou family. So she, like Liu I, is pushed into a social catastrophe: he by failing the exams, she by a disastrous marriage. The princess is prevented from having a career in the human realm, and she is pushed out of her royal role in the Dragon King's lake. Yet, although this lowers her in the realm of human beings, it exalts her in the realm of the gods.

We see here a compensatory movement: the pulling away from the conscious human realm toward the unconscious is compensated by an advance from the unconscious toward consciousness. There are European fairy tales where princesses who are similarly ill-treated by their fathers meet a simple Dummling from the lower layer of the population who redeems them and becomes a prince. In these stories too, we have that double movement—a lowering of the level of consciousness toward the unconscious, while simultaneously there is a movement from the unconscious toward consciousness. This latter is demonstrated in our story by the fact that the dragon princess is expelled from the Ging Chou kingdom.

We must now look at the lake from which the princess comes, her home. In another story, called "The Dragon Princess" (also in the same volume), a fish-

---

[34] MDW, *Märchen aus Turkestan und Tibet,* no. 9 (Jena: Diederichs, 1923).

erman falls into a cavelike hole in the ground and disappears for many days. In that cave dragons come to him and he eats green algae that tastes like rice. When the fisherman returns, he tells about this. His story intrigues the Chinese emperor, so he consults a wise old man who explains what has happened. This subterranean cave has four corridors or tunnels. The first tunnel leads to the southwest shore of the Dungting Lake. The second leads to a valley in the four-stream land. The third ends up in a cave of some mountains, and the fourth comes up in an island of the Eastern Sea.

So you see, there is a subterranean cave and this would the way to the Dungting Lake. Then there is an island in the sea, which typologically would be the fourth function, being more or less cut off from the rest. And there are the mountains and the valley. These are opposites: water, fire, valley, mountain. Here there is a water hole in the firm land; there, an island in the water. There is a kind of subterranean mandala structure, and according to Chinese thought the Dungting Lake belongs to one of those ends.

We had a similar structure in the Danish fairy tale of the princess with the golden shoes, where there were four different kingdoms, and there are many others like that. The four kingdoms represent different "compartments" or realms within the unconscious. Only, these Chinese kingdoms are in the water; they are not like human countries. They therefore refer to the quaternary structure of the Self. So it is an aspect of the archetype of the Self that Liu I encounters at the Dungting Lake.

I'm jumping about a bit in order to pull the structure together, but as we learn later, there is trouble not only in the Ging Chou Lake, where the evil husband has expelled the dragon princess, but also, at the same time, great trouble in the Dungting Lake. Namely, when Liu I arrives, there is the problem that the king is on the coral tower discussing important matters with the sun priest. The sun priest is a human being, not a ghost or a dragon. And they are talking about the Holy Book of the Fire, discussing how they can reconcile fire and water.

So deeper down, below that tragedy of the rejected dragon princess, there seems to be a still deeper and more cosmic problem, namely that fire and water are fighting each other. We therefore have to look at what fire and water represent in China.

In the *I Ching,* water is represented by the trigram K'an, the Abysmal, of which it is said:

> The trigram K'an means a plunging in. A yang line has plunged in between two yin lines and is closed by them like water in a ravine. The trigram K'an is also the middle son. . . . As an image it represents water, the water that comes from

above and is in motion on earth in streams and rivers, giving rise to all life on earth.[35]

So moving waters are also like the dragon, which represents movement:

> In man's world K'an represents the heart, the soul locked up within the body, the principle of light inclosed in the dark—that is, reason. [The sign itself] has the additional meaning, "repetition of danger." Thus the hexagram is intended to designate an objective situation to which one must become accustomed, not a subjective attitude. For danger due to a subjective attitude means either foolhardiness or guile. Hence too a ravine is used to symbolize danger; it is a situation in which a man is in the same pass as the water in a ravine, and, like the water, he can escape if he behaves correctly.[36]

If you look at the commentaries in the second section of the *I Ching*,[37] you find that K'an also means heart disease or difficulty in hearing. It has to do with dark passion and with the dangers of a passionate nature—with the dynamic, creative aspects of the unconscious, to put it in psychological language, and all its terrible closeness to the instincts and the passions.

The trigram of fire, Li, appears in hexagram 30 of the *I Ching*, called "The Clinging." Whereas K'an is a masculine figure, the second son among the heavenly family of the trigrams, fire, when it is represented by the trigram Li, is feminine. It means to be conditioned, to depend, and it means rest, brightness. But Li means much more in Chinese. It also means order, not in a rational sense as we would see it, but as an orderedness of nature. The whole logos side in the Chinese civilization, the whole idea of "order," is not about an order imposed by human consciousness onto nature, but rather of order that human consciousness deduces from nature, or reads into nature. Therefore it is an order that is completely contained in the mystery of nature.

Li has to do with the designation of a *pattern,* and one of the oldest patterns from which the Chinese deduced order was the surface of the tortoise shell. The tortoise shell displays a roughly laid-out matrix of little squares, and when one put such a shell in the fire, it cracked the shell along these squares. According to how the fire cracked the tortoise shell, the priests read the future and what had to be done. That was an ancient form of oracle used even before the yarrow stalks of the *I Ching*. It is historically the oldest form of oracle in China, and this pattern on the back of a tortoise shell is also designated by the word "Li."

---

[35] *I Ching*, pp. 114-115.
[36] Ibid., p. 115.
[37] Ibid., pp. 277-278.

So Li represents that secret pattern of nature into which you can put the fire of your human participation, your concern. And when you do, that pattern cracks open and shows a definite path. "A dark line clings to two light lines, one above and one below."[38] Well, we already know that water, the sign K'an, is like that. But with Li this is reversed to become

the image of an empty space between two strong lines, whereby the two strong lines are made bright. The trigram represents the middle daughter. The Creative has incorporated the central line of the Receptive, and thus Li develops. As an image, it is fire. Fire has no definite form but clings to the burning object and thus is bright.[39]

We are tempted to see fire more as a male, dynamic force. But the Chinese emphasized the fact that fire is dependent on the material it "clings" to. If the fire has no more material, it goes at out at once, thus it is passively dependent. In the Chinese way of thinking, therefore, it is feminine. "As water pours down from heaven, so fire flames up from the earth. While K'an means the soul shut within the body, Li stands for nature in its radiance."[40] Water, K'an, has a downward movement, and Li has an upward movement. Therefore it is very important to bring the two together.

If you look at hexagram 63 of the *I Ching,* you find water above fire. It is said that they are in perfect equilibrium. This hexagram pertains to the period after completion—after the opposites have been united. But this state will lead to trouble: when there is perfect harmony, watch out!

Then, in the last hexagram, number 64, you have a complete reversal of this situation. You have water below Li; the fire is now underneath. But again there's trouble. Before, we had togetherness between the fire and the water, but in a harmony which was about to fall apart. Now, because water naturally sinks down while fire goes up, they separate more and more, and do not yet form a harmony.

This is the situation described in hexagram 64, Wei Chi, "Before Completion," where the opposites are not yet united but where they may be united. In our fairy tale, we are at this stage where there is not yet harmony: the fire and the water do not agree.

Now, the interesting thing is that here something is brought in that is not in the *I Ching.* In the *I Ching,* K'an and Li both represent pure nature forces that

---

[38] Ibid., p. 118.
[39] Ibid.
[40] Ibid.

sometimes unite in nature and then sometimes separate in nature according to the rhythm of Tao. But our story is slightly different in that it is said that Li—orderedness, the feminine, the fire—belongs to the human world, while K'an—the water, the creative dynamism—belongs to the dragon world. So there is a split between the world of human beings and the world of the gods, and these two worlds have to be reunited. That is what the Dragon King is discussing with the priest.

You see, the sun belongs to Li, and that means again that the fire is not a consuming dynamic phenomenon, but nature in its radiance. Li has much more to do with the light of cultural consciousness, while the dragon has to do with the nature of the unconscious. What the Dragon King is discussing on the coral tower is nothing more nor less than the problem of reconciling the human world of civilized consciousness with the deepest, abysmal powers of nature.

We must assume that once more, as happened so often in Chinese history, the civilized world has become too refined, too bright, too differentiated, too sophisticated, and because of this, has estranged itself from the basic instinctual nature of man.[41] Chinese civilization has repeatedly reached a level of highest sophistication, with a tremendous amount of formalism and artistic differentiation. But generally, these periods have been followed by periods of destructive revolutionary movements or by invasions of the northern barbaric population. In other words, there is a tendency in Chinese culture toward overdifferentiation, over-aestheticism, too much formalism. You see it even in descriptions in their fairy tales, where there is so much politeness surrounding their behavior toward one another. Now, that is just wonderful, but it also stifles brutal nature, so to speak. And in these phases of overcivilization and overdifferentiation of art, philosophy and music, etc., there was too great a social gap between the higher and the lower layers of the population. Such refinement leads to the situation in which certain leading families and clans are really the sole participants in civilized culture, and the poor rice-planting peasants in the country could gain nothing from it. They remained in their nearly Neolithic folklore customs, and had no part in the great differentiations achieved by the royal courts.

So what appears on the subjective level as an estrangement between cultural consciousness and the instinctual forces of the unconscious gets mirrored outwardly in a too-great social fission between the upper and lower layers of the population, and thence always leads to those crises that have repeatedly shaken

---

41 The seventeenth-century novel, *Dream of the Red Chamber*, trans. Chi-chen Wang (New York: Anchor Books, 1932), gives a good idea of the refinement of Chinese civilization, although it describes a period much later than that of our story.

Chinese history. And such crises are usually connected with the most basic psychological problems.

In our story, it is an essential problem to unite consciousness with the unconscious, to unite the human world with the world of nature, and to unite the male and female opposites. That basic problem underlies the fact that in the Dragon King's family household, his daughter is pushed into an unhappy marriage. You see, if those basic forces of K'an and Li are not in harmony, then everything is out of Tao. Then the father *will* do the wrong thing toward his daughter, and the daughter *will* hurry into the wrong marriage, and the same is true for the human world. For instance, it is unlikely that Liu I failed the exams because he was incapable. He is an elected man. The whole human world was failing its exams, in a manner of speaking; the exams themselves weren't right. At that time, Chinese society probably demanded too much Li—too much refined, specialized knowledge. And no human being who had a high potential for individuation or for heroic deeds could acquiesce in the fulfillment of such demands.

So a whole human world is wrong, and because of this the unconscious is disturbed as well. It is a great catastrophe, but it is in the unconscious. It is the Dragon King who is now working to reunite the opposites. Into this situation, Liu I explodes like a bomb with the catastrophic message of the unhappiness of the Dragon King's daughter, and the whole court begins to howl in despair.

It is interesting that it is the entry of an ordinary human being into the dragon world that gets things going. In terms of an individual, we might say that if there is a neurotic attitude in consciousness, then the unconscious has a compensatory one-sidedness—also an unhealthy attitude. And that leads to a neurosis. But if we do not make a connection with the unconscious, then neither we nor the unconscious can move forward, for the unconscious is blocked as well. The unconscious depends on our participation to produce its healing forces. Otherwise it has to produce a neurosis to force us to concern ourselves with the unconscious and then make a connection. The unconscious seems to be unable to make the connection directly. It makes endless attempts to do so by sending us dreams. But we are generally in a situation where we don't notice them, so the unconscious cannot show its healing power.

So, it is only after Liu I takes the information into the unconscious that the dragon princess is unhappy and rejected, that the unconscious gets stirred up and that first big unhappiness breaks loose. It is as if only then can one realize one's unhappiness.

Sometimes people who have strong will power and the capacity to put up with adverse circumstances endure a neurotic situation with great courage for years, not admitting to themselves how unhappy they are. Then, when they go into analysis, and only then, do they fall into the depression or conflict which had been latent for all that time when they did not want to acknowledge it. This is why sometimes the beginning of analysis brings a worsening of the situation, and the family or the marital partner says, "Oh my God! He has begun analysis and now he is much, much worse than before!" This is because only when one realizes what is wrong does an emotional reaction occur.

The same thing can happen collectively. Sometimes, for years and years, certain layers of the population put up with impossible social or economic conditions without complaining. Especially in the Orient, there is a great demand that people be patient and that they put up with impossible situations, often for a long, long time. But naturally, one day the whole force of their misery breaks out and the revolution comes.

And now, when Liu I brings the bad news about the princess, all the anger and misery surfaces: Tsian Tang, personified as the dragon of rage, explodes and goes out to avenge the daughter of his brother. When he gets loose there is a tremendous thunder storm with cloudbursts and hail. In China, the dragons represent the water principle, the rain and the clouds in heaven. They represent the dynamic power of nature, and, we would add, also of the unconscious. In China the play of rain and clouds also means sexual union, so you can also say that the fact that the princess, the anima figure, is shepherding rain servants and cloud rams refers to her tremendous hidden erotic potency. This gives the hero a hint that she must be a goddess.

Liu I then has the difficult task of transmitting to the world of the dragons the princess's letter of despair. You remember how he is admitted to the court of the dragons in the Dungting Lake, and how he had to wait a certain time because the Dragon King, father of the princess, was occupied on a coral tower, discussing with the human sun priest how fire and water could be reconciled.

Recall what water and fire mean in Chinese civilization. Water, K'an, is a male principle, the dynamic principle par excellence. It is also the passionate nature in humans. You see how, later in the story, the passionate outbursts of Tsian Tang and the passionate nature of the dragons come to the fore.

Li, the fire, in Chinese mythology is feminine. It means the yielding, the soft one, the oldest daughter among the family of the trigrams. It means dependence, submission to the facts. For the Chinese, what struck them most in the nature of the fire is the fact that it depends on some underlying material. If the straw or wood is used up, the fire cannot survive. The trees and plants, which also belong to Li and which produce the underlying material for the fire, are also dependent.

They depend on being rooted in the soil. So the whole substructure of the possibility that there is Li, fire, is based on the fact that it is dependent on material without which it cannot subsist.

Li represents the principle of cultural consciousness. It means nature in its radiance. It also means order, the orderedness of the conscious world, but, in a typically Chinese way, this is understood as existing in constant dependence on its underlying ground. We would say it depends on the unconscious; the Chinese would say, on nature. This shows that in the Chinese civilization, consciousness has never become, as with us, a kind of independent, anti-natural or partly anti-natural principle. We have used and developed a consciousness that goes against nature. It rapes nature; it corrects or reorders nature by force. We think consciousness is there to *subdue* nature, whereas in China the idea is much more that consciousness *completes* nature. Their view is more like that of the alchemists' idea of *ars naturam perficit*—consciousness serves nature and brings out its best; it helps nature along by fighting its imbalances. In that way consciousness, Li, is a feminine, passive, yielding principle.

The masculine, emotional, active principle is relegated to K'an, the water principle, and its "fiery" nature (as we would call it) is represented by the fact that K'an in China also means blood and the color red. Thus the dragon uncle of our princess is described as having "burning eyes and blood-red tongue, blood-red skin and a fiery beard." Blood was considered, as with us, to be a symbol of the emotional nature, the seat of emotional psychic reactions. In China that goes together with K'an, the water. Naturally, if you study foreign fairy tales, you have to take into account their own mythological representations. You can't amplify a Chinese story with, for instance, European or Anglo-Saxon associations. You always have to begin by amplifying as much as possible within the cultural environment of the story itself.

As in most fairy tales, the need for a reconciliation of fire and water means that there is a disturbance in the cosmic balance of human consciousness and the unconscious. Again we have an aging king, and it is his trouble and the trouble in his kingdom that gives rise to the problem of reuniting the opposites.

The eight trigrams of the *I Ching* are arranged in two orders. The first is the older heavenly order that was introduced by the legendary Fu Shi; the younger heavenly order is attributed to King Wen. Now, in the arrangement of the eight trigrams under the older heavenly order, heaven is situated on top, and at the bottom is the earth, K'un. But in the younger heavenly order, in the North—on top—is K'an and at the bottom, Li.

The older arrangement of the trigrams is outside time and space. It is an eternal heavenly order. It underlies the cosmic order in an invisible form but does not enter into action. But in the younger heavenly order, the eight trigrams enter time-space and become temporal. In China, time is understood as cyclical. Therefore, when the heavenly cosmic order appears in the cyclic form, it is the younger order, K'an, the water, taking the place of Ch'ien, heaven; and Li, the fire, takes the place of K'un, the earth. (This may seem a bit sophisticated, but I need to explain this in order to take up a certain problem we will encounter later, namely why the uncle of the dragon princess has been fettered.)

As you remember, when Liu I delivers the letter, the Dragon King promptly confesses his guilt. As father of the princess, he feels it was his haste that caused her to have an unhappy marriage. He wanted to marry her off early to the dragon of the Ging Chou Lake, and presumably he made the typical arrangements, selling his daughter for political gain, so to speak. This he now very much regrets.

It is not uncommon for humans to sell their daughters for political reasons, but we wonder that divine figures, which represent archetypal powers of the unconscious, should do the same. How can an archetype do such an awful thing?

At first, you might be tempted to say it's a projection of the Chinese consciousness, but I think that is a rather cheap explanation. Instead, I think it points to the fact that when consciousness has a wrong attitude toward the unconscious, when we are not in tune with our unconscious, then the unconscious can reach its goal only by intrigue, by arranging mischief.

You find such a thing happening, for instance, when you have to analyze someone who is too arrogant, too high up, too sure of themselves. Since such a person does not listen to the unconscious and does not want to know about his or her own shadow, in a mischievous way the unconscious arranges something to make that person trip and fall—*bang!*—into the dirt. For example, it might make one fall in love with an absolutely unsuitable person. The unconscious will do this in order to humiliate this arrogant consciousness and force one to listen, to change course.

These "intrigues" of the unconscious are sometimes very disturbing; they don't feel right. Seen from a distance or from an onlooker's standpoint, such goings-on are most unfortunate, but in spite of that one realizes it's the only way the unconscious can penetrate the armor of such a personality. At bottom, it is the unconscious that is unfortunate, that isn't listened to and isn't taken seriously, so it is not difficult to understand why it is forced to voice itself in devious ways.

Another way in which the unconscious sometimes forces its purpose to the surface is to make the person physically sick. Or it might arrange a bad car accident or something of the kind in order to place us in the kind of catastrophic situation that will finally make us willing to listen to our dreams. So when the unconscious makes someone neurotic, we must not assume that is really the intention of the unconscious to make that person sick; it is simply forced into it by the wrong attitude of consciousness.

Therefore, we can say that underneath the fact that this father dragon sold his daughter lies a deeper fact—that fire and water are not in harmony. Consciousness and the unconscious are not in harmony, so the dragon world, which represents the unconscious, cannot act properly either. It too is disturbed. If a person has a devious and disturbed conscious attitude, then the unconscious is devious and disturbed too. It is out of balance because it has to overcompensate. But we are not yet finished; we must go one layer deeper still.

When the rest of the court hears about the dragon princess's misery, they begin to howl and lament loudly. The Dragon King then says to a servant, "Go in and tell them they shouldn't cry so loudly, because Tsian Tang might hear." Liu I asks, "Who is Tsian Tang?" The Dragon King replies, "That's my beloved brother. He was once the ruler of the Tsian Tang River, but now he's deposed." "Why shouldn't he hear the crying?" asks Liu I. The Dragon King answers:

> He's so wild that I'm afraid there could be a great catastrophe if he did, just like the flood he caused many years ago. At that time, my brother was annoyed with the Emperor of Heaven, so he sent a flood that covered the five big mountains and lasted nine years. The master became angry with him, and since then he has been chained to a pillar in my palace.

We begin to see that the world of the dragons doesn't seem to be almighty after all. They are not the ultimate powers of the Chinese cosmos. Above them is the Emperor of Heaven, whose name is Tien Ti. This name is not mentioned in our story, but it signifies the ultimate cosmic ordering principle which is also often called "the will of heaven," and which is found in certain Chinese philosophical systems, sometimes also in Taoism. (This is a Taoist story, as you may have realized.) "The will of heaven" refers to that element which keeps all the cosmic powers in order.

So, in the temporal world, there is not only a disturbance between fire and water, human civilized consciousness and the collective unconscious; there is also a deeper, anterior disturbance between the younger heavenly order and its ruler and the older heavenly order and its ruling principle. And that is an even deeper conflict than that between fire and water. The temporal order of the cosmos is no longer following the will of heaven, and on account of this Tsian Tang is now fettered.

The greatest task of the Chinese emperor was to keep the numbers of the calendar in order. He was the maker of the calendar, and he had to see that the days coincided correctly with the will of heaven. In the imperial Chinese civilization, every day of the calendar had its astrological connotations. It had its own ritual, its own food; it had its own ceremonies in the imperial household and in the administrator's household, in the mandarin's house as well as in the peasant's house. On every day of the year, they had to put on certain clothes, make certain sacrifices, play certain music, eat certain food. The days of the calendar marked the whole order of civilization. Everything was time-bound, so to speak. You couldn't eat bean soup on a certain day. You could only eat bean soup on another certain day. Even such absolutely banal facts were all ordered. We have lists of the menus of the imperial household: what they had to eat and cook at certain times. We also know how many robes they had to wear and of what color, and what music had to be played or what must not be played on certain days. All of this was fixed in holy books which the master of ceremonies knew. These lasted for the duration of a whole dynasty. When one dynasty fell into decay and chaos, the ruler who introduced the new dynasty would reform the calendar. As the texts say, he would "bring the calendar again into harmony with the will of heaven."

Whenever there was a disaster in the empire, one had the feeling that the emperor wasn't functioning according to Tao. If the situation was very bad, this indicated that the emperor ought to reform the calendar again in order to make the temporal order of the world coincide with the extratemporal eternal order of the universe. So you see that our story describes a period of catastrophe when the calendar was in disorder, and Tsian Tang, brother of the Dragon King of the Dungting Lake, had revolted: K'an had revolted against the will of heaven. The Chinese people had a very deep problem.

Now, all this is quite clear from the perspective of the Chinese world concept. But how shall we translate it into our psychological language? I think the only way, though it leads us into difficult thinking and into a paradox, is to say that the older heavenly order refers to what Jung calls the Self. And the younger heavenly order would refer to the collective unconscious as it is constellated *at a certain moment*, and also as it is constellated in a single human being *at a certain moment*.

This does lead us, however, to a paradox, in that Jung defines the Self as the oneness of the collective unconscious. Therefore, in a way, he does not distinguish between the concepts of collective unconscious and Self. But in another way, we must distinguish them because we know that the Self is the superordinant regulating center in the collective and personal unconscious, and is a more decisive factor than the collective unconscious as it is constellated at a certain moment. This is because when the collective unconscious is constellated, or appears in a constellation of a certain moment, it can be one-sided: for, at any specific moment, it might be overcompensating a one-sidedness in consciousness.

Now, whenever this happens, Jung advises us not to blindly follow the advice of dreams or the unconscious. We cannot blindly say, "I had such-and-such a dream, therefore I must do such-and-such," as though looking at that one dream was all we had to do. If we did this, we would be giving in to the unconscious, doing what it seems to want at the moment, when all the while this might actually conflict with the will of heaven or what the Self wants at that moment. The will of heaven, or the Self, can only manifest in a human being if the ego is firm too. The ego must take a critical stand toward the single temporal manifestations of the unconscious.

Jung discussed a situation like this in one of his seminars. He had a patient who was an overspiritualized middle-aged lady with a rather peculiar theosophy. She lived in the stratosphere of the spirit and never realized she had a body or that something so ugly or dirty as sex could even come near her. Accordingly, she was highly neurotic. When she came into analysis, she dreamt frequently of prostitutes rolling drunkenly in the gutter. And Jung said, "Yes, yes, that is your sister, you see. Everybody has that side too. You should consider that seriously and not reject it. Love they neighbor as thyself!" But his advice didn't sink in. She was too far away to be able to accept that; perhaps it would have been too great a shock.

Then Jung had to go away on a trip. Now, he knew this lady had a habit of taking long, soulful walks in the woods, and he thought that in the present constellation this wasn't very wise. He told her so and made her promise she would not go walking in the woods while he was away. But she did and she was sexually attacked. She was severely wounded, had to go to hospital with several broken ribs and a big shock. You see, when such a prostitute shadow, possibly with a "come hither" look, was constellated, such a situation was unconsciously attracted.

Now, one certainly couldn't say that this woman's dreams of drunken prostitutes meant she should have gone out to get drunk and pick up a man. That would be falling into K'an, not following the will of heaven. You may laugh, but I find this mistake again and again among students of Jungian psychology. They do the most impossible things and say, "But I had a dream that told me to." Then I say, "Well, well, well! There is still ego consciousness to consider!" When we take account of such dreams, we must not excuse ourselves from having to use our critical faculties and moral judgment. We must take a stand and reflect on such a communication from the unconscious, and take reasonable measures in response. It is not a question of just blindly, primitively acting out our dreams. We have to obey the Self, but we do not have to obey a momentary constellation of the unconscious.

Now you may say, "Yes, but how can we make the correct distinctions?" You can make these distinctions only by attending to a series of dreams. That's why it is so absolutely immoral to interpret single dreams for people, or to act in response to a single dream. The will of heaven, or in our language the purpose of the Self, is something one can find out only by using one's critical faculties, not by acting out the dreams at once. We must wait and see, taking only very small steps until, over a series of dreams, we get a hunch as to what is really needed.

This illustrates in psychological terms why the Chinese make a distinction between the two representations of the total order of the unconscious, one that is momentary and temporal, that changes through the seasons, and one that is outside of time, eternal. It is only the eternal order that one has to obey absolutely, for that is the will of heaven. In Chinese philosophy, the will of heaven is the ultimate authority. No one, not god nor demon nor genius nor human being can resist it. But on the other hand, one can still have one's reservations about the temporal order. One can view it as a momentary constellation with no absolute validity. Since it has a certain temporal validity, in that sense one must take it into account, but it must never be the sole or final source of practical decisions.

To come back to our example, the lady who dreamed of the prostitute could not simply sit back and say, "Aha, yes, that's my shadow," and be sad about it. That would not be sufficient, for her shadow demanded more than just a theoretical acknowledgment. However, to invite it to be acted out as she did is to go to an extreme in the other direction.

In our fairy tale, there had been a catastrophe in the past. We can assume that it was one of those big political catastrophes, because the story takes place during the seventh to ninth centuries, some time after the literary and cultural peak of the age. Already, the civilization had become estranged from the cosmic order and so there had been a flood, which is interpreted in the story as an outburst of the Tsian Tang dragon.

The great rivers of China, as you may know, all have the bad habit of overflowing their banks from time to time, causing terrible floods. In earlier times these floods were never understood merely as nature catastrophes, but as reactions of nature against a wrongness of the human order and of the cosmic order.

In Chinese historiography, for instance, one reads chronicles that go like this:

> In the Year of the Hare, the empress flirted with the first general. On account of this, a dragon was seen in Lake So-and-So. The Yangtze Kiang flooded its borders and destroyed the rice fields. The emperor decided in August to perform certain mending ceremonies. He didn't sleep with his wives. Music was banished from the court. He wore dark robes and ate only this and that. After that, in September, . . .

And then it might go one to tell how the empire recovered politically.

Here you see synchronistic thinking, pure and simple. Naturally, the Chinese weren't so stupid as to think that the Yangtze Kiang River overflowed *because* the empress flirted with the first general. They would no more think of connecting these two events causally than we would. But for them, as Marcel Granet puts it, "Every year is an ensemble of events which as a whole gives a meaningful picture of what sorts of things always seem to happen together."[42]

While the Western scientists were interested in what causes what, the Chinese also had a real science, one based on a different but equally legitimate question: "What events 'like to' happen together?" The Chinese knew about causality quite well and used causal principles in the practical concerns of life, but they thought causality was not nearly as scientifically interesting as the question of how to understand synchronous events, even those not causally related. That is why, when they wrote down the historical facts of any particular year, they would try to give a meaningful picture of that year, its constellation. That is the essence of Chinese synchronistic thinking.[43]

So, we can assume that at the same time the river flooded in the Year of the Hare, the angry dragon had been overstepping *his* bounds as well. He was obviously called to take revenge for certain misdeeds of humans, but he went too far. In our story the dragon princess must be avenged, and it does seem implicitly fitting that she should be. But Tsian Tang destroys too much of the land and he kills too many people, besides eating the princess's frivolous husband. Now, that's going too far!

Tsian Tang seems therefore to represent the passionate nature of the water principle K'an, the blood-red nature that tends to overstep its bounds. And this,

---

42 *La Pensée Chinoise* (Paris: Albin Michel, 1968).

43 [For a more extensive commentary, see von Franz, *On Divination and Synchronicity: The Psychology of Meaningful Chance* (Toronto: Inner City Books, 1980), pp. 7ff. In North America this way of thinking is reflected in attempts to predict movements in the stock market, such as that it usually goes up in years when one football league or other wins the annual Superbowl, or in months with a so-called blue moon (a second full moon) and so on.—Ed.]

as you may know, is one of the great psychological conflicts in Chinese civilization: they tend in their conscious life to overdo formality and correctness. They overemphasize "saving face" and politeness. And because of that, being normal human beings, they accumulate rather too passionate and disorderly a temperament in the unconscious, which then explodes wildly from time to time, politically as well as privately. They repress their innate "wildness" too much by being overly concerned with formality.

My father, who lived for some time in Manchuria, once observed a scene that illustrates this. He took part in the Japanese-Russian War in 1905, and he was quartered in a Chinese-Manchurian peasant house, a farm house. There was not enough room in the farm house, so one of the sons had to live outside with the cattle in a little hut. They took turns staying in this hut.

Now, my father didn't know Chinese very well so he could only guess, more or less, at the conversation, but one day he overheard the older brother saying it was now the younger brother's turn to go, although the older one had come back too early. Of course, the younger brother was none too pleased with this idea, so the brothers began to quarrel. The older brother grabbed the younger one by the plait—they still had plaits at that time—which was the greatest insult for a Chinese man. So the younger brother simply exploded! He fetched a hatchet and went for the older brother. And my father thought, "They are going to kill each other!" But then the old grandmother hobbled out of the house and pulled the *older* brother by the plait. She showed him that he had to leave, not by speaking but by simply making this gesture. And the older brother, who had been furious and ready to kill, meekly put his head down, bowed deeply, and returned to the hut with the cattle. So ended the quarrel.

This incident illustrates the ever-present tension within the Chinese psyche: on the surface level of behavior, there is much civility and politeness (Confucian filial piety in this case). But underneath there is a wild, passionate nature that is repressed and therefore explodes from time to time in violent outbursts. On a larger scale, again and again in Chinese history you hear of incredibly violent massacres. I think I need not allude to contemporary events; we all know this still happens.

So, Tsian Tang is really a symbol of this passionate nature in the unconscious which in China is too repressed and therefore tends to break out violently. And then, naturally, comes the counteraction. This time—after devastating the land and people and eating the dragon princess's former husband—Tsian Tang is not imprisoned but takes part in the evening festivities. They all get drunk, and Tsian Tang gets *very* drunk. The next morning, having a hangover, he insults Liu

I by haughtily and arrogantly recommending that he marry his niece, the dragon princess. Liu I's pride is hurt and he refuses. He does not relent even the next day, although the Queen of the Dungting Lake expresses her regrets and the dragon princess herself cries and clearly shows she loves him.

Here we have a conflict common in folk tales of any country, but one that in our story has an interesting, specifically Chinese twist. As you know, in China it was (and in general still is) absolutely essential not to "lose face." Although to us Tsian Tang's offer may not seem offensive, if Liu I had accepted it he would have lost face. That is why he would not accept it even though his heart told him that the princess loved him and he loved the princess. And it is right there, as we know from the context of the story, that he makes his fatal mistake. He should have sacrificed his persona pride for the sake of love, but instead he's stuck in the formalities of the Chinese way of life. He misses his chance, with the result that the suffering dragon princess has to follow him into the human world, making a second detour, as it were.

What has happened in the story to this point is a variation of what happens again and again in Chinese novels and folk tales. The message is that Liu I has made a fatal mistake, the same mistake often found in European parallels, where the hero goes home and forgets his bride, whom he found in the Beyond, or on his way home he falls asleep while his bride is taken away by evil powers.

It is a basic archetypal motif for the hero to find his divine anima figure and then lose her again. You find it with different variations in fairy tales all over the world. But here, the fact that the hero loses her because of persona pride, is a nuance I haven't found anywhere else. It is specifically Chinese to exaggerate the persona aspect of life, and to fanatically subscribe to the dictum never to lose face. But this, in itself, is only a variation of a universal conflict that takes place in everyone, namely the conflict between power and eros.

Power and eros exclude each other totally. Jung writes, "Where love reigns, there is no will to power; and where the will to power is paramount, love is lacking."[44] You cannot combine the two; it's either one or the other. Jung said that no man can ever assimilate or even get to know what the anima is before he has overcome power—schemes in connection with feminine contacts, purely sexual drive or purely aesthetic considerations. As long as a man looks at a woman for sex or for her good looks, or maybe for her bank account, there is no question of love and therefore no question of getting to know what the anima could even be.

---

[44] *Two Essays on Analytical Psychology,* CW 7, par. 78.

For a woman it would be if she falls off course in her search for the truth. You see, the animus in its positive essence is a healing spirit, a spirit of truth. So if a woman falsifies her inner search for truth by getting enmeshed in power games, or by pursuing a man simply because he has money, the same catastrophe will ensue. For example, you go to university and have to write a thesis. You have an idea for that thesis but you know it's one your professor will not accept. If you don't write about that idea because it is more important to you to get good grades than to write what you believe is true, then you have betrayed your truth—just as a man betrays his love by having an eye on the woman's bank account. Again it's power.

So, Liu I refused to marry the dragon princess because his pride was hurt and because the dragon Tsian Tang behaved rather arrogantly. Now, think back to the uppermost line of the first hexagram of the *I Ching,* where it is said that "arrogant dragon will have to repent." This seems to be the inherent danger of the dragon principle in China—the pride or arrogance that prevents the inclusion of the feminine. Repentance indicates moving on to the next phase, namely the second hexagram, "The Receptive," which concerns the feminine, the earth principle. But if the dragon principle resists the enantiodromia into the feminine, through arrogance, or where the hero finds his destiny, his true bride, and then for some reason or other forgets her or leaves her and becomes engaged to some other powerful princess for worldly reasons (money, social status, whatever, a "false bride")—then, at the last minute, the true bride turns up again, sometimes even at the church door, to remind the bridegroom of their former love.[45]

Seen in light of the anima problem of men, the question ultimately becomes that of having to decide between love—one's heart, one's feelings—and social status or some other worldly value. This touches a very deep problem which confronts analysands and analysts and poses a serious dilemma. In his autobiography Jung says that group identity and individuation are incompatible; you can't have both:

> It is really the individual's task to differentiate himself from all others and stand on his own feet. All collective identities, such as membership in organizations, support of "isms," and so on, interfere with the fulfillment of this task. Such collective identities are crutches for the lame, shields for the timid, beds for the lazy, nurseries for the irresponsible.[46]

---

[45] [For more on the false and true bride motif, see Nathan Schwartz-Salant, *Narcissism and Character Transformation* (Toronto: Inner City Books, 1982), pp. 67ff.—Ed.]
[46] *Memories, Dreams, Reflections,* ed. Aniela Jaffé, trans. Richard and Clara Winston (New York: Vintage Books, 1963), p. 342.

In other writings, however, Jung made it clear that he did not advise people to become antisocial eccentrics. Always he insisted that his patients adapt to reality and not disappear into the unconscious, so to speak.

So here we have one of those seeming contradictions or sources of conflict that arise in every analysis. In one way, it is certainly necessary—and especially so when one gets in touch with the unconscious—to keep in touch with reality and to maintain one's social adaptation. If you treat borderline cases, it is even essential that their persona holds up. I have had analysands who, when they let their persona go in the analytic hour, were absolutely, honestly mad. But at the end of the hour, they more or less cleaned away their tears and picked up their persona and walked out pretending to be normal. And that was a tremendous help, because in time, naturally, their so-called madness could be normalized or improved, but in the meantime their social adaptation, like a corset, kept them together so that outwardly, at least, they didn't fall apart. Later they normalized inwardly and were held together by something more substantial than just the persona, but even the persona in such a moment can be life-saving. These are extreme cases, but we always see that social adaptation, for the sake of both society and the individual, has to be maintained.

And yet—and here comes the real paradox—to say the absolute opposite would be just as true. There are crucial moments in every analysis when one has to choose between the world and God, or, to use our language, when one has to choose between following the call of individuation and retaining one's social adaptation. There *are* situations where it amounts to an unavoidable, mutually exclusive either-or. And the one who decides for social adaptation has lost everything. As Jung says, at such times the two are incompatible.

But such situations are even worse than that: if at such a crucial point one chooses the wrong thing, namely worldly adaptation, one buys this adaptation with a life-long neurosis. Jung compares this with the fact that Jacob wrestled with the angel, commenting that "no claims were ever made that the angel, too, came away with a limp."[47] You see, the angel was the stronger. So, whenever it's a question of wrestling with the messenger of God, when it comes to this crucial moment in individuation, then one has to know who is the stronger. And although one is free to choose, it is clear that everything will be lost by opting for social adaptation.

Liu I is in such a situation. He can't go on, for he is meant to be the bridegroom of the dragon princess. Fate kills the women, his first two wives, with

---

[47] Ibid., p. 344.

whom he tries to escape. The dragon princess now approaches him as an alleged daughter of a Taoist.

This whole folk tale is obviously a literary novel written from a Taoist standpoint. I will go into that later. Now, all the alchemy that was practiced in China was practiced in Taoist circles, so that Taoism and alchemical philosophy in China are practically identical. And the Taoist religious philosophy influenced Chinese alchemy to conceive of its goal as the creation not of gold, as in Western alchemy, but of the immortal body.

In Western alchemy, the Philosophers' Stone was also interpreted to be the resurrected body. According to official Christian teaching, after death our physical body will decay in the grave, but in the end-time we will be resurrected with another body. That teaching has puzzled people no end.

But the alchemists had a completely different view. They thought that the resurrection body was a kind of subtle body which was slowly forming within the material body, or which you could form or become aware of in your own earthly lifetime through meditation. This made it possible for you to move your psyche from your mortal body into your immortal resurrection body during this lifetime, so that at the moment of death, the mortal body would fall off like a shell and you would survive at once in your immortal form. But even the immortal psyche, they believed, needed a certain material substratum. This is what they called the Philosophers' Stone, and they represented it by different mandala symbols and all the other symbolism you can study in Jung's books on Western alchemy.[48]

Now in Eastern or Chinese alchemy, the basic pattern is similar, only they called the resurrection body the "diamond body." In one of their texts, "The Secret of the Golden Flower,"[49] there is detailed advice on how to build this diamond body through meditation in one's lifetime. It was believed that the great sages and Taoist alchemists did not literally die; they merely moved their psyches into the subtle body, the diamond body, and then their mortal bodies withered away, falling off like dust—without you seeing it happen, of course. There are innumerable folk stories where the old sages just recede away or disappear: one sees them riding on a dragon carriage up to the heavens and then they are gone. They have become immortal. They have joined the many other immortals

---

[48] See especially *Aion,* CW 9ii; *Psychology and Alchemy,* CW 12; *Alchemical Studies,* CW 13; *Mysterium Coniunctionis,* CW 14; and "The Psychology of the Transference," *The Practice of Psychotherapy,* CW 16.

[49] Trans. Richard Wilhelm; commentary by C.G. Jung (New York: Causeway Books, 1975). Jung's commentary is also in *Alchemical Studies,* CW 13.

in the Chinese Beyond, and death is only a rather insignificant, irrelevant moment when the dust of the mortal body falls off the already fully blossomed diamond body in which they move away.

In our story it is asserted that the dragon princess is the daughter of such a Taoist. With her comment to that effect, the marriage broker alludes to the fact that Liu I was about to come into contact with an outstanding personality, the daughter of a semidivine father. But she said no more, because she didn't want to admit that the girl was the dragon princess. So our hero marries the dragon princess in this human form, and only after a year, when she had given birth to a son, does she dare to tell him who she really is. She says, "Now that I have given you a son, I hope you will transfer the love you have for him also to his mother."

At this point, we see that the dragon princess had all along been feeling rejected. She was rejected once already by her first husband, and then she felt rejected by Liu I. She was so deeply hurt that she completely doubted his feelings for her. In a way, she had a certain right to do so, because in the past he did betray her for the sake of his stupid pride. Therefore she tries to get him back—and this again is typically Chinese—by giving birth to a son.

If you know what it meant in old China to have a son, then you understand why she could count on its bringing him back to her. In China, since the ancestral cult is the cornerstone of religious ritual, it was of vital importance that every man had a surviving son who could then offer the ancestral sacrifices. If this was not done, there would be a danger that the spirit of the dead father would become anonymous, unknown; its memory would not continue in the society of the living, and it would scatter in the cosmic void. The only ones who were independent of these rituals of the ancestral cult were the Taoist immortals. They had reached the highest level of consciousness and had acquired a diamond body, so they were no longer dependent on the ancestral cult for their postmortal well-being. But all the ordinary human beings were sustained in their postmortal lives only through the memories of their living descendants. Therefore, having a son was a matter of vital interest for every Chinese man.

This is not a general archetypal motif. It is specific to China. I have never found a fairy tale outside China where the loving woman buys back her husband by giving him a son. In the European variations, she generally buys three nights in her beloved's bedroom. For instance, she asks the false bride if she could have the three nights, and she generally pays for this time with all the worldly goods she possesses. Then, in the night, she pleads and tries to reawaken her destined husband's memory so that he will remember her and realize that she is the one he should marry. Usually, the false bride gives the bridegroom a sleeping drug so that on the first two nights he doesn't listen. But on the last night, he becomes suspicious so he doesn't take the potion. Then, he is reawakened at the last moment and switches to the right woman. In European fairy tales, that is the most frequent method by which the loving woman overcomes all obstacles to regain her husband. But in our story, it is through giving birth to a son that she hopes to win back his love.

So, Liu I woke up as though from a deep sleep, and after that he and his wife loved each other very much. We don't know how long their happy life on earth lasted, but one day the woman said, "If you want to live with me always, we cannot continue to live in the human world. We dragons live to be ten thousand years old, and it is fitting that you should become as old as I. So please come back with me to the Dungting Lake."

Then they go back to the Dungting Lake, and ten years later a cousin of Liu I comes there. He sees Liu I disappear back into the lake. We can assume that they lived there for some time, that Liu I's son grew up and that they had more children, but all that is passed over.

Here, the dragon princess wants to impart her longevity to her husband. It's not quite immortality, for we're talking about a finite although very long time-span. But this again belongs to a concept in Taoist alchemy. Not only did the alchemists have the necessary means and meditation exercises to build an immortal inner body, they also had certain alchemical elixirs by which you could indefinitely prolong your life. You have the same thing in Western alchemy, where the Philosophers' Stone is often called the elixir of life. Some elixirs were known as *aurum potabile,* "drinkable gold," for example. It was believed that whoever drank them could become very, very old. Some alchemists supposedly lived not merely 10,000 years, but 150,000 or 200,000, by using "drinkable gold" or the elixir of life.

In Taoist alchemy, the elixir was usually a red pill made of quicksilver. Now quicksilver, or mercurius, was the basic mystical element of Chinese as well as Western alchemy, and with such a pill you could live for hundreds or even thousands of years. We have many Chinese recipes that are literally parallel to the recipes of Western alchemy, and almost always they call for some combination of quicksilver with gold or some other substance in order to produce a pill of longevity. In our story the pill of longevity, which is also sometimes called a pearl, is in the hands of the dragons. This is not unusual, for in Chinese art you often see the heavenly dragon holding this pearl of immortality in its claws.

So the whole mystery of Taoist alchemy in this story is linked up with the mythology of the dragons, who represent the water principle. In Chinese civilization, alchemy formed the undercurrent of Taoist philosophy. Its main goal was to maintain contact with what we call the unconscious. As you know, Jung says of Western alchemy that it was not an anti-Christian movement but rather a compensatory undercurrent which preserved many things that were discarded, forgotten or underestimated in the developing Christian world-view. In China, the two great movements were Taoism and Confucianism. In the conscious social world it was Confucianism that took official precedence over Taoism. Confucianism was the philosophy on which most of the outer civilized life of China was based, while Taoism has a more complicated history. In fact, at times Taoists had to go underground because of persecution. Yet Taoism always constituted that undercurrent which kept contact with the living development of the collective unconscious, as opposed to surfacing in conscious rules of behavior. That is why its ideas have been preserved in folklore and linked with alchemy.

In my opinion, Taoism, by not uniting with Confucianism, became a bit too other-worldly. It took to an extreme the ideal of disappearing into some mountain hermitage, retiring with a beloved man or woman and leaving the world. Many people reproach Jungian psychologists for the same thing, charging that we are antisocial and attend only to our individuation, ignoring our social responsibilities. That charge, I think, is absolutely ungrounded. But it does seem to hold true for Taoist philosophy and alchemy. They are extremely introverted, individualistic disciplines, and they endorse a program of complete abstention from the concerns of the visible, social, human world.

So it is in this sense that the dragon princess takes Liu I away into her blissful, eternal dragon world. After several years his cousin discovers that Liu I really reached immortality and is living now under the Dungting Lake. The cousin had been only a witness to this fact, but then he too was pulled over to the other side, retiring from the world forever.

To retire from the human social world is a one-sided solution. We find this in certain Western stories as well. For instance, the magician Merlin disappears from the world in the loving embrace of a water fairy. Jung calls this the hermetic ideal of the lonely person who follows the way of individuation and leaves the world to persist in its own dirty turmoil. It seems to me that this attitude, which is propagated in our story, begins to be justified, at least in very old people. I have seen that in the dreams of old people who were approaching death, the unconscious took exactly this kind of turn in order to concentrate on building the diamond body, on dying properly by shedding the mortal body and surviving the change and shock of death in a certain state of consciousness. But I have never seen it in dreams of people younger than sixty or sixty-five. So it looks as if only in old age is it natural and right, ethically and socially justified, for people to leave the outer world.

On the other hand, to retreat in this way at a younger age is a bit too one-sided, too introverted. But the great tension in China between Confucianism and Taoism, which ultimately is the tension between extraversion and introversion, goes through this whole story and is visible in this form. It is even exaggerated in that the question of what happened to Liu I's son is completely ignored. This runs very much against the official conscious Chinese viewpoint.

So this fairy tale has the same compensatory role to the official collective viewpoint as our European fairy tales have for us. Of course, we have to know the collective official viewpoint in order to find that out, and we have to compare. That is why I think it will take perhaps a hundred more years of study by a whole team of specialists to write a history of the national differences among fairy tales. But by doing so, we could establish a history that would clearly show the consciousness of a given population and the compensatory role of their fairy tales. It would show how consciousness and the unconscious function against and with each other, and it would be a wonderful tool for comparing this interplay with the similar interplay between consciousness and the unconscious as we find it in individual dreams.

4
The Nine Brothers Who Were Changed into Lambs, and Their Sister (French)

Now I want to discuss a French fairy tale called "The Nine Brothers Who Were Changed into Lambs, and their Sister."[50]

There were once nine brothers and a sister, and they were orphans. They were very rich and lived in an old castle in the forest. The sister was called Lévène, and was the oldest. When their father died she took over the household and the brothers obeyed her as if she were their mother. They always went hunting in the forest, and they lived from the hunt.

One day, as they were pursuing a hind, they came to a hut made of twigs and bits of earth. They had never seen the hut before. They thought they would tell whoever was in it that they needed water because they were thirsty. So they went in, and there they saw an old woman.

Her teeth were as long as her arm, and her tongue could be wound nine times around her body. They were terrified and wanted to run away, but the old woman said, "What do you want, dear children? Come in." "We want a little bit of water, grandmother," said the oldest. "My dear children, I'll get you clear water, but come in and don't be afraid." She got some water for them, and she stroked their hair and said, "Now you must pay me for the little service I gave you." "We have no money, grandmother," said the children. "I don't want money, I want the oldest of you to marry me."

The poor boy was horrified and didn't answer. She said again, "Answer! May I not become your little wife?" "I don't know," said the oldest. "I'll ask my sister." "Oh, all right, I'll come to the castle tomorrow and ask for your answer."

The poor children went home shivering, and the oldest asked if he should marry the old witch. But Lévène said, "No, we will try to resist her." The next morning, the sorceress came to the castle, and they answered that the oldest would not marry the witch. Then the witch became furious. Here eyes became like two glowing coals, and the nine brothers trembled, but they held firm. Then the old witch took a twig and murmured a magic verse, and the whole castle collapsed in one terrible bang. Not one stone remained upon another. And then she said another magical verse, and the nine brothers became nine white lambs. And then she said to the girl (who had kept her normal form), "Now you can be the shepherdess of those lambs, but don't tell anyone that these lambs are your brothers, for if you do, I will trans-

---

50 MDW, *Französische Volksmärchen*, vol. 2, no. 34 (Jena: Diederichs, 1923).

form you too into a lamb." And then, laughing, she went away.

The beautiful gardens of the castle and the big forest around it were turned into an arid steppe. Lévène stayed there with her brothers, and she tried to get them some fresh grass. She stroked them and talked to them as if they understood—and they did seem to understood. One lamb was bigger than the others. That was the oldest brother.

Then Lévène made a little hut from stones and earth and moss, and when it rained she stayed there, and there she sang songs to her brothers and said prayers for them. One day, a young nobleman, named Gulden, who was hunting in the country, heard her beautiful voice, and he found her. He fell so much in love with the beautiful shepherdess that he went there often. He finally convinced her to marry him, and they had a great feast.

The nine lambs were brought to the garden of the castle. Lévène always stayed with them, making flower garlands for them and helping them however she could. Her husband was astonished, because these animals seemed to be reasonable beings. He asked if they were true lambs, but Lévène didn't answer.

Then Lévène became pregnant. She had a maid who was in love with the gardener, and this maid was also with child. The maid was in truth the daughter of the old witch who had turned the brothers into lambs, but that, too, no one knew.

One day when Lévène bent over the edge of a well in the garden, the maid took her by the feet and threw her into the well. Then she ran to Lévène's room and went to bed and shut the curtains. She pretended to be having labor pains.

Lévène's husband wasn't there at the time. When he returned, he did not find his wife among the lambs, so he went to the bedroom. "What's the matter with you?" he said to the woman who was lying there. "I'm very ill," said the maid without opening the curtains. "Please don't open the curtains, I can't stand the light." "But where is your maid?" "I don't know, I haven't seen her." Then she added, "Oh yes, I'm terribly hungry, and the only thing that could cure me, I think, would be for me to eat a piece of the big white lamb in the garden. That's the only thing that could put me right again."

Lévène's husband went and ordered the gardener to kill the big white lamb and roast it for his wife. The gardener tried to kill it, but the lamb always ran around the well very quickly, so that the gardener couldn't catch it. The lamb also moaned and made signs toward the well. So Lévène's husband said, "What's the matter there? What is in the well?" He looked into it and found his wife at the bottom of the well. So he pulled her out, and from the fright she at once gave birth to a boy, who was very beautiful. And she said, "We must baptize this child at once, and I want the big white lamb to be its godfather."

"What! You cannot give your son a lamb as a godfather!" said the husband. "But I want to," said Lévène. "So please don't ask any questions!" So Lévène's husband agreed, although he was very puzzled.

They went to church. The big white lamb went quite happily along with the father and the godmother, who was a beautiful princess. The eight other lambs followed. Everyone was astonished when they came into the church. The father then said to the priest, "Don't bother about the godfather looking like a lamb, just begin the baptism."

The priest made no further objections because such transformations at that time were not as extraordinary as they are today, and he began to baptize the child. The lamb stood on its hind legs and held the child and everything went perfectly. At the end of the ceremony, the lamb who was the godfather turned back into human shape, and everyone saw that it was the oldest brother of Lévène. She told how everything had happened.

Now the magic was broken, and the witch had no power over them. The priest said, "Then those other lambs are your brothers?" And the oldest said, "Yes, they are my brothers, and they, too, can now return to human shape. You must put your *stola* [stole] over them and say a prayer, and then they will become human again."

The priest followed this advice, and at once the other brothers also returned to their normal shape. And then the oldest brother told about what the maid had done and that she was the daughter of the witch. Eight of the brothers returned to the castle, and one brought the old witch back from the forest. And when they had all come home, she and her daughter and the gardener were torn apart by four horses, and then they were thrown on a pyre and burned to ashes. But Gulden and Lévène lived happily from then on, and they had many children. The oldest brother also lived happily ever after.

The main figures of this fairy tale are ten children—nine brothers and one sister. And they have no parents, they are orphans. Very often, as you know, the hero or heroine is an orphan or at least one parent has died. Then, generally, in the place of the father or the mother comes an evil figure that gets the action going. Here the figure that comes in negatively to replace the dead parents is this terrible witch who has those long teeth and that enormously long tongue.

Witches very often have a phallic attribute: they ride on a broom, or they have an enormously long nose, or as here, a long tongue. Our witch figure is a hermaphroditic creature. It is a male and female in one. The gnostic philosophers would call her the "father-mother" or a "mother-father" figure. Erich Neumann would call it the "father-mother uroboros."

The witch here represents an aspect or personification of the unconscious in which male and female qualities are not separated into a polarity but are still one, in a most regressive negative form. In general, when the parents of the hero or heroine have died, this shows that the prevailing conscious attitude relating to logos or eros has become lost or receded; its energy has moved into the unconscious, where it activates a replacing figure that is usually negative.

This happens, for instance, in "Snow White,"[51] where the queen dies and is succeeded by a wicked stepmother who curses the heroine. There are many other fairy tales in which a king has children, his first wife dies, and the woman he marries next is a wicked stepmother who persecutes the children. The closest Grimm parallels to our French tale are stories such as "The Seven Ravens" and "The Six Swans."[52] In "The Six Swans," the mother dies, the father remarries, and the stepmother, because she wants to make room for her own children, curses the six sons of the first woman and transforms them into swans. And in "The Seven Ravens," it is the father himself who in a moment of annoyance curses his sons to become ravens. In both of these cases, as well as in our French story, the sister redeems her brothers from their animal shape.

In the French story the situation is extreme because as many as ten children are not only motherless but fatherless as well. The father generally transmits spiritual values, while the mother transmits eros and the life-habit values, of a civilization. But since both are gone, that would mean the entire traditional continuity of civilization has died away; a complete stagnation has taken place. The conscious forms of life are no longer alive.

The number nine is important in this story, so we must consider its significance in a wide context. For instance, I would like you to look at this figure of the famous "magic square":

4	9	2
3	5	7
8	1	6

The magic square is used for many different purposes, in Chinese mathematics, in the Islamic world, and in all parts of Africa. The mathematical properties of this square are such that any column or row adds up to fifteen, no matter which direction you choose. Even the diagonals give the same sum. That's the puzzling magic of this so-called magic square: all the sums of all the rows are always fifteen.

This purely arithmetic property has always fascinated people, and therefore it

---

[51] *The Complete Grimm's Fairy Tales,* p. 249.
[52] Ibid., pp. 137, 232.

has been used to represent the totality of the temporal world—not the eternal world, only the temporal world. It has been used in games, in magic formulas and so on. According to the Islamic interpretation, it is said that these numbers are the powers through which the energy of Allah flows into the world of creation. So the creative energy of the godhead manifests itself in its totality in that magic square. The numbers are qualities, so to speak, of divine energy, and through them this energy becomes manifest in the world. The number ten is "outside" the square and signifies either a new beginning or an end.

In antiquity and also in the Celtic world, which would be related to our fairy tale, the number nine is connected with the moon or with any sacred time period associated with the moon. Most sacrificial animals in antiquity and in the Celtic world were brought in groups of nine, especially those offered for the dead. The number nine plays a role in the sacrifices of Dionysus, of Demeter, the earth goddess, and in all sacrifices to Hades and the gods of the underworld. It definitely has a lunar and chthonic quality about it.

In medieval number symbolism, nine was mainly understood as three times three—the square of the number three—and therefore was associated with the Holy Ghost, the most dynamic manifestation of the Trinity. So it came to signify the dynamism of the Holy Spirit. This is not unlike the Islamic conception that nine symbolizes the flow of energy and represents the dynamic manifestation of Allah in the world.

In the German parallels, the brothers are transformed not into lambs but into birds. Birds are symbols of unconscious spiritual contents, so with respect to our French tale we can also assume that this transformation of the nine brothers into animals must have to do with the dynamic chthonic forces in the unconscious that serve consciousness. Their transformation therefore means that these forces have regressed to a point where they cannot be contacted any more. What it means more specifically, we will see later.

The sister—the feminine, the tenth (which in number symbolism means a re-beginning or an end)—is Lévène, the heroine of the story. I have found no amplifications for the name "Lévène," so I can't tell you what it means.

This fairy tale was collected in the eighteenth century, a time when people were very careless about how they picked up these stories. They do not give their sources, so we only know it was picked up as a folk tale at that time and that Lévène is the heroine's name. It's unfortunate that for a long time the French thought that fairy tales were merely childish nonsense or a pure play of fantasy, so that one needn't write them down. They had no strict rules about passing these tales on, so in many cases several stories were mixed up with one another. And in the earlier publications of fairy tales, the publishers or writers would often alter them to suit their own liking. Even the Grimm brothers did that; sometimes they thought, "That fairy tale isn't very nice, so we'll just mix it with another one." But the Grimms at least annotated their work and told us what they did to the original stories.

Only for the last forty or fifty years have the French taken a scientific attitude toward collecting their folklore, finally taking care to record their stories authentically, as they were told. Since our story comes from before that time, we can't be sure that even the name of the heroine wasn't an invention of the person who wrote it down. We know that at least some parts of the story were interposed by the collector, for example the remark that "such transformations at that time were not so extraordinary as they are today," meaning it wasn't unusual for lambs to go to church; certainly that was added—it just doesn't fit in with the way the original story proceeds. The French editions of fairy tales are full of that kind of pseudo-novelistic nonsense, so we have to sort through such interpolations and keep to the basic patterns.

We can make a guess from what we know about number symbolism that the nine brothers represent deities or archetypal powers which point to the pre-Christian Celtic world (and in the German parallels, to the Germanic pagan world). They are, so to speak, the gods of pre-Christian paganism that live in the forest, beyond the borders of civilization.

The Christianization of Europe has never quite penetrated completely through to the agricultural population; in the country, Christian thought has always been blended with pagan folklore traditions. Even now, part of the pagan polytheism in Christian Europe has been integrated into Christianity in the form of the different local saints and angels. These figures satisfy the need of the people to pray to a special god to whom they feel closer than to the great metaphysical godhead in heaven. They also fill their need to pray to a god who "specializes" in certain specific concerns. That's why in the Catholic calendar you have all those saints. Each one is a specialist: St. Anthony gives you back things you have lost, St. Florian protects you from fire, and so on. Each has a function. That is a vestige of the former polytheistic state in which the different gods represented different archetypal aspects of the unconscious to which one could turn in particular situations.

One advantage this half-way polytheism in Catholicism brought with it was the need to construct the "Church year." Although this practical Church calendar was lost in the Protestant Reformation, when they propagated a strict monotheism and did away with all the Catholic saints and angels, the Catholic Church still makes use of this Church year, where every day has its saint, its function, its rules of behavior and its special uses of certain instruments. You have a time for sowing beans, for washing the vinegar bottle, etc., and for each such practice there is a little legend telling you why you should do it. For instance, you have to prepare the vinegar bottle on Good Friday because vinegar was given to Christ on the cross. Therefore the "mother" of vinegar has to be washed on Good Friday and on no other day of the year.

If you look at any peasant calendar, you will see how many customs are regulated in their relationship to the right moment, the change of seasons and the cycles of life. Such practices put people in touch with cyclic time, helping them to honor the rhythms of nature.

Underlying all these customs are traces of many pagan traditions. Of course, these things have little meaning unless we understand them psychologically, otherwise they would be mere habitual superstitions, and they would be most irritating to the rationalist: "Why on earth should you prepare the vinegar bottle on Good Friday?—I can see why you should do it when it's necessary or when you change the vinegar bottle, but why just on Good Friday?" If one loses sight of the deeper psychological meaning of such practices, they become purely mechanical, and in that case they *would* be rather stupid!

In our story the parents, the ruling powers of consciousness, have died away. So now the plurality of archetypal contents comes to the fore, and their "nineness" refers, as I said, to underworldly lunar and chthonic powers. Therefore we may guess that they represent or hint at pre-Christian gods who *should* function in an integrated way with the ruling attitude. But they are now in the forest with their sister; they live only from the animals in the forest, completely isolated from any other human contact.

Isolation always invites an attack by the powers of evil and the dangerous aspects of the unconscious. That is why, with the exception of hermits and shamans, people who have a specific religious call and the power to overcome attacks of the unconscious, it is always dangerous to put oneself in such an isolated position. In many archaic religions one is advised not to live alone, especially not to live alone in nature. There are innumerable primitive stories that begin by stressing the perils of so doing. For instance, in a South American Indian story,[53] the family wants to go to the village feast and one of the girls says, "Oh, no, I want to stay home." The others say, "That is dangerous!" But they leave her, and as soon as they have gone a strange man appears at the door of the

---

[53] MDW, *Indianer Märchen aus Südamerika*, no. 52 (Jena: Diederichs, 1921).

hut. He snoops around and asks for food, and suddenly the girl realizes with horror that this is Kurupira, a man-eating ghost of the forest. The girl knows, "Now I'm in for it," and then through all sorts of tricks she barely escapes being murdered and eaten.

There are similar stories from Indian countries and from all over the world. When one lives alone, separating oneself from the rest of the tribe, this at once attracts the nature spirits in a negative form. They attack you, and if you are not a called medicine man or shaman, you do not have the magic to defend yourself, and so you succumb to the powers of the unconscious.

If you want to know what that means psychologically, just go and live for several weeks alone in a forest or in a mountain hut, and then you will know. The devil attacks from every side.

There is a certain amount of unconscious energy that normally flows into human contacts; when this energy gets dammed back into the unconscious, it overflows in a flood, so to speak. This flood of unconscious energy usually surfaces first in the form of the shadow or negative animus or anima, especially if the unconscious has been repressed or ignored before. In our story, what has been ignored is obviously the witch. The brothers come to this witch while they are hunting, by following a hind. They come to her hut and enter her realm.

This is a very widespread European fairy tale motif. But it is archetypal everywhere, not only in Europe. For instance, some magical animals lure a hunter into a place where he has never been before. In eighty percent of the stories this has a positive outcome. Usually the hunter comes upon a beautiful princess in distress, or in some other way he discovers his heroic task. Such scenes very often describe the beginning of a process of individuation.

In alchemy the stag and the hind represent the fugitive god Mercurius who lures the adept into the unknown. These animals always have the quality of being elusive, difficult to catch, and yet at the same time they function to bring about renewal.

Already in classical antiquity it was believed that the stag held the secret of self-renewal; the actual hook for this projection was the fact that it sheds its antlers and then grows new ones, as though undergoing a partial death through which it becomes beautiful again when it grows new antlers. Aelian tells a story according to which the stag, when it grows old and tired and begins to lose its antlers, goes to a cave of its bitterest enemy, a poisonous snake.[54] There it inhales the snake, which bites the stag, and then the stag expels the snake in the

---

[54] *De natura animalium,* ed. Rudolf Hercher (Paris, 1858).

right way and becomes even sicker. The stag nearly dies, but then renews itself. This shows that the secret of self-renewal is to integrate one's own opposite. The poisonous snake is the stag's absolute opposite. By ingesting its opposite, the stag can renew itself and find the secret of new life.

This legend gave rise to the world-wide idea that the stag is a kind of hero who has the healing secret of self-renewal, but there is also one negative quality attributed to the stag, and that is pride. We have to concentrate on this negative quality, because the hind in our story is negative; it lures the brothers to their doom. In medieval allegories, the stag was a symbol of pride, and again the hook for this projection is very obvious, if you have ever seen a beautiful stag carrying its antlers in a majestic way.

As Adolf Portmann has said, the antlers of a stag are a nonsensical invention of nature because they are not very good as weapons; good pointed horns would be much more useful. Portmann used this example to show that in nature there are not only utilitarian constructions, but also a certain amount of what he calls *Selbstdarstellung,* "self-exhibition" or showing off.[55] That is, sometimes it seems that certain animals just naturally exhibit certain qualities that tend to be used as symbols, and that these features cannot be explained solely by utilitarian principles. This view is not generally accepted by other zoologists, but it shows that even Portmann—he especially mentions the stag in this connection—can become caught up in the archetypal feeling man has about the stag, that it represents beauty and pride.

So these ten children lived in a certain state of isolation, and isolation, we know, often leads to pride—the feeling that one is special. If you live among other people, from morning to night they will take great pains to teach you that you are nothing but a common, ordinary human being. Quite rightly. But if one lives alone, one easily gets lost in fantasies about oneself and the world. So the children's pursuit of the hind would mean they were pursuing some wishful desire or fantasy.

In hexagram 3 of the *I Ching,* "Difficulty at the Beginning," one oracle states, "Whoever hunts deer without the forester only loses his way in the forest."[56] And the commentary says that means that "he desires the game."[57] It says there that if one is in difficulty and simply follows one's desires or wishful fantasies without the necessary correcting wisdom, one can run into trouble.

On the other hand, in the many other stories where the pursuing of the hind or

---

[55] *Das Tier als soziales Wesen* (Zürich, 1953).
[56] *I Ching,* p. 18.
[57] Ibid., p. 402.

the stag leads to the process of individuation, one could just reverse this wise saying and say, "No, one *should* follow one's wishful desirous fantasies, one's drives, and then take what comes."

It would not really be inconsistent to say that, because what one ought to do in such a situation depends on whether or not one has the companionship of "the forester," a certain natural wisdom. Those who do not have the forester with them don't know how to deal with the witch. It's similar to what I said before: only the shaman or the medicine man can stand loneliness in the woods without getting into trouble. If one risks an encounter with the unconscious, one needs a certain nature wisdom and a certain kind of knowledge in order to avoid succumbing to its impact.

Our evil witch has phallic teeth, and she has a tongue that winds nine times around her body. That points to her underworldly qualities. In antique mythology, the River Styx winds nine times around Hades. Also, Cerberus has nine heads according to certain stories. Since the number nine is found in the symbolism of hell, the underworld and the realm of the dead, this puts our witch into that realm also: she is a creature of the waters of death in the underworld.

What this witch wants is to be married to the oldest brother. Needless to say, the boy's refusal is quite understandable.

The proposal of marriage by a witch is very unusual. In most other fairy tales these destructive wood-witches want to enslave people, to make them their servants. They want to make them the cook or the kitchen maid in their house, or they simply want to eat them. Proposals of marriage are very infrequent, but there are some parallels which show that this could be a variation of the general theme that the powers of darkness long for the light. The dark powers want the human being for nourishment, or for service or companionship, for they cannot subsist alone. They long for some connection with the human world.

Our witch goes so far as to want a love union with a human. We don't know what would have happened if the eldest brother had agreed. For all we know she might have improved her manners, but she probably would have destroyed him. However in the actual story this question does not arise.

When this fairy tale took its final form, the dark underworld powers, the chthonic powers, were not sufficiently integrated. They were expelled and left out, and the people had lost sight of them. Therefore there is a dynamism in those dark powers toward consciousness. In this connection we must remember that in the milieu in which this story takes place, we come across several noblemen and owners of castles. Lévène marries a nobleman. Her family is also from the noble aristocracy. So the story makes a point about this aristocratic class within the prevailing French civilization. Living in their castles, they formed a small feudal clique among themselves from the Middle Ages right up to the eighteenth century. And during this time there was a tremendous social gap between the lifestyle of the nobility with its rather lofty idealism and spiritualism on the one hand, and the powers of darkness and the power of the earth on the other. And this gap was much too wide. The rest of the population were serfs, completely doomed or drowned in the dark, so to speak, in mother nature.

France is a tremendously fertile country; the people call their country "The Garden of God." It really is a paradise in the still unspoiled rural parts of France, and in its positive form this feeling of bounty and richness has led to "La Douce France"—the wonderful agreeable ways of life the French people know. They have led the world in the art of good living, in questions of love, of food, of wine, of cultivating beauty. But the dark shadow of this way of life is that one tends to lose sight of the negative powers of existence. Whenever one is happy, one loses sight of the dark side of life. We are all made that way. Perhaps it has a meaning, but I can say about myself that I'm like a cork: when nothing depresses me, I just float happily on the surface of the water until the next dark or negative thing bangs into me. And as far as I see, most of my fellow human beings are the same way. If you are happy, you just unconsciously lose sight of the disagreeable and dark aspects of existence.

You see one result of this in the French Revolution. The peasants killed their nobility in masses, chasing after them with guillotines. And when the *tricoteuses,* the proletarian women, sat on the tribune, they knitted calmly all the while: "Oh there, look—it's the Duc du Subise who is being beheaded . . ." "Oh, ah! Marie Antoinette, she's very attractive. She looks quite pale! Oh, doesn't she look beautiful!"—and they went right on knitting, taking great pleasure in the beheading of their ruling class.

Jung once said that the French have not yet recovered from this catastrophe. They still haven't really found a form of democratic life. They haven't quite recovered from that sudden outburst. The Revolution did not arise from nothing— it had to come because the upper classes completely ignored what was going on in the depths. They ignored the problems and the suffering of the people. They lived happily on the surface in a kind of fool's paradise. So you can see in the history of France what happens when the dark side of human nature is not taken sufficiently into account.

That is the state of affairs behind the passionate wish of the witch to be accepted, to be integrated. But her wish is not fulfilled, as we see at the end of the story. She is simply executed. In other words, the desired connection of the underworld with consciousness does not come to pass.

It is interesting that the size of the witch's tongue is emphasized. The tongue is the instrument with which we form our words. In French, both "language" and "tongue" are signified by *la langue*. So the tongue signifies the logos principle, the Word. And when it is negative, it means mainly the misuse of words, as in slander. That's in many representations of devils and demons: they have very, very long tongues.

A Jesuit Father of the sixteenth century, Picinellus, says that there is a wheel—a fiery wheel of evil—going round in human society, which is kept turning and turning by the slandering tongues of people who constantly gossip and talk and fan hatred. The tongue there represents the devilish principle that keeps this wheel of evil going. It brings up the shadow, and that is not always a bad thing. If one *can* still poison someone by making him or her feel inferior or distrustful or jealous or envious, then you know that person still has such a complex. If you have really worked on your complexes, you become more or less untouchable and you are no longer influenced by poisonous gossip. As long as poisonous talk can get to you, it means there is some shadow element around that isn't yet integrated. And so the wheel is not quite so deplorable, because it keeps you on your toes.

The nine-times wound tongue of the witch reminds us of the darkness we have to accept; we cannot just repress it. Without the witch's tongue, people will try to do just that: they will embrace too fully the Christian ideal of perfection and become too aloof about their ideals and their striving to be good. They will have a too-lofty idea of what individuation is, and because of that they will repress the dark side.

In the social milieu of France we find evidence of the shadow everywhere. For example, refined political intrigues have always played a great role in French politics, which we see in the way French ministers exchange their seats so quickly: that is all arranged behind the scenes. But there is also another area where we encounter this witch in French history, and that is in the realm of materialism. France is a naturally rich country. Although this may no longer be quite as true, it has for a long, long time been relatively easy to live in France. So the French tend to fall for a very narrow-minded, materialistic set of values. It is the witch, it seems, who lurks behind all this—in those tight-lipped French women who make political marriages, who sell their daughters and sons to neighboring families and discuss the inheritance in detail. France, the country of love, is also the country where marriage politics are constantly at work, and questions of money and inheritance play a tremendous role. I have never analyzed a French person without having to discuss money problems for ever and ever. These problems seem to be linked up with the witch, who is not outwardly accepted and who therefore rules in the darkness of the forest.

In our story, the witch, because she is rejected, turns the nine brothers into lambs. She spares the girl from this fate as long as she doesn't tell anyone about it; otherwise, she would be turned into a lamb too. Why the witch spares the sister is not clear: perhaps it is only because she is of the same sex, so naturally she could not have refused to marry the old witch. Lévène was outside the domain of the witch's marriage wish, so to speak, and therefore she was not hit so directly.

Now we have to ask why, of all things, the witch chose lambs for her transformation of the brothers. That's quite unusual. I haven't found any parallels where the cursed ones are turned into lambs; the animals chosen are usually some kind of bird or some woods animal. The fact that lambs were chosen must indicate that this is a local form connected with a local problem.

We have to look at the negative aspects of the lamb. Although in Catholic countries we think of the lamb as the Christian symbol of the *Agnus Dei,* in our fairy tale it is obviously a curse to be a lamb. Even the priest hesitates to accept the lambs into his church, so we must eliminate the Christian idea of the lamb and see what else it represents in folklore.

In folklore lambs and sheep are thought to be mediumistic, to have hunches of what's going to happen. They know the weather, they know the death of their master, they know of coming catastrophe, and they show all this by a panicky reaction. On the other hand, they are also thought to be primary victims of black magic and witch work: if you want to work black magic on your peasant neighbor, the easiest way is to bewitch his lambs. They are more easily bewitched than any of his other animals. No matter what black hex you put on them, they will fall victim to it. It is because of their innocence. They are so innocent that they have no defense against powers of darkness.

In Greek, sheep were called *probaton.* That's a beautiful word. *Pro* means "forward" and *baton* comes from *beino,* "to walk." The lamb is the forward-walking animal. I think that is so beautiful. A flock of lambs on a plain will just walk and walk and walk, one after another, grazing stupidly. They don't look where they walk; they just walk with the flock. A large herd of sheep sometimes is like a flow of water; they all flow in the same direction.

Lambs are also terribly gregarious, and that is one of their great weaknesses. They are panicky animals, and if, for instance, a dog chases a leading lamb so it jumps into an abyss or does something else out of panic, the whole flock will follow suit. You read again and again in our papers that dogs or tourists in the

Alps frighten just a few sheep, or a single lamb that jumps into the abyss and the whole flock follows! Then the peasants have to kill all of them. Once they had to kill three hundred sheep who had all jumped over a cliff after the leading ram. Completely idiotic!—their gregarious instinct blinds them completely; they just walk forward behind the leading sheep.

So the lamb has always been an appropriate picture for the "herd person," the "mass man"—our gregarious side that makes us indiscriminately do exactly what all the others do no matter how stupid an action it is. It's like going to a sale in a big department store. In these sales the women just grab everything, and then they come home and they don't know why they bought the things they grabbed. They did it because the others were doing the same! That is a beautiful example of this type of human reaction. You can see it already in little children. So often when one child does something, all the others have to join in: "Me too! Me too!"

Another explanation of the selection of sheep in our story as the animals of transformation lies in the fact that the French as a nation are predominantly a feeling people. Feeling is their dominant function, and therefore there is a certain unwillingness, or inability, to think.. Characteristically, when the French do think, they show a tendency toward schematic, abstract thought, which is typical for the inferior thinking of feeling people.

Jung once gave a lecture to a society of French physicians and philosophers. He was young at the time and he explained his concept of the unconscious to them in a very simple way, yet he got nowhere. The message simply didn't arrive. Then he tried to explain it in a rational, philosophical way, and again in a medical way, but still nothing sunk in. Then finally one member of the society (who was Jewish and therefore may have had a broader viewpoint) said, "Ah, I understand, you are talking about religion!"

You see, religion is a subject that's in another drawer. One doesn't think about it. It's considered to be a self-evident truth that one lives by but never reflects on. One uses one's mind only for playing with little rational details, not for asking deep questions. The deep questions are forbidden. They are in the drawer for religion, and that is the affair of the Church and the priests. The ordinary person doesn't think about such things.

I've given lectures several times in Paris. It was very difficult to convey what I wanted to say, because I felt a kind of blockage. Once I did a very stupid thing. I thought, "The French are rationalists, schematic rationalists," so I gave a lecture on my book *Number and Time*. But there are some real thoughts in it, not just schemata, so I got nowhere. The only discussion they seemed interested in revolved around occult number symbolism. That was the one subject I hadn't touched on—I didn't want to have anything to do with it, but that's the subject they brought up. Occultism!—that, they liked! I was very disappointed, but afterward they commented rather favorably on my feminine qualities, so that comforted me and I went home quite happily. But I had to put my mind in my back pocket; I couldn't convey any real thoughts to them, or so it seemed.

That is the "sheepification" which has again and again threatened French culture. Naturally there are exceptions; there are always geniuses and other personalities who break through this curse. I hope you realize that when I make such sweeping statements they are only meant as the kind of generality that always has many exceptions. But the collective tendency against deep thinking is strong, so I believe that partly explains the sheep symbolism that is so striking and so special in this fairy tale.

Now, Lévène lives with her sheep brothers in a little hut, and she sings them little songs, and she says little prayers, and after she's married and at the castle, she sits in the garden and makes little garlands for her brothers and sings more little songs. You see here the whole scenario of Daphnis and Chloe, the rococo garden, the erotic, pseudo-back-to-nature phase, the end of the feudal system in France where people actually played at being amorous shepherds and shepherdesses, completely ignoring the subterranean rumblings that led to the French Revolution. And right to the end, they almost playfully let themselves be killed. It was a world of degenerated, sentimental playfulness which even played with the "back-to-nature" slogan. It became popular for one to be more natural, but what naturalness—the most unnatural naturalness there is! They made everything sweet and sentimental, so that even the pigsties no longer smelled! This is the unreal world in which Lévène marries a young nobleman.

While Lévène plays around in the garden with her lamb brothers, she is pushed into the well by the jealous maid who is the witch's daughter and the wife of the gardener. Both of the women are pregnant, so the maid puts herself in Lévène's place, and then she demands to eat the eldest lamb.

There are two Grimm parallels for this motif. One is called "The Goose-Girl,"[58] and the other is "The White Bride and the Black Bride."[59] Very often you find a princess or a noble girl whose maid puts herself unexpectedly in her mistress's place by deceiving the husband. He thinks she is his wife, but the real wife is either killed or turned into an animal, or expelled in some other way.

---

[58] *The Complete Grimm's Fairy Tales,* p. 404.
[59] Ibid., p. 608.

Here the true wife is pushed into the depths of the well.

Since Lévène is the heroine of the story, she represents the redeeming factor, that feminine feeling attitude through which the curse on the brothers could be lifted. She therefore symbolizes an impulse toward a differentiated and human feeling which has a the right connection with the spiritual values of the depths. But here she is pushed into the well by the maid, the false bride.

The false bride is always a jealous female. Her motive for doing what she does is envy and jealousy. I tend to take that quite literally, because, as Jung once said, envy or jealousy is the primary flaw of feminine nature. It is not only a flaw of feminine nature in women, it is also the shadow of the anima in men. As soon as a man is anima possessed, then he too is touched by jealousy and envy. You can see this, for instance, in scientific discussions. When a man no longer discusses for the sake of facts or the truth, but begins to discuss with a feminine undertone as though to say, "Now you must listen to *me* . . ."—then you know he's in the anima and is acting out of vanity and jealousy. He's no longer interested in what is true, he only likes to hear himself talk. So although we can call that a flaw of feminine nature, it refers to both men and women. It simply means that the shadow of the feminine is an indiscriminate envy or jealousy. It is similar to what I described earlier, the "me-too" reaction, the not knowing one's own needs or values, not being able to differentiate them from everyone else's. This leveling out, I-want-it-too-because-the-other-has-it reaction is one of the great hindrances to individuation.

The witch has another potential latent in her. She has the healing quality. The tongue is an instrument not only of talk, but also of discernment of tastes. Many times when we cannot find out what a thing is with our eyes or by touch, we can put it on our tongue where, as you know, we have a tremendous number of nerve endings. Then we can discern what it is. So the tongue is a symbol of discernment and therefore of making qualitative distinctions. That is precisely what is lacking in this sheep's world.

The negative side of the witch, the maid, acts out of envy. Enviousness is one of the greatest enemies of human civilization everywhere. That's why envy and jealousy are always evoked in negative political propaganda. One has only to write, "Look, *they* have it and we *don't* have it!" and everyone's emotions are aroused. That witch trick has been used throughout history to lure people out of themselves and into mass movements.

The gardener, who is the maid's husband, is ordered to kill the oldest lamb, but he cannot because it keeps running around the well. By doing this the lamb points to the fact that his sister is down there, and that's how she is saved.

This is another singularity in our fairy tale—that the gardener is a negative figure. That almost never occurs. Gardeners in mythology are generally very positive figures and are usually linked with the idea of the saving hero. In Egypt, Osiris was represented as a gardener. After the Resurrection, Christ appeared as a gardener to the women who came to the empty tomb. This probably has something to do with the Osiris connection. And in most other mythological contexts, very often the hero becomes a gardener at the king's court and lives there for a while until he is revealed as the true hero.

So the gardener here is a latent form in which the hero survives until he is recognized in his higher form. You could also interpret Christ's appearance as a gardener in that way. He is in a time of latency, the three days after His entombment when He is invisible and has not yet resurrected, when He appears in the form of a gardener. Only at his transfiguration does He reveal His true divine being. Since our gardener is negative, therefore, we must look into this very closely.

Remember that the beautiful garden in our story represents civilized nature but with a negative connotation because it is too much of a paradise. You know that paradise is a garden, so our gardener would be the creator of a fool's paradise, so to speak; he has made this nice little garden where the lambs play about and the girl plays with the lambs. It is just this state of innocence that is harboring the evil side of nature. Here too, the evil deed of the maid gets things going. It is because of her insistence on eating the lamb that Lévène's husband ultimately discovers that his true wife has been pushed into the well. And it is through Lévène's fright in that situation that she gives birth to the child. And it is through the baptism of this child that the brothers are redeemed. So although the child is completely anonymous and purely instrumental in the story, through it we have the baptism and the possibility of the brothers' redemption.

That child is the decisive factor. Generally in other parallels, the sister of the bewitched brothers gives birth to a very special child who has a star or a sign of the sun on its forehead, by which it is characterized as the new redeemer or the healer, or the new king, or the divine child which represents a renewal of life.

Through the evil deeds of the maid and through her act of pushing the heroine into the well, into the depths, Lévène brings forth the child, the redeeming or renewing factor. So we see that Lévène is that feminine element which is meant to produce a new possibility of life that will overcome the stagnation and lead toward the future.

Lévène says, "We must baptize this child at once, and I want the big white lamb to be its godfather." Usually one baptizes children "at once" only when they are weak or when their lives are in danger. Otherwise, one waits one or two days. So this divine child, this possibility of life-renewal, is still in great danger. It is still possible that the dark forces of the witch, the gardener and the witch's daughter might harm it, and therefore the baptism has to be performed at once so that it doesn't die before its soul has been accepted into the community.

The white lamb becomes the godfather. Now this is interesting. In the English language, you have a "godfather" and a "godmother" for a child. In German, it's *Pate* and *Patin,* words that don't reveal much of their meaning. But the English words reveal the function. The godfather and the godmother at the baptism remind us of the fact that we all have not only two mortal, incomplete, all-too-human parents, but that our true parents are the archetype of the father and the archetype of the mother. And if you are a child's godfather or godmother, you must say at the altar that whenever the parents are unsatisfactory or if they die or in any way fail in their function, you will take their place. And so the godparents are a kind of life assurance for the child.

Although this is not done so much in reality, we can see in analysis that whenever someone has an unsatisfactory father or mother, or a negative relationship to them, there are still in the background of that person's psyche the healing forces of the positive mother and the positive father. And if one wants to be healed of whatever the personal father or mother has done, one must fall back on those archetypal powers that are *not* sick and that can restore what the actual parents had ruined.

By choosing the eldest brother as godfather, the sister demands that within the Church system this leader of the pagan gods be acknowledged. Notice that he is redeemed by being made a godfather, while the other brothers are redeemed by the priest putting his stole over them. In giving them his stole, he makes them brethren—priests, so to speak. He gives them a part of his priestly adornment and thus recognizes them as priest figures. So the eldest brother is recognized in a very veiled way as a god, and the other eight brothers are accepted as priest figures, and by these actions they are all redeemed, restored to their human shape.

This shows that, as so often in Catholic countries, the collective unconscious tries not so much to overthrow the prevailing conscious form of life as to enlarge it "downward" toward a deeper and more meaningful integration of the pagan substratum. The Church has already taken on much paganism in its outward forms and cults; but in order to survive and not petrify, it seems necessary that it absorb and integrate even more of the pagan underworld. But that naturally leads the Catholic Church to the same problem Protestant Churches meet in another form, and which is not solved in our story, namely the problem of absolute evil.

In our story, anything of Celtic paganism, anything of nature, can still be taken in. By the broadmindedness of our priest, who doesn't reject the idea of the lamb carrying the child and acting as godfather, these elements can be integrated. If that were the end of it, we would have a more satisfactory solution.

But that is not the end of the story: the problem of evil still remains. When the story actually ends, we have two triads. First we have Lévène and her nobleman husband and their child, a positive triad. But we also have a negative triad, that of the witch, the maid and her gardener husband. This latter triad is not reconciled with the first. It is cut apart, eliminated; its members are torn apart by four horses. Everything positive is triadic; there is a positive triad and a negative triad, but the negative triad is removed.

That is a most unsatisfactory solution to this fairy tale. Or rather, it is unsatisfactory to me, from a psychological standpoint, because it disposes of evil, so to speak. Such executions of evil figures are quite common in fairy tales, but as we all know, no sooner is the witch executed in one story than up she pops immediately in the next one—so we know how effective such executions really are! They are only momentary. What they means is that *for the moment* the destructive activity of this dark mother archetype is stopped. But in eternity it is not really stopped at all. It has been defeated only in this one constellation and for only this one moment. It will therefore reappear soon in some other form.

Whenever an evil figure is executed in a fairy tale, a specific neurosis-creating, destructive impulse has disappeared from the lives of the people. It has lost its activation and returns to a latent form, but it is never gone forever. It is only exorcised for the time being from the realm of consciousness.

So our present fairy tale, too, ends with the same strange question mark as do many others: the redeeming processes go only so far, then they simply stop, so one is left with a question. I have found this to be the case most often when we have predominantly triadic formations—nines and threes—but not with fours. I even begin to think that triadic formations are more frequent in fairy tales than quaternarian formations. On the other hand, however, in all religious mythologies and in alchemy, quaternarian formations predominant. That throws a strange light on what fairy tales are by contrast. They are images of processes in the collective unconscious *when consciousness does not understand them.* They are like not-understood dreams that are not integrated into the cultural consciousness or that are integrated only partially.

As to the folk tales, the people just enjoy telling these stories and leaving them at that. They feel refreshed by them, for they have a positive healing effect, but they are not assimilated; they are not reflected upon, as are mythologies that form the basis of religious systems or civilizations or alchemical philosophies. Man concerns himself with them. He tries to construct a conscious philosophical or dogmatic or theological or theosophical system from them. He tries to explain why these things are so. Through them, man enters into a kind of *Auseinandersetzung* or dialogue between collective consciousness and the collective unconscious. But as for fairy tales, they are a pure nature product. They show how nature plays with itself. They are like the dreams of those who write down their dreams but never think about them. Therefore, through fairy tales you can see how compensatory processes form: how destruction surfaces and how a solution forms, how another destruction and then another solution follow. But there is no end to this process.

What is lacking is the human individual. That is why so many stories have a slightly sad or questionable ending. And it's interesting, as you will see when we look at an African story, that the closer we come to the early material of so-called primitive populations, sad endings are more frequent. If you read African or South American Indian fairy tales, you find that very few end happily.

I will discuss later what that means, but I want to prepare the way by showing you that even in more developed cultures, when a fairy tale has a satisfactory ending, there is always a sad question left over: "Yes, but what about . . . ?" In our case, for instance, what if the evil witch comes back? She hasn't yet married. So what about that demand of darkness? How will it come up in some other form? This problem is linked up with the fact that since the Middle Ages we have completely repressed the problem of evil. We have tried to pretend that evil doesn't exist, or that it can be exorcised by religious or scientific means. But this delusion must one day come to an end.

5
The Tale of Mrile
(African)

Now we will look at an African fairy tale. It's called "The Tale of Mrile."[60] It comes from East Africa, from the Dschagga tribe, one of the Bantu group. The tale goes like this:

A man had three sons. The oldest, whose name was Mrile, went with his mother to collect kolokasia seeds. Mrile saw such a seed and said, "Oh, is this a seed? It is as beautiful as my little brother!" Mrile's mother said, "How can a seed be as beautiful as a human being?" But the boy hid the seed in a hollow tree, saying, "Masura Kiriviri chacambingo nakasanga" [one would not be able to understand this even if one knew the language], and they went home.

The next day Mrile went back to the hollow tree and saw that the seed had turned into a little child. Now, his mother always cooked the food. Every time she cooked a meal, Mrile would hide away his portion and secretly carry it to the child, but he himself became thinner and thinner. His parents became very worried, and they wondered where the food had gone.

Mrile's younger brothers saw one day that Mrile was hiding his food away, so they followed him to see what he did with it. They watched as he gave his food to the child, and they reported back to their parents afterward: "He goes to a hollow tree and puts the food in there. And there seems to be a little child there." Then they led their mother to the place, and the mother saw that there was indeed a child in the tree, so she killed it.

Mrile did not know of this, so the next time he took his food to the tree, he found the child dead. When he returned home he began to cry. His family asked him, "Mrile, why are you crying?" but he only answered, "Oh, it's just the smoke in the hut that is bothering my eyes." So his family advised him to sit on the other side, but when he did so he still cried, and he would not tell them why. Then the family said, "Take your father's chair and sit outside in the courtyard."

So he took his father's chair outside the hut, sat down and said, "Oh chair, go up like the cord of my father when he hangs up the honey pot in the trees." And the chair went up about 50 meters. It got stuck there. Then Mrile said a second time, "Oh chair, go up like the cord of my father when he hangs up the honey pot in the trees." This time, one of his younger brothers saw him. He called the others, crying out that Mrile was going to heaven.

---

60 MDW, *Afrikanische Märchen*, no. 9 (Jena: Diederichs, 1921).

His mother came outside and said, "Mrile, return, return, my child!" She said this six times. But Mrile answered, "I don't return. I don't return, mother. And I don't return, and I don't return." Next, the younger brothers called, "Mrile, return! Come home!" But Mrile answered, "And I, I will not return." Next his father said, "Mrile, here is food! Here is your food!" But Mrile replied, "I don't want any more food. I don't want any more, my father, and I don't want any more." Then all the tribe came and said, "Mrile, come home!" And his uncle called up, "Mrile, come to your home!" But Mrile sang the answer, "I don't return, Uncle, and I won't return any more." And so he disappeared and was seen no longer.

Mrile then met many different people: one who collected wood, one who sowed millet, one who herded the cattle, and so on. He asked those people, "Where is the way to the Moon King?" They all answered, "We will show you the way to the Moon King if you help us a bit." So he helped all those people, one after another, and slowly he found his way through this to the so-called Moon King.

When he came to the Moon King, he saw that the people were eating uncooked food, so he said, "Why don't you cook with fire?" They replied, "What is fire?" Mrile was very surprised: "Do you know nothing about fire? Food is much better when it is cooked with fire!" So the Moon King said, "We will give you a lot of cattle if you show us how to cook with fire." So Mrile instructed the people to collect much wood. Then with a drill borer he made a fire. Then he roasted some bananas and gave them to the Moon King, saying, "Now isn't this much better?" The Moon King was delighted. Next Mrile gave the people cooked meat, and again they were all delighted. So the Moon King called all his people together and said, "This is a medicine from the other side. Yes, from the other side, from your people!" [All of the dead ancestral spirits go to the Moon King, so when the Moon King said, "It is from your people that a man has come," he was probably addressing Mrile's ancestors.]

Then the people gave Mrile great riches, but suddenly he felt homesick and wanted to go home. He tried to send many birds down to tell his people that he was coming, but the birds all made the funniest cries, and not one of them arrived. Finally a thrush came, and she flew right down to Mrile's people and said, "Mrile will come home on the day after tomorrow; save some fat in the spoon for him!" Then the thrush went back to Mrile and said, "I've done it!" But he did not believe her, so he ordered her to go back a second time, but this time she was to bring back a stick from home to prove she had been there.

Finally Mrile was convinced that the thrush had warned his people that he was coming back, so he started on his long journey home. Since it was such a long journey, he soon became very tired. So the bull said, "If you are so tired, I'll carry you on my back, but what will you do for me in return? If I take you on my back, will you eat me when I'm killed?" Mrile replied, "No, I'll never eat you." So he got up on the bull's back and began singing, "I have great possessions. All these cattle are mine! I have great possessions, all these cattle are mine!"

Then he arrived home, and his father and mother gave him a lot of fat and meat. But later, the bull became too old, so the father killed him. His mother said, "Should my son, who had such trouble with this bull, not eat some of his meat?" So she hid the fat from the bull in a pot, and when she knew that it was finished, she took some flour and mixed it with the fat and gave it to Mrile. But when he put it in his mouth, the meat talked to him and said, "Do you dare to eat me although I carried you on my back?—Then you will be eaten too, as you ate me!" Mrile sang, "My mother, I told you not to give me the meat of the bull!" But when he took a second bite, his foot sank into the earth. He sang again, "My mother, I told you, don't give me the meat of the bull." But when he ate all of the flour and fat, suddenly he sank away into the earth. And this is the end.

In the beginning, Mrile secretly puts away one kolokasia seed. He hides it in a hollow tree, and by magic he turns it into a little child. The whole tragedy of the story then is linked up with the fact that the mother discovers him and kills the little child.

This is a widespread archetypal motif. We find it also in another African fairy tale called "The Tale of Chuveane."[61] In this case, Chuveane also breeds such a little magical child in secret. His parents also discover it, but they don't kill it; they only hide it from him. Then he cries and becomes so desperate that they permit him to find it again and keep it. The child becomes a great medicine man, and later he becomes even a godhead. So we see from this fairy tale of Chuveane what great potential rests in this little seed child.

I want first to discuss the fact that this is not only an African theme. Among the Grimm fairy tales there is one called "The Tale About the Toad,"[62] where a little girl secretly finds a toad and brings milk to it. The toad gives her crowns and jewels and gold. And then suddenly her mother discovers the toad and kills it, and on account of that the child dies too. So again, a mother kills a child's secret magical companion. Mrile is only badly damaged, as we will see, but in the Grimm tale the little girl is killed outright when the toad is killed by her mother. This gives us a general idea of what can happen when a child has such a friend, be it a seed child, a magical toad or any other divine magical companion.

We know for a fact that between the ages of one and a half and five years, children very often attach themselves to a doll or a toy animal which becomes a kind of divine object for them. They can't sleep if they don't have the toy in bed

---

61 Ibid., no. 22.
62 MDW, *Kinder und Hausmärchen*, Die Gebrüder Grimm, vol. 1, no. 1 (Jena: Diederichs, 1922).

with them; they are afraid in the night without it. We could say these objects are a first projected form of the Self. Later such things become less important to the children. They usually replace them with other toys as time goes on, and by the time they reach school age they already know that the toys are "dead." Thus the projection slowly dissolves; but in very early childhood nearly all have some link to a magical divinity that is their double. They talk to their teddy bear or their doll exactly as their mothers talk to them. They want to share with them not only their food but many other day-to-day experiences as well.

To have a magical or divine double is an archetypal motif in the life of children. It is like having a little brother or sister who has divine qualities. This comes from the fact that small children mainly live in the realm of the collective unconscious. Since their egos have not yet developed, they are very close to the Self and the contents of the unconscious. We can see this in part through their dreams, which are often very archetypal. We could say that they still have one foot in eternity; they are not yet completely incarnated into an ordinary, earthly human being, and their eternal personalities continue to hover around them. This timeless personality is what lies behind the "double" of small children.

In many primitive societies, especially in Africa, the belief is widespread that every person has such an eternal double. It is identified materially with the placenta. When the placenta is discharged as the after-birth, they dry it in the sun and form it into a fetish which they then hang around the child's neck. This represents the child's other half which has remained in the ghost land or in heaven and which now has to accompany the person through life in this form. But if ever a man should see his double, for example meeting it suddenly in the woods as an hallucination, this is a sign of death.

We find this superstition even in many European countries: if you see your double, it is a premonition of death because it is one's "other half" who remained in heaven during one's life but is now coming to fetch one back. And, at the moment of death, you meld with it to become whole again. It is only in the moment of death, therefore, that you reach wholeness, by reuniting with that half of your personality that remained in the Beyond, the ghost land, the land of the ancestors.

Now, Mrile breeds a little seed at an age rather beyond the normal time for playing with toys; he turns that seed into a living child that even other people can see is real. This shows that Mrile is an extraordinary personality; he has a call to become a medicine man. In primitive societies, very often medicine men from earliest childhood are characterized by the fact that they never quite lose their connection with the ghost land and the Beyond. Later, in their initiation, they again contact certain helpful familiar spirits. These are very often dead ancestors or magical animals, and with their help medicine men can perform healing rituals and other functions that they could not have done by the power of their egos alone.

The egos of medicine men are just as ordinary as our own. But, unlike ordinary people, they have the extraordinary gift of being able to relate to and constellate the helpful figures of the unconscious. They keep a connection with the depths of the collective unconscious which normal people usually lose in their first school years. For instance, once your children reach a certain age, if you try to tell them fairy tales or myths, they will say, "Oh, no! Don't tell me such stuff, I want to hear the *real* thing!"—namely, they want to hear about trains and automobiles and so on. Whenever such instances arise, you can see the forming of the ego complex, the entering into *this* world, the world of the adult, and a rejection of the fantasy world.

But among adults, too, there a few people who somehow keep this connection with the unconscious; we say they have a call to become creative in some way. And if for any reason they are prohibited from following that call, their connection with the collective unconscious will come to the surface in a destructive way, perhaps by leading them into madness or an early death.

Whether or not one has this connection with the collective unconscious is not a matter of choice but of fate. Yet, if one has this gift and doesn't know how to cope with it, or if one's personality is weak, there is a great danger of psychic illness or physical death, for one is then lured back, so to speak, into the ghost land, the land of death. If a gifted person is healthy and strong enough to enter into earthly life all the same, then it is also likely that he or she will develop a double personality. Such people have a normal ego, which functions in the adapted, three-dimensional world, but they also keep up the connection with their eternal personality.

Jung himself confessed quite openly to having such a double personality; in his autobiography he describes how he felt that he was actually both a Personality No. 1 and a Personality No. 2.[63] He very clearly felt that No. 1 was just the ego of an ordinary school boy, but that No. 2 was his eternal personality. It comprised the whole collective unconscious; it gave him the feeling that the whole ghost world, the ancestral world, was living in him. He mastered the transition to form a schoolboy ego without losing the magical double. But normally the latter becomes lost to us in an abrupt transition when we go to school.

---

[63] *Memories, Dreams, Reflections,* p. 45.

I think the transition in Africans of Mrile's area is more gradual than ours. The African parents simply begin to include their children in more of their adult activities—hunting, getting seeds, finding honey, etc.—as they grow older. So the children then have increasingly greater opportunities to listen to the profane chatting of their parents, and so they are pulled very slowly into the world of adult life.

Also, if one is brought up in a community which still retains its religious beliefs intact, then one has a better chance to keep one's No. 2 personality, because the entire community believes in the special realm. But as you see in the story of Mrile and in the parallel story of Chuveane, it seems that even among many African tribes, the adults are far from pleased when their children keep too close a connection with the eternal. In the case of Chuveane, they say, "That child is a magician." No one who is normal can turn a seed into a little child, so this boy is a magician and the people become frightened. At one point, they even try to kill him because they are so afraid of him. In our story of Mrile, too, the mother must have had similar apprehensions. On the surface, she is worried only because she doesn't want Mrile to get too thin by not eating his food. So, on the surface it looks like we have just a simple case of very strong "motherly love." But obviously there is more to it than that. She also feels this magical child is uncanny, and therefore she kills it.

Something similar still happens among us today. If a child shows extraordinary behavior, the parents only rarely have the sense to realize that the child might have an unusual gift. Only if the parents are similarly gifted and have some connection with the unconscious do they understand. Otherwise they become terribly uneasy. We have a story that illustrates this nicely: when a hen broods little ducklings, she will walk with her chicks along the lakeshore. But if suddenly one of her ducklings ventures out into the water, the hen loses her head! She becomes extremely upset, even desperate, because *that shouldn't be!*

It is this way all over the world. The parents of unusual children are afraid; they think their child is abnormal or psychologically sick, and they run to the child therapist or the teacher. We then have to tell them, "No, your child is just an extraordinary little person with some gifts that you yourselves don't have."

I'm sure you have heard the expression, "black sheep." According to perfectly natural laws of genetics, sometimes in a very fine, normal family a "black sheep" will suddenly appear. Someone is born into that family who is a half-wit or has criminal tendencies, who brings out the shadow and the tragedy of the whole family. But sometimes the black sheep in a family is not really black at all; he or she is actually whiter than all the others, and that whiter-than-usual sheep in a normal family is just as frightening to the parents because it is *above* their level. So, the gifted children cause the same kind of excitement and projections as do the black sheep.

Naturally, the main excitement for the African parents in these stories is the problem of magic. About Chuveane, the people even say openly, "He is a magician." In the Mrile story it is not so clear, but probably the motif underlying the mother's killing of the magical child is also her fear of magic. In neither story do the people take the trouble to wonder if it is black or white magic. They just display the usual fear of magic of any kind. It would be exactly the same if we had a child with an extraordinary gift and did not ask ourselves if it was a gift or a deficiency, but became frightened simply because the child was different.

Everything unusual frightens people. They don't know how to relate to it because they have no previous experience of it; therefore there is a tendency prematurely to judge the unusual in a negative way. We see in the life histories of gifted people how often this is the case.

I once read the biography of a Swiss woodcutter who was quite well known for making strange wood carvings from roots, but also more conventional, very beautiful things. He came from a small, hard-working peasant family. From his earliest youth, he always kept a knife with him and began to carve whenever he found a bit of wood or any workable object. And his parents got so upset about that! They called him a lazy, no-good dreamer, etc. But he did work hard on the farm; he was not one of those inflated future artists who feel they are better than the others and therefore have the right to lie in bed until eleven in the morning and do only their art. According to his biography, he worked just as hard on the farm as all the others. The only difference was that at any spare moment, in the evenings or on Sundays when there was no work to be done, he always carved. And that alone was enough to set his family against him.

So when he was nineteen, he ran away from home and by chance came to another farmer's family in the Toggenburg, in St. Gallen, and this family finally understood him. They took him in as a servant and paid him wages, but they allowed him to carve as much as he liked. They admired his work and encouraged him to go on. And then finally when he was twenty-five, he bought an old dilapidated house, married, and set himself to repairing the entire house. He made every bit of furniture himself, and established himself as a woodcarver. He had a very hard life, but he maintained his independence and became quite a well-known artist in Switzerland.

You see, his parents just couldn't understand why one of their boys was constantly taking a knife and carving what they thought were strange figures. They are very beautiful, but it upset them even though they couldn't find any other fault with him. He simply wasn't normal: one *did not do that.*

The animus of the mother especially seems to have such a destructive, inhibiting effect on creativity. Jung himself told us once that when he was a student of sixteen, he became very excited about something—chemistry or physics—and he drew enormous charts in his room. He put them all up on the wall. Then his mother came in, looked at them suspiciously and said, "Is that of any use?" And Jung was so upset by this that for three days he couldn't go on with the project. Finally he pulled up his socks and said, "Damn it all, I'm not going to be hindered by her remark," and went on again with his charts and figures. But for three days he was completely lamed by that remark, "Is that of any use?"

Now Jung's mother was not evil, and she didn't kill the magical child, but even so, because she did not understand, she badly wounded his creative impulse. Any creative person who has a minimum of sense, therefore, knows from earliest childhood that they must keep the beginning stages of their creative work completely secret, even from their very best friends. It is so delicate, it is so sensitive, that if you show it even to a good friend, and that friend says or even hints of something derogatory, that alone may be enough to deter you from going on with your project.

When you've finished, it doesn't matter. At least I, when I've finished something, don't mind the criticism so much. Oh, I like praise and I dislike criticism, but basically it doesn't affect me after the work is done, because by then I know what it is worth in myself. But in the beginning stages, creative projects are like an egg without a shell; one must not touch them. One should keep them absolutely secret.

Now the great difference between Chuveane and Mrile, and the thing that marks Mrile's tragedy, is that he doesn't protect his secret well enough. Chuveane succeeds in keeping his secret much longer, and he hides it much better, much more shrewdly than Mrile.

Mrile is slightly naive. Thus, Chuveane is able to save the magical side of himself, but Mrile doesn't. His little brothers spy him out, and the mother destroys the child. Then, in his terrible sorrow, Mrile cries and cries, but *now* he hides his reason. He says he's crying only because of the smoke in the hut. But at that point it is quite unnecessary to hide the truth. It seems Mrile is therefore deficient in his ability to distinguish what to keep secret and what things are unimportant enough that they can be made public. That is one of the greatest, more important instincts one must nurse and develop in oneself—namely, this ability to know what should be kept secret at all costs as opposed to what one can expose to the comments of others.

In one letter,[64] Jung even goes so far as to say that analytical understanding of a human being should only be as deep or extensive as the neurosis of that person; otherwise, psychological or intellectual understanding can kill the delicate, private aspects of that person's life. It is good to understand the neurotic mechanisms of the patient, to pull *them* into the light of understanding so that one can kill them. But on the other hand, there are always many secrets one should not understand about one's analysands. One should not even try to understand. One should respect these aspects of their lives and leave them alone.

Sometimes people tell me a dream and I have a strong feeling, "Now for God's sake, don't interpret that!" If it is really a dream that contains something of the essence of that person's being and fate, then one should not interpret it. One should refuse any comment, even if the person wants one. I say, "I prefer not to touch that. In fifteen or twenty years, you will know what that dream means." Because with such a dream, one grows. One goes along, one puzzles, and then bit by bit, by becoming oneself, one also becomes that dream, and then one understands it. But if the person is intellectual and a thinking type, or an intuitive, always wanting to *grab* the material, then one should flatly refuse to interpret it, because it is a mistake to expose such material to the light. Instead, like this seed child, it should remain in the hollow tree as a personal secret. And if, by ways of the heart, one sometimes guesses the other person's secret, one should pretend not to have seen it.

Mrile lacks that instinct. He keeps up his crying even after it is too late to save his little seed child. The child is killed, and nothing matters any more, but he still won't say why he cries. Before, he did not take sufficient care to see that the child remained a secret.

Now the family says to him, "Take your father's chair and sit outside in the courtyard." This is probably because in the courtyard there is such an abundance of goat and sheep dung that you cannot sit on the earth as you can within the hut. That's why they give him the chair to sit in outside, away from the smoke. But there's more to it, because as you see afterward, Mrile sings to the chair and says, "Oh chair, go up like the cord of my father when he hangs up the honey pot in the trees." We can therefore say that he identifies with the father when he sits on the father's chair, and that shows the other reason why he has fallen victim to his mother. Old Freud would be in seventh heaven here, because this time we really do have an Oedipus complex, clearly. Mrile is identifying with the fa-

---

[64] *C.G. Jung Letters*, vol. 1, p. 31.

ther, and therefore, secretly, also with the husband of his mother. He's too closely tied to the mother, and now this goes to the extreme of identifying with the father as the bridegroom of his mother. This Oedipus complex, this mother tie, estranges him from reality so he just goes away to heaven.

What this means practically is the following: Very often when a son has a negative mother complex the mother will have a destructive effect on the son, on his vitality, on his virility. This is expressed here when Mrile's mother kills his child, his creative fantasy. As a result he can no longer bring his creative impulses into concrete reality. He cannot play; he cannot act out his fantasies any more. He has to keep them within, with the result that he begins to drift away into the unconscious. And that is often the very clear beginning of a neurosis.

The creative impulses in a child are normally kept not only introvertedly within, but they are also acted out in play, with other children. But if that is hidden and kept inside, the child becomes silent and sulky and bored in the daytime; and at night he lives his creative fantasies, generally by masturbating and building up a second fantasy world which he now really hides from the parents. Since he can no longer carry them out concretely, these fantasies cannot be corrected, so they can become completely morbid or neurotic or crazy. If the child could act them out in play, then when they became morbid or neurotic his parents or his playmates could correct them: "No, don't do that!" It's enough to say once, "Oh! No, don't do that!" to stop any morbid deviations. But when the child's fantasy world is completely hidden, it blossoms in the dark and estranges the child from reality. At that point his teachers begin to complain that he doesn't pay attention in school. He just sits there in a kind of dumb way, isolates himself from his comrades and lives in his own neurotic fantasy world.

I call it "neurotic," but not every such child is neurotic; if he is a divine child, then although he may hide his creative fantasies, his creativity can survive even in this retired form. If at a later point in life he can again contact it and create from it, no neurosis results and he experiences only a temporary estrangement from so-called normal reality. His creativity has not died completely.

This kind of situation also accounts for many of the strange states into which young men can fall, which I described in my book on the puer aeternus.[65] The puer aeternus does not always have a neurosis, and when he does it is not always due to a positive mother complex. A negative mother complex can also cause a similar state of estrangement from reality. Sometimes boys whose creativity or

---

[65] *Puer Aeternus: A Psychological Study of the Adult Struggle with the Paradise of Childhood* (Santa Monica: Sigo Press, 1981).

essential personality has been negatively hit by the mother can also become high-flying intellectuals. They become very good in school, even brilliant. They use their minds for high flights, for example reading philosophy at a very early age. But at the same time they become lame and inefficient on the physical side. They are generally very bad in sports, and don't like to play or have any social contacts with their schoolmates. They live completely in a realm of premature intellectual brilliance.

Now this is not necessarily to be condemned; it is simply a way to escape the destructive effect of the mother, because *there* she cannot follow. So these young boys go into a masculine realm of the mind where the mother, if she is not brilliant herself, can't go, and there the young man can build up an empire where he is the ruler, where he's free and gets away from his mother.

But later, when he's away from home, he will suddenly discover that he wants to return. And then the whole negative mother complex explodes again. When he wants to connect with a girl, he encounters the problem of his sexuality and of touching reality in any way that requires contact with his instincts and his body. Then the catastrophe becomes manifest. There's nothing there.

In their private, intellectual world, such people feel marvelous, like they are flying high in an airplane, above everything. But on earth, where physical encounters are inevitable, the dragon of the mother complex still waits for them, and they can't get into this kind of reality without having it out with that negative mother complex. And that's why they hover in mid-air for such a long time, unable to come down to earth. Usually only when they are thirty or so and their reality problems become truly urgent do they come into analysis. They *have* to, because they can't go on hovering in mid-air forever.

I use the metaphor of the airplane because I have found it in innumerable dreams. I remember the dreams of a young man who was in that situation. He always dreamt he was in an airplane and he was the pilot. Behind him there was only one passenger seat, as in the smallest aircraft. But there in that passenger seat was a coffin full of rattling bones. One half of his personality had been killed by the mother. And he would have trouble landing on earth again until that coffin—that other half in the coffin—had been resurrected and brought back to life. It was a very long and painful process.

The mother kills the creative fantasy in the child sometimes by fear of magic or lack of comprehension, but often also by a genuine hatred of the creativity and the masculinity of her boy.

Once I had neighbors where I had rented a room, a family of three. The mother was a fat, vulgar woman who had married late and then had a son when she was thirty-eight. One saw it coming that she would eat that poor creature, but it was none of my business, and I pretended not to notice what was going on in the house. But then one day I heard her beating up the little boy, and he was howling so badly at the top of his voice that I couldn't refrain from rushing out of my room and saying, "What are you doing!?" And the mother said, "Imagine! Imagine! He wanted a sprinkling can for Christmas, so we gave him one and said, 'But you can't use it in the flat, you must use it only in the springtime, in the garden.' And just now when I was out of the house he took the sprinkling can, filled it with water and sprinkled all the flowers on the carpet! Imagine!"

So I said to her, "Listen. First, you put that idea into his head yourself. You suggested it to him. And second, that's the most innocent, natural thing to do. Anyone would do that. You can't scold him for it." And she said, "Yes, but you see, if he does that now, he'll kiss the girls when he's sixteen!"

There you are! You see how her fantasy took off about that sprinkling can, which is a nice symbol, a first manifestation, of that little boy's virility, and of the creative fantasy that goes with virility. And already she hated it; she pounced on it because she saw that it was the element that one day would lead the boy away from her. It had to be stamped out right then when he was only three or four, so that by the time he was sixteen none of it would remain. He walks about now at thirty-two, unmarried. He works in a bank, looks pale, and after work he sits with Mama at home. I see him in the street and I think, ""Oh my God! That's how it's done!"

Returning to our story, on his father's chair Mrile goes up to heaven and looks for the way to the Moon King. He finds many different stations where he has to work for certain people who show him the way. That's a completely international, archetypal motif. Very often in European fairy tales, the hero goes, for instance, to the sun, the moon, the stars and the night wind. Or he comes to a three-headed, a six-headed and a nine-headed giant and asks for the way. Or in Russian fairy tales, he comes three times to a wood brother or to a hermit, and he always has to do something or make some sacrifices to find the way. I will therefore skip this and not go into the details except to point out how it shows that each time, Mrile has to do some work, and he does it.

That makes the difference between him and someone who just neurotically retires in the way that little boy retired after his mother had cut him off from his creative fantasy with the sprinkling can. He became completely neurotic, and had much difficulty in school because he was lamed.

Mrile is only partially lamed. He's like the young man I described with the rattling bones in the back seat of his airplane. His ego is still intact, and he still has a purpose and is going somewhere, but Mrile cannot survive on earth any more. He transposes his whole vitality now into the Beyond, and he does hard work there. He collects wood for one, digs for another and so on, which is to say that he keeps up a certain activity toward the contents of the unconscious. He doesn't just drift along, and that redeems his retreat from the earth. He does the work he would have done in one way on earth, but he does it now on the other side. That shows he is a called medicine man or a creative personality: he does not fall into lamed laziness. Because the mother prevented him from doing his work on the outside, he now becomes active inside; he works hard, performing whatever task he meets, which comes from the unconscious. But his goal is to go to the Moon King.

As in Greek, Roman and certain other European mythologies, the moon is the place where the dead go. And there the ancestral spirits become protectors, living with the Moon King and certain gods. So gods, ancestral spirits and the Moon King are all in the realm of the Beyond.[66]

The ancestral spirits are called *mzau ya aümu*, or simply *aümu*. They live on the moon with the Moon King. They are immortal and bestow rain and fertility on the earth. They are the protective gods of the tribes. The Dschagga tribe prays mostly to such ancestral spirits, and most of their sacrifices are offered to them.

Now what is interesting here is that the Moon People do not know about fire. This is all the more remarkable because a neighboring tribe has a Prometheus myth that says humans were immortal and didn't know death, as long as they lived like all the other animals. They ate their food raw and had no knowledge of fire. But then a very shrewd man and his wife stole the fires from the *aümu*, the ancestral spirits, and then on earth humans began to cook their food and to melt iron and make weapons and other implements using fire. As a result, humans became estranged from the rest of creation and also became mortal. The *aümu* and the gods became so angry that they put the curse of death on humankind.

So it is a general mythological theme that only through becoming conscious do we become mortal. This is not to be taken in a literal sense, but rather it means we become aware of death. As long as there is no strong ego consciousness, death is no problem. You enter this world and you leave this world, always keeping one foot in eternity. Therefore, death is only a slight transition. That is why many primitive people can die very easily and without making as much fuss

---

[66] There is a picture of the land of the Moon King in Joseph Campbell's *The Hero with a Thousand Faces* (Bollingen Series XVII; Princeton: Princeton University Press, 1974), Pl. XVIII. It is based on a story from a different tribe, but it still shows the bull and the cattle living on the moon as they do in our story.

as we do. They die quietly and with dignity. They even tend to die too easily. For instance, if one imprisons a Bushman for more than a day, he dies from discouragement. Primitive people can easily die from discouragement if they feel life isn't worthwhile. They just fade away. I read once that a man hurt an African Negro's feelings, and the African became very angry and said, "You just wait!" And the next morning, when the man walked out his door, there before him hung the corpse of his enemy. The offended man had hung himself to hurt the other back.

In that man's view, hanging himself was like saying, "Now I'll make myself into a ghost, and as a ghost I can haunt you much more than I would have as a living being. You will really be in for it when I come back as a revengeful ghost!" The fact that he had to die in order to do this was only a minor detail.

The more ego consciousness becomes focused, the more it has continuity and brightness. The stronger our ego, the more does death, which is a giving up of the ego, become a problem. This is especially true if we don't trust our instincts.

In analyzing the dreams of dying people, I have seen that sixty to seventy per cent of them communicated this message: trust the animal. In the beginning of life one should trust the animal, one's instincts, to guide one into life, and this is just as true at the time of death. One must trust one's instincts to guide one out of life. Our instincts can teach us how to die properly. These are animal instincts; therefore if we trust the animal, if we trust our body, then we are led out of life as harmoniously as we were led into it.

Many myths say that only with the stealing of fire and the birth of consciousness did mortality come into the world. And according to a variation of this same Prometheus myth, the African tribes say that up until that point heaven and earth were quite close to each other. You could touch the sky with your hand. But after the people stole the fire and created human civilization, the sky and the heavens rose up very high and were no longer reachable.

You see therefore that the conscious and the unconscious, the opposites of the psyche, are torn apart through consciousness. Thus an original unconscious totality or harmony is disturbed, and that is how these people believe it happened, this tragedy of mankind in discovering consciousness.

But in our story we have a most amazing, reversed myth. The Moon People and the ghosts of the dead have no fire until Mrile teaches them to use it. He brings the achievements of human consciousness into the heavenly world of ghosts and gods. That is a very puzzling motif. It means that he carries the light of human consciousness into the unconscious. He is a light-bearer, not for earthly mankind and his tribe, but for the unconscious. We may conclude, therefore, that he is not meant to be a cultural hero but instead he is meant to be a medicine man, so our earlier suspicions of this are now confirmed.

Some medicine men, like the Eskimo shamans, don't achieve much on this earth. Some do healing ceremonies and so on, but these healers are usually believed to have a lesser status compared to the true medicine men who carry light into the unconscious; they not only make a connection with the unconscious, they also illumine it for others.

In our story, then, the powers of darkness are longing for the powers of light; in psychological terms, the unconscious is longing to be understood.

According to Mircea Eliade in *Shamanism,*[67] African, Melanesian, Australian and other initiations and tribal rituals are very similar. But he does distinguish shamans from priests. He claims that among the Eskimo tribes who have priests, the priest is a preserver of rituals, ensuring only that they are done correctly. But the shaman is the "specialist of the soul." His function is to deal with cases of possession and to see that the dead find their appropriate place after death. He is a psychotherapist more than a ritualist. And those differences within Eskimo culture seem to be true as well for many tribes in Africa and Australia. They have specialists for the rituals; they have magicians who do minor magic like tracking down thieves, and then they have the greater ones who are the wise men, so to speak, concerned with what the gods want, the future of the tribe, or the decision of the ancestors when a question of going to war arises.

Medicine men are often initiated by torture, similar to the experience of the shamans. The difference is that not all medicine men use ecstasy to contact the Beyond, while the shamans mostly do use an ecstatic frame of mind. The medicine men don't need it because they are usually people who can enter into such a state without going into a trance. They are the mediumistically or parapsychologically gifted personalities of the tribe who have an immediate contact with the unconscious. Many of them don't need ecstasy as a bridge to go over.

So Mrile enlightens the world of the Beyond. While he has left his visible surroundings and retired into a creative dream world, he has worked on understanding the unconscious. In other words, he has really brought light into the other world, and therefore he is rewarded with tremendous riches and finds no difficulties in returning home. The Moon People do not try to detain him.

This is very unusual. Normally if you go to the land of the dead, the spirit land, you are held back from returning to the outer world. But because Mrile has

---

67 Bollingen Series LXXVI, trans. Willard R. Trask (Princeton: Princeton University Press, 1974).

done all this active work with the powers of the Beyond, they let him go and they even give him a large herd of cattle and a bull. He can move back freely.

So up until now we can say that Mrile has not been ultimately damaged. Perhaps his mother had even been *meant* to kill the seed child, because through that Mrile moves on to his destiny. Now he can return to his tribe as a rich medicine man, a man who has experienced the gods and the ghosts of the spirit world and the Beyond. And everything is all right. We know he has become a medicine man from the fact that the birds obey him. He has advanced to the rank of a semidivine being.

In the other African story, "The Tale of Chuveane," the hero keeps his divine child. He has very few heroic exploits to his credit, but the fairy tale ends with somewhat of a surprise: Chuveane, as you remember, saves his divine child. The parents give it back to him, but then the people think he's a black magician and they begin to play tricks on him. They even try to kill him. They dig a pit along the path where he leads his cattle, and they give him poison. But Chuveane, in contrast to Mrile, is not naive. He always notices their plots. He pours out the poison, he goes around the pit, etc., so the village people become angrier and angrier and more and more afraid of him. Finally, however, they give up. Next, Chuveane himself becomes angry and begins to play nasty tricks on his tribe out of revenge. He becomes quite a nuisance, but then he too finally gives this up.

At the end of that story we hear that Chuveane became very famous. Some say he was even the great god who created the mountains, rivers and woods. Other tribes say that is not true, that the great god whose name was Chuveane disappeared after creation and was never heard from again, and the hero of this story is only his son, Hutsveane, who will one day come back and lead mankind to happiness and riches.

Either way, suddenly at the end it is revealed that the story was actually about a very high deity, either the highest creator god himself, or at least his son, the future savior figure of all the tribes. At first one feels they are ordinary men, but they often turn out to be divine figures.

The transition from the human to the divine is not as great in the representations of these people as it is for us. A great medicine man or a great wise man can, without much transition, become an incarnation of a godhead and be venerated as a god. On the other hand, we believe—or at least Christians do—that Jesus was the only incarnation of the divinity. It is even forbidden to think that anyone else could approach that state. For example, if the more naive parts of the population begin to venerate a local saint too much, the Catholic Church takes the trouble to insist that that saint is only a mortal human being and comes nowhere close to being an incarnation of the divine

But this enormous gap between the human and the divine exists only in our Christian civilization. In Hindu mythology and religion it is quite possible that a yogi, at the end of his life, will be revealed to have been an incarnation of Shiva or Krishna. And in African tales too, the trickster, Chuveane, is suspected of being the highest god himself, because of his tremendous deeds. Certainly, Mrile is approaching the state of deity when the second catastrophe happens in his life. It happens through the killing of the bull.

In most parts of Africa and until the year 3200 in Old Egypt, the bull was the king and the Moon God in one. In Egypt, for instance, the Moon God, Min, was the protecting godhead of the Pharaoh, the Egyptian king, and it was only with the beginning of the so-called Old Empire that the Sun God, Ra, became the incarnation and protector of the Pharaoh. Before that there was a kind of lunar bull kingship. But the bull, being a representative of the king's life and potency, of his mana, remained important throughout classical Egyptian times.

When the Pharaoh went into his wife's bedroom for the first time to generate a successor, he transformed himself into the Sun God, Ra. The title one gave him on that day and in that night was Kamutef, "bull of his mother." As a bull, he was committing incest with his wife, that is, with his mother, and as a bull of his mother, he regenerated himself. You see, he had to marry his mother on that night symbolically, in order that the newborn son would be himself. His son was then his continuation. In eternity there is only one king and one queen, and the Kamutef has the same function in Egyptian theology as the Holy Ghost has in Christianity. He is the link between father and son and the generating power that enters the mother of the new god.

That is one meaning of the bull. Perhaps if you have been in Egypt you have seen in Abydos those enormous coffins of embalmed bulls, royal bulls. They were special. They had certain white marks on their forelocks and were believed to embody the source of the health, generation and creative power of the king.

What in Egypt became an elaborate cultured form of representation spread throughout Africa in a simpler form, but in many ways the bull has always represented the power of the chief and the medicine man, and the god of fertility. In all Bantu tribes including the Dschagga, the bull was the highest sacrificial animal. That is why Mrile should not have eaten the meat of that bull. The bull in the story came from the Moon People, from the ghost world. He was a supernatural bull, so obviously he should not have been eaten; he should have been given back to the gods.

Now among the Bantus, when one has dedicated a sacrificial animal to the ancestral spirits, it is not permitted to let that animal die from a disease. For instance, a Dschagga man might vow to sacrifice a bull to the *aümu* if his wife gives birth to a son. And if for any special reason the owner wishes to sell or kill such a bull, a substitute must be found and an important ceremony has to be carried out. The original animal and the substitute are tied and thrown on their sides, touching each other. Some hair is cut from the forehead, the chest and the tail of the original beast and placed on the substitute. The animals are then released. Next the ghosts or the *aümu* are addressed, and it is explained to them that owing to pressing reasons the original beast has to be killed or sold as the case may be, but that a suitable substitute has been provided. Some beer is brewed and a libation of it is poured out in the hut of the village head.

So you see how important it is never to kill or sacrifice an animal that belongs to the Moon People; and strictest of all is the rule never to eat such animals, for to steal from the ghost world in order to eat this meat yourself is one the greatest violations of the taboos.

This ceremony of the substitute is interesting, because according to the Dschagga, in the hair of the forehead dwells the soul of the animal. If you move the soul of one bull into another bull's body, you can kill the original bull, because in that case he's no longer the same bull. His soul has moved into the other animal.

Now, Mrile finds himself in a very delicate situation: even though it may be permissible under certain circumstances to kill a bull belonging to the ghost world, as his father did when the bull became too old, Mrile's particular bull had specifically reminded him not to eat from his flesh. That is where Mrile breaks the taboo.

We can only explain this as a kind of inflation: because he had been living with the Moon People and the ancestral spirits, and because he could credit himself with bringing fire to them, Mrile feels identical with them. He feels like a superman who, like the Moon People, can eat the Moon People's bull. Therefore, at the end of his life, like so many mythological heroes, he oversteps human boundaries and human limitations. As a result he is devoured by the earth. It is even said, "You will be eaten too, as you ate me." The flesh of the bull says this to him and the earth opens, and he is devoured.

So Mrile is one of the many tragic heroes who, after many great achievements, fail in the end. Think, for instance, of Gilgamesh, who goes to the end of the world in the Beyond, to Utnapishtim. He gets the herb of immortality, but on the way back he puts the herb aside in order to take a bath in a pond, and a snake steals it from him. All for nothing! Or Heracles, who after his great deeds puts on the robe given to him by his wife, Deianoira, and is burned so badly by it that he has to burn himself. He becomes immortal through this act, but at the same time he succumbs to the trap of his jealous wife. And Maui, the great Polynesian hero, after many brave deeds and stealing fire and God knows what, finally creeps into the mouth of the Great Mother, Hine-nui-te-po. Then a little bird sees him and thinks he looks very funny with his behind sticking out of Hine-nui-te-po's mouth and his legs dangling, so the bird begins to laugh. Hine-nui-te-po wakes up, shuts her mouth and swallows Maui, who disappears forever.

It seems that in many, many stories a hero performs great deeds all along, but then suddenly there is a tiny little mis-step, a little mistake that marks a tragic end to the hero's life. This little mistake always has to do with inflation, with transcending human limitations. It is as if it even *belonged* to the archetype of the hero to always go beyond mortal limitations and therefore to meet a bad end. And it is very, very important that that bad end be told because, you see, when you listen to a hero story, you identify with him. You feel *like* the hero and you naively identify with him. But the hero is not an ego. The hero is an archetypal force, and only if one does *not* identify with it can it carry one through difficulties. But if the ego does identify with it, then that ego must also share the hero's end, which is almost always tragic.

So the bad endings must be told in order to warn us: "Don't identify! It's the hero, not you; you can survive, but the hero himself will come to an end!" A hero is abnormal, divine, beyond human limitations. It also exists in the human being, as a mood. The archetype of the hero seizes one from time to time, like a mood, and one needs this mood in order to do heroic deeds.

The archetype of the hero always comes up when a person should do something outstandingly courageous which, in the ordinary ego mood, one could not do. For instance, I knew a young man who had to move away from home and take a room for himself at the age of twenty-two. Anyone who knew his mother knew what a heroic deed that was! This young man actually had a dream during that transitional time when he was looking for rooms, as he approached that terrible moment when, over the lunch table, he planned to say, "Listen, Mother, I'm going to take a room in town and not stay here any more." He was trembling, wavering back and forth, still trying to decide if he should or could do it. And then he dreamt of a hero slaying a dragon.

Now that's very funny, and you might say, "What an exaggeration! Just to stand up to the silly animus of his mother. What a mythological exaggeration!" But no, it's the other way around. The unconscious used that tremendous heroic image to give him courage, to put him into the mood of feeling like a hero, like

Siegfried or St. George at least. He needed to be carried by that kind of mood in order not to falter at the last moment and go back.

So, you see, the hero is an archetype, and therefore a function, and it appears at crucial moments in people's lives to carry them over difficult transitions. The hero carries you over the river, so to speak, when you can't cross it yourself. But you should not identify with him. The hero should disappear again when his work is done; he *should* sink back down into the earth. He is not something you can use for everyday. If you hang on to the heroic attitude, then you become inflated and you will suffer the same fate as the hero, namely catastrophe. That is why it is very meaningful and in a deeper sense not ultimately negative that the hero stories so often end tragically. There is always this strange slip-off in the end, but it is there to jolt the hearer out of identification with the hero, to put one back in touch with human limitations and one's will to survive. It is there to prevent one from playing the hero wrongly.

So in this deeper sense, Mrile's end is not a negative end, but one which the tribe needs to hear, because it places them back in that frame of mind of respecting their taboos and not eating the flesh of the bull, who is dedicated to the Moon People.

I think that is most important, because as Jung pointed out, among the people still living in nature one of the greatest problems is hunger, much greater than sexuality, for instance; in fact, it is the number one problem. Accordingly, food has a divine quality. The gods are food. For example, certain Indians talk about their bison as though they were divinities. They say, "Its flesh keeps us alive. Its bones give us needles and weapons. Its hide gives us clothes," and so on. They enumerate all that the bison gives them, for he is the god who gives life, so to speak. Therefore the killing and eating of the bison is regulated by religious rules of behavior.

As another example from the primitive world, in the case of some sacrificial animals one had to reassemble the bones and the hide. Then the animal resurrects, but only if none of the bones are missing. That is why you may not eat any of the bones. You must garner them with the head, say a magical verse, and then the animal resurrects. If you don't do this, all the animals of that kind will diminish in number, and then all the people will starve.

You see, this is a very meaningful regulation which we have broken. That is why we are going to run out of resources and food one day. We ignore this religious regulation of how much we may take from divine creation and how much we must give back or not touch. We have lost our instinctive respect. If you don't understand from the feeling standpoint that food is divine, I advise you to do the same thing I did once in my youth.

I did it involuntarily. I had no money at the time, and I went with a friend for a very long hike in the Wallis Mountains. Foolishly, we decided we would eat only once a day, but when you walk eight hours a day this is impossible. I became weaker and weaker, but I still held on because otherwise we would have had to go home. So we hiked on, and one day I bathed in a very cold river, which also takes the calories out of you. Then, toward evening, I felt absolutely faint and miserable. I pulled up my socks and dragged myself on and on, and finally we came to a miserable little inn and ordered two portions of spaghetti.

When the hot spaghetti arrived, I passed out. After awhile, I came back to consciousness, covered with sweat, and the spaghetti had disappeared. My friend said, "Well, you certainly have eaten!" I had devoured the spaghetti in a religious trance. When I came to in the inn, sweating, I felt I was dead, and now I was alive again! Suddenly I felt how the warm blood was streaming into my arms and legs, how my mind began to work again. I had been literally dead, and then literally resurrected. I felt a god had given me life.

If you have ever been in that situation, you understand that the giver of life gives life to you through food. Primitive people knew that the great Creator stood behind their food, and they knew, therefore, that they owed some of it back. You don't take it all. As an act of gratitude and so that the food keeps coming, you give some of it back. That is why it would be breaking a taboo if you stole from the gods. It would be as if you went to a church, broke in and stole the money there. It is sacrilege.

6
The Straw, the Coal, and the Bean
(Grimm)

Now I want to discuss "The Straw, the Coal, and the Bean."[68] In the field of German literature, stories such as this are called *Schwank,* meaning they are more or less funny. Although this is a German term, *Schwank* stories can be found in every country. Some are almost like the funny stories you find in the *New Yorker,* complete with their drawings, caricatures and so on. People tell each other such stories as a kind of joke. Many are obscene, and many give an impression of being completely nonsensical.

I have always avoided these stories in the Grimm collection for two reasons. First, in a sense, jokes are things one shouldn't interpret.

We had a colleague in the past who was most amusing. She did not have a great sense of humor, so whenever you told a joke she made a very serious face and said, "Now what is the psychological meaning of that?" Then, of course, everyone would laugh all the more because although jokes do have meanings, one cannot put them into serious psychological, theoretical terms.

The other reason why I avoided these stories is that I always felt they had an especially deep meaning. They were not superficial jokes as you find in newspapers, where you get the point and the fun of it immediately. Unlike such jokes, these very often had a macabre background that reminded one of death and the transitoriness of life, or of the futility and ridiculousness of our existence. They all seemed to have the same sad undertones you find in very good and very deep jokes. That is why most internationally famous clowns are very melancholy if not suicidal personalities. This doubleness, the combining of the deep sadness of life with the humor of it, is one of the pairs of opposites in the unconscious.

Many such jokes are also cruel and gruesome. They portray a world similar to the one we find in certain dreams. Sometimes when we sleep deeply, or are exhausted, we wake up from a dream as if coming from great depths under the sea. We try to remember the dream, but all we can catch are utterly nonsensical bits and pieces, so we say, "Oh, I won't write that down. It's too complicated and meaningless." But in spite of this feeling, if we do write down such a dream and meditate on it, we always find an especially deep meaning. These are

---

68 *The Complete Grimm's Fairy Tales,* p. 102.

dreams that come right out of the body, so to speak, from a very deep layer of the unconscious, and they are quite unformed. Very often one is unable to interpret them; they are too far away from consciousness.

Such dreams depict the same kind of world one finds in Lewis Carroll's *Alice in Wonderland,* where you encounter many gruesome, macabre, cruel, funny nonsensical situations. Stories like this give you the feeling that you shouldn't meditate on them—but nonetheless, they tease you.

Adults can rarely invent such stories unless they try to compose them especially for children. Lewis Carroll himself was a mathematician, a very funny man, and a bachelor. He obviously had a huge anima problem, a feeling problem. He wrote *Alice in Wonderland* for his little niece, and in the context of his "wonderland," he could relax. He approached the story with the attitude, "This needn't be meaningful; it needn't be beautiful. It must only be fun and nothing more." That attitude gave him the freedom to write some very subtle nonsense.

This *Schwank* story from the Brothers Grimm kept teasing me to find a meaning. I was unable to decipher it at first, but after I had made a great effort to look up many amplifications, I think I discovered its meaning. Here is the story:

In a village dwelt a poor old woman, who had gathered together a dish of beans and wanted to cook them. So she made a fire on her hearth, and that it might burn the quicker, she lighted it with a handful of straw. When she was emptying the beans into the pan, one dropped without her observing it, and lay on the ground beside a straw, and soon afterwards a burning coal from the fire leapt down to the two. Then the straw began and said: "Dear friends, from whence do you come here?" The coal replied: "I fortunately sprang out of the fire, and if I had not escaped by sheer force, my death would have been certain,—I should have been burnt to ashes." The bean said: "I too have escaped with a whole skin, but if the old woman had got me into the pan, I should have been made into broth without any mercy, like my comrades." "And would a better fate have fallen to my lot?" said the straw. "The old woman has destroyed all my brethren in fire and smoke; she seized sixty of them at once, and took their lives. I luckily slipped through her fingers."

"But what are we to do now?" said the coal.

"I think," answered the bean, "that as we have so fortunately escaped death, we should keep together like good companions, and lest a new mischance should overtake us here, we should go away together, and repair to a foreign country."

The proposition pleased the two others, and they set out on their way together. Soon, however, they came to a little brook, and as there was no bridge or footplank, they didn't know how they were to get over it. The straw hit on a good idea, and said: "I will lay myself straight across, and then you can walk over on me as on a bridge." The straw therefore stretched itself from one bank to the other, and the coal, who was of an impetuous disposition, tripped quite boldly on to the newly-built bridge. But when she had reached the middle, and heard the water rushing beneath her, she was, after all, afraid, and stood still, and ventured no farther. The straw, however, began to burn, broke in two pieces, and fell into the stream. The coal slipped after her, hissed when she got into the water, and breathed her last. The bean, who had prudently stayed behind on the shore, could not but laugh at the event, was unable to stop, and laughed so heartily that she burst. It would have been all over with her, likewise, if, by good fortune, a tailor who was traveling in search of work, had not sat down to rest by the brook. As he had a compassionate heart he pulled out his needle and thread, and sewed her together. The bean thanked him most prettily, but as the tailor used black thread, all beans since then have a black seam.

A poor old woman had some beans and wanted to cook them. And in order to cook them faster, she put some straw on the fire. Now, you will find such a poor old woman in many fairy tales. Generally she has a double aspect: either she is an old witch who bewitches the hero or heroine or captures them, or she is a wise old woman living in the woods who gives the right advice, or she gives the hero a thread or a ball. She thus leads him to his way, giving him the right warnings about the danger he's going to encounter.

In spite of her modest appearance she represents the archetype of the wise old woman, the wisdom of Nature. She cooks her own meal so she represents Nature not in her giving form but Nature circling in herself without progress. So something is bound to happen.

Now, cooking is one of the greatest landmarks in the history of civilization. By cooking food, you are able to preserve it longer. You can expand your menu because you can eat many foods cooked which you would not have been able to preserve raw. So, in times of starvation man greatly enhanced his chances of survival through the use of fire and cooking. And you remember from our African story that Mrile taught cooking to the creatures of the Beyond.

To cook is to transform food through the agency of fire; therefore the kitchen is like an alchemical laboratory that transforms matter, putting it into human service and enabling mastery of a wider domain of nature. Through cooking, matter is transformed and integrated. In our African story, I gave you some amplifications where the discovery of fire and cooking was even identified with the beginning of human consciousness and thus becoming mortal. Before that, we lived like the animals, eating everything raw. But the moment cooking was invented, we began to separate from the animal world. This was also experienced as a falling out of that paradise of oneness with nature, and as a sin against it.

I also explained that only when humanity attained consciousness did it become difficult for us to accept death. Before that, we died as easily as the animals. This doesn't mean that animals die with complete resignation: they too put up a death struggle, and if you have ever seen cattle going to a butcher you can see they know something is the matter; they are depressed and full of anxiety. So I'm not saying that animals like to die; only that the more consciousness one has, the more difficult it is to accept death.

Cooking, according to African myths, has contributed enormously to the increase of collective and individual consciousness. So perhaps we could say that the poor old woman represents an incarnation of great Mother Nature in her double aspect, representing a feminine humanity that is based on an aspect of nature that promotes consciousness.

Nature invented us as intelligent beings. It was nature that imposed on us the progress of consciousness. It came from the unconscious. We didn't especially want it—it came to us. But we have it, with all its advantages and disadvantages. So we could say the poor old woman represents Mother Nature's design for humanity. That wish of nature promotes our becoming civilized and conscious.

But the old woman is tottery; she drops a bean. And she's sloppy; she drops some straw. Considering this from the purely human standpoint, the older one gets, the more careful and slow one should be in one's actions. Jung even went so far as to say that senility was to a great extent a facultative curse. In other words, it could be avoided. If old people restricted themselves to a small rhythm of life and concentrated on doing everything slowly and carefully, they could avoid becoming senile.

One of the worst mistakes is to be hasty. If in old age one still wants to go fast, then naturally, because one has slowed down physiologically, one will forget to perform even the most obvious, habitual tasks—old men forget to zip up their flies and other such charming things. They become hasty and then they can no longer cope with the situations of daily living. That is quite an accurate picture of a tottery, senile old person.

So this old woman, in my opinion, is not quite all right. Haste, as one says, is of the devil. It becomes a serious problem in old age, but it is also a problem in youth. *All* haste is of the devil. With haste, you feed the underworld. You give the shadow a chance to pop out. Whenever you see that you have done some awful shadow thing with your left hand, you can be fairly certain that you did it when you were under pressure of haste or stress or fatigue, for at such times the shadow has the upper hand. You say the wrong things, put letters into the wrong envelopes, dial the wrong number, and so on.

The old woman dropped that bean, and thus she created an opportunity for renewal. When one feeds the underworld and the unconscious, they become activated; then the unconscious can come up. That is why as an analyst one is not dissatisfied when analysands "put their foot in it," because then one has something to analyze, to bring to consciousness. That is when change becomes possible. If we were always correct, life would be stifled.

Now we must consider the fire. Fire is used in many folklore rituals and has many amplifications, but I want to mention only one aspect that fits nicely into the context of our story, namely that fire in folk rituals is often used to chase away the ghosts of the underworld—the dead, spooks and so on—because of its purifying quality. It is therefore understood as being hostile to the underworld because it brings light and the warmth of life.

Fire is often used in this positive sense of chasing away the powers of darkness. If you have ever gone into a hut that hasn't been inhabited for a long time, you immediately open the windows. The room feels damp and moldy, spiders are around and you are overwhelmed by a rather depressing, cold feeling. There's no breathing space; you have the feeling that ghosts have taken over. Then you make a crackling fire in the fireplace and at once you are at home. Now it's warm, now the hearth lets you feel at home, as if you have spread your own atmosphere into the room. Or, after you have been in the rain, you immediately warm yourself by the fire and suddenly all the depressing, moldy evil that was lurking about is gone.

In primitive societies, fire was a tremendous salvation from the attacks of wild animals. Bushmen, every night, no matter how hot it is in the Kalahari Desert in summer, make a fire to keep the lions away. And the light of the ring of fire forms a barrier; the lions never come near it. One man must always stay up to tend this fire, putting more twigs on it. Sometimes you see or hear those lions moving about; you see their eyes in the dark, but they don't come near as long as the fire is burning. So the fire banishes the danger of death, the powers of evil. That's why in primitive households the hearth is the center of the house.

In Russia, the *domoboi,* the ghost of the house, lives in the stove. He protects the house and one gives him something to eat in return. He makes the atmosphere of the house good or bad. He provides the warmth of life and the feeling of relatedness for the family that gathers around the hearth. He keeps away the dangers that come from the unconscious and from the outside.

The blade of straw boasts that he slipped through the old woman's fingers. The bean says she just escaped, and the coal jumped out of the fire. The bean escaped by being dropped, a lucky accident. But there is a definite motif in the fact that two of them, the straw and the coal, really wanted to escape. This shows a certain resistance; they didn't want to be burned up. They didn't want to serve the old woman; they wanted to remain themselves.

Now I will tell you some amplifications of the straw, the coal and the bean.

Straw is that part of the corn which is thrown away. In the past it was either burned or plowed under the soil. Viewed negatively, it is useless and to be thrown away, but viewed positively it is the part we give back to nature. Very often after the harvest, one made a puppet of straw and burned it up as a sacrifice to the vegetation spirits. In many countries the people believe there is a spirit living in the corn. This spirit is responsible for the harvest and for the fertility of the fields. As soon as the corn is cut, the corn spirit retires into the cobs. It is immortal. It stays in the cobs through the winter and then sprouts again the next spring with the new corn. So the straw is the corn when it is in its dormancy, its underworld phase, latent and hidden but not dead, still holding the promise of a new crop for the next season.

In many countries there are also festivals of the May bridal couple or the Whitsun bridal couple; or in England they hold a festival for the May Queen. During these festivals puppets are made from straw and sometimes also from spring flowers, and burned up. In Poland, the Guild of Tailors made a straw sack which was then burned, as our Zürich *Böög* at *Sechseläuten* is burned in a spring festival, to chase away the spirits of death and winter and as a sacrifice to revive the spirit of the corn and the fertility of the new year. So you see how things begin to fall into place. We even have a connection with the tailor.

The straw has to do with the underworld. In more modern times, straw has the negative connotation of futile, meaningless, worthless nonsense. St. Thomas Aquinas, about four or five weeks before his death and during the writing of his famous *Summa,* came to the chapter about penitence. At that time he had an overwhelming experience of the unconscious. Suddenly he sat in his cell, completely confused and upset. Then he put the pen away and said, "All I have written is straw." Later on, in order to prevent misunderstanding, Church historians added, "All I have written is straw in comparison to what I saw and experienced." I think that is true. Thomas had an overwhelming experience that made him see that the scholastic, intellectual, theological way in which he exposed the Christian truth was only straw compared to what he had experienced inwardly.[69]

In many religious texts of the gnostics, and also in the Bible, separating the

---

[69] [For more detailed comments on Aquinas's experience, see von Franz, *Alchemy: An Introduction to the Symbolism and the Psychology* (Toronto: Inner City Books, 1980), pp. 180f.—Ed.]

wheat from the straw means to separate what is to be immortal, what is going to survive, from the unwanted portion which is to be burned away. The alchemists also said that in the alchemical process, all futilities and superficialities had to be removed or burned. Straw has that utterly negative connotation of being something that must be discarded.

Now, it is very irritating when someone comes for an analytical hour and then tells you for the entire sixty minutes about some futile quarrel with a neighbor or something like that. Other people, out of fear of touching their own complexes, sometimes spend sixty *hours* prattling on about utter nonsense, and they do so with a kind of unemotional "bla-bla-bla-blah" voice; there's no emotional melody underlying such speeches, so I suspect that they themselves think it is all nonsense. They know it is, but they won't touch the real problem, so they talk and talk and talk nervously about all their trivia. I even had one such man who always began to yawn when he talked like that. He himself was bored. I almost said to him, "Have you noticed you are yawning? Why?" You see, he knew it was all straw. He was merely beating the straw, but that was a clue that he was hiding something very hot inside.

This negative aspect of the straw shows up in our story: the straw cannot make a solid bridge. It's too insubstantial. It is the cheap, useless aspect of the straw that is displayed in our story. It is incapable, and it is also a boaster: it offers to make itself into a bridge, but when the hot coal touches it, it collapses entirely. It cannot do what it wants to do.

Next we come to the coal that jumped out of the fire. In antiquity, the only form of coal widely used was charcoal. Real coal was known only in the Orient. In Western alchemy the charcoal was mixed with carbuncle and quicksilver. They believed that quicksilver, especially in its combination form as cinnabar, was identical with coal. So you see, the Western people had only a vague idea of what coal was. In early alchemy it was called "anthrax." That is still a name for certain coals, and anthracite comes from it. The theory was that it was the basis of certain types of *prima materia,* the basic matter of stones and of the earth. According to certain early alchemical theories, the basic material of the metals was water, and the basic material of the stones and the different types of earth was that mysterious anthrax. So coal was the very essence of concrete reality.

Because of its blackness coal was naturally associated with the underworld. Later, a rich folk tradition arose that the coal miners, because they were "black" men who worked in dangerous conditions, were great magicians from under the earth. They knew the secrets of Mother Earth. Even today, miners sometimes bring up the most marvelous crystals or they discover a precious metallic ore.

Thus they are the ones who discover and dig up the treasures from under the earth. They are like the alchemists, the great magicians of the past, in having something uncanny and underworldly about them because they work in the dark. Miners were also believed to be slightly devilish, because one felt that it was a hubris—a devilish boldness—to dig into Mother Earth and rob her of her hidden, secret treasures. So coal, a most basic material of life, is associated with Mother Earth or nature. It represents the secret essence of the visible world.

Many alchemists claimed that coal also contains a hidden fire. You see, if you light a coal with a match, or with a handful of straw as in our story, it slowly begins to glow. And since it glows inwardly and doesn't quickly burn away like wood or straw, the idea emerged that coal contains a burning fire hidden under its black surface; you could bring out this hidden fire by putting some fire from the outside in contact with it.

As a result of this association with hidden fire, coal came to represent the passionate nature of man. It is especially associated with the hottest passion, namely repressed, unexpressed passion. We have a German proverb that says, "Nothing burns as hot as a great love nobody knows about." Such is the nature of the coal fire. When you burn inwardly from love or hated or a seething grudge and keep it inside, it becomes much, much hotter than if you had reacted externally. Such burning stays in the bottom of your body. It can also lead to many somatic diseases.

So, the hidden fire of the coal therefore has to do with the devil and the with the black demons of the underworld. But we must remember that they are also the keepers of treasure.

And now we come to the bean. In the Greco-Roman world, the bean belonged to Hades, the realm of the dead. It was the food of the dead. In the Pythagorean communities, the eating of beans was strictly forbidden; beans were taboo because they belonged to the ancestral spirits. We found a similar taboo in our story of Mrile, who shouldn't have eaten the bull because it belonged to the Moon People and the spirits of the dead.

In Switzerland we have what is called the *Sälige Lüt,* the wild hunt. Here and in many other European countries, the dead go about with Wotan in the dark of the night from the last days of October until the second day of November. That is always the time when there are big storms and the wind god is very much in evidence. Under the guidance of Hermes-Mercurius in the antique realm, and of Wotan on the other side of the Alps, the dead come from the underworld and wander about. And they eat only beans!

On the other hand, beans were also believed to be an aphrodisiac. They improved one's sexual powers. In antiquity, therefore, the Romans and the Greeks sang certain so-called "obscene bean songs" which were supposed to increase one's sexual potency. So we discover the strange fact that the realm of sex and the realm of the dead belong together, mythologically speaking. That is why the philosopher Heraclitus said of the Dionysian processions in the street, where one carried red wooden phalli and sang obscene songs, "If it weren't Hades, the god of the dead, for whom they make this procession and sing the phallic songs, it would be an obscene thing; but Dionysus and Hades are one."

Behind this tie between sex and death lies the archetypal fact that clowning and macabre fun, the enjoyment of wild, uncivilized exuberance, are really very close to death. In our country, especially in the villages, it is still quite usual that people have real fun at funerals! At first, you are very sad. But then you begin to drink, and since a funeral is a big family gathering of people who often haven't seen each other for years, the dinner parties after the funerals end in absolutely marvelous festivals.

This is not as heartless as it might look. Jung once said to me, "It is because these people are still very much like the primitives, who felt the danger of death, of being gripped by the coldness of death." Therefore, they assert life by getting drunk and being vulgar and funny. One asserts life and one's connectedness with one's fellows in order to chase away that cold shiver one feels after having borne a loved one to the grave. It is as if one were saying, "We are still here! We must go on! We must live! We must now love each other and be together with each other in order to chase away that cold hand of death still hovering over the ceremony." So it is not heartless.

This double experience of death and exuberance belongs to the world of the Great Mother. All the rituals for Hades-Dionysus had to do with Mother Earth and the earth cult of the gods of the underworld, the maternal world.

Beans have another interesting quality: they grow so high! In many European countries, one plants beans on Ascension Day so that they may grow high and go up with Christ when He ascends to heaven. In many myths and fairy tales, a hero plants a bean and climbs up to heaven on the stalk. So the bean has not only a strong underworldly quality, but also the capacity to connect us with the Beyond; the bean is a better bridge than the blade of straw.

The bean is the only one in our story who is wise. The coal is a fool because she is so hot tempered. And the straw is a superficial boaster. But the bean has wisdom, and the bean can connect heaven and earth. Like everything connected with the land of death, the underworld and the unconscious, the bean also has to do with luck and oracles. In many countries, one puts the seeds of beans in a coffin and then takes them out again and throws them like an I Ching and counts them to discover the lucky number to pick for the lottery.

So you see here a whole realm of things that belong together: undeserved luck, death and the pure nature aspect of the unconscious, with its not understandable meaning or its meaninglessness. We have, therefore, an underworldly triad assembling at the hearth of the old lady. All things which belong to the underworld realm—death, the unconscious, the gods of sexuality and Rabelaisian wildness—that triad of straw, bean and coal assembles at her hearth and then they decide to go away together.

I think the important thing here is that this trio is all vegetation, because coal, too, comes from decayed trees. All three, therefore, have to do with the vegetative aspect of the psyche, that aspect of the unconscious quite low down in the body, where we just exist as bodily beings and aren't even animals yet. In some layers of the unconscious we are just like plants.

The three go on their way and come to a little river where there's no bridge, and they don't know what to do. The straw says, "I will lay myself straight across, and then you can walk over on me as on a bridge."

It's time we looked at the history of this story for a moment. If you look up the extensive commentaries on the tales collected by the Grimm Brothers,[70] you will find that this is an especially old story. There is even a printed Latin version of it from 1548. When a story is written down so early, that means it must go back to the early Middle Ages and probably even to antiquity; the first printing by no means indicates the time the story first came into being. So this is a very archaic story and very widespread. In every European country there are parallels and little verses alluding to it, so we may assume it is very important.

In some of the early versions of this story the bean is replaced by a mouse. Otherwise the story is the same. This shows that when the fantasy of the people replaces one symbol with another, it generally does it along the right lines, which is to say archetypally, because it is done unconsciously.

You see, in most countries the mouse is taken to represent the soul of the dead. In many early medieval pictures illustrating scenes of death, one finds either a little bird or a mouse coming out of the mouth of the dying person—that's the soul leaving. And in many, many folk beliefs one finds the idea that the dead continue to live in the house as soul animals. They make funny noises and appear only in the night. They personify the dead who reappear in this form so that

---

[70] See J. Bolte and G. Polivka, *Anmerkungen zu den Kinder- und Hausmärchen der Brüder Grimm,* 5 vols. (Leipzig, 1913-1927).

they can still live hidden, sneaking about in the dark.

In contrast to the bean, however, the mouse has a more negative connotation. It is more like a demon of death or a death ghost, disturbing and haunting. But the bean is like it in that both belong to the land of the dead. Both represent a psychic component that lives as a more or less definite unit in the collective unconscious, but one that is not accepted. For a thing to be dead means that it is not accepted, not integrated into the conscious view of the people; therefore it has an autonomous life in the Beyond of the unconscious.

Now we have to amplify the bridge, but we also have to ask ourselves from what shore to what shore do those three beings want to go? We must remember too that they do not succeed.

In many medieval parallels, they want to go to church to confess their sins, and on their way their tragedy with the bridge happens. That would confirm the theme that they want to cross the threshold toward collective consciousness. They are now active. First they were discarded by human consciousness, now they want to be recognized in human consciousness. They even want to go to church. That means they want to be accepted within the realm of the religious Weltanschauung. They are obviously sinners, because their goal is to go to confession. So they are the unaccepted sinners who want to be accepted in church. In my opinion they represent those features that have not been well enough accepted in the Christian Church: the obscene, the macabre, the carnivalesque, the sexual—all the somatic areas of life. They have been discarded, thrown into the hands of the devil instead of being integrated into our religious outlook.

In the Middle Ages, the aging Church began, like a tottery old woman, to drop these things. For instance, in southern France, up to the eleventh or twelfth century, once each year in spring the people held a carnivalesque black mass. A little boy of four or five, called "the Pope of the Little Boys," went around saying blessings and sprinkling everyone with water. His great pleasure was to imitate the Pope in this way. The clergy drank the mass wine until it was completely gone, and the people then brought a donkey into the church and sang songs that ended with "He-haw, he-haw!" instead of "Alleluia!" Everyone had fun, but then the next week, the solemn, aesthetic mass would be resumed.

You see, for one day in the year the people gave religious recognition to the lower powers. This was not done surreptitiously or shamefully, but rather in a way that openly showed a religious integration of these darker powers. It would be quite a different matter, for instance, if I were to commit a sin once in a drunken state and then go immediately to confess it. That would not indicate my acceptance of it, really.

So, although Christianity was becoming increasingly aestheticized and spiritualized, in its earliest form it was still marvelously pagan. It blended with pre-Christian rituals, as in the donkey festival where the powers of darkness had their place and were properly acknowledged every spring.

In Native American religions, too, you have a sacred group of merrymakers, the clowns. Among the Uglalas, for instance, there were the *heyoka,* about whom one would tell obscene, funny stories.[71] In rituals, they acted for fun in contrary ways: when everyone cried, they laughed; when everyone laughed, they cried. They are a type of priest, counter-priests with a sacred mission, who serve the dead and break any rule and counter any ritual.

In the book of Lame Deer's visions,[72] we read about this interesting institution in his tribe, that of the so-called clowns or *heyoka.* If people dream about the thunder bird in their initiation, they have to become *heyoka.* They have to act out concretely anything they dream! If they dream that they walk about naked in public, they have to do it the next day. If they dream they are hitting someone over the head, they have to do that the next day, too. The people see this as a terrible fate; they hate being *heyoka.* Imagine if *you* had to act out your dreams, what difficult situations that could put you in! There is also a ritual through which you can be freed from this fate. By great sacrifices you can be freed from it in spite of having dreamt of the thunder bird.

Even in these societies, you see, ritual and convention tended to become so repressive that they had to be loosened up from time to time and seen in their whole ridiculous relativity. The *heyoka* had this function. Jung called them "trickster clowns." They represent the shadow; they kept alive a living connection with it, so that it would not be repressed.

We must always keep in mind the opposite of what we believe in, the opposite of our highest ideals, even of our most serious and holiest convictions—for all of these have another side. We should always be able to think in terms of paradoxes and opposites, what both is and is not. Those clowns do that; they keep people aware of the opposites.

They also keep the door open for the unconscious and thus for creativity, because without this natural dark side of the unconscious, there is no creativity. Every renewal comes from that side, not from above.

According to one of the Latin tales, beans have a bad smell. When the coal

---

71 See Paul Radin, *The Trickster,* with commentaries by Carl Kerényi and C.G. Jung (New York: Schocken Books, 1978).
72 See John Fire/Lame Deer and Richard Erdoes, *Lame Deer: Seeker of Visions* (New York: Simon and Schuster, 1972).

falls into the water, the mouse says, "This isn't good incense." It makes an awful stink. Then the coal says furiously, "That is not your business; it is the affair of the gods to judge the smell of the incense." Bad smells are usually attributed to the devil and evil. The devil stinks of sulphur. That's why incense is used to purify a church from the influence of evil demons. So you can see how close those merrymakers are to the sinners and the realm of the devil.

But we must come back to the bridge. Why this transition over a bridge? The story could have said just that the three wanted to go to church and something funny happened to them on the way. But everything happens on a bridge.

In early times bridges were numinous because they were the only places where you could cross the larger rivers. There weren't many ferries or boats in most countries. To cross the water, you had to walk up the banks of the rivers to the bridge, then back down on the other side. Bridges were numinous because they offered the only means to reach faraway countries.

On the other hand, bridges were highly dangerous because the enemy could invade your country from them. If you look at military history, you find there were always great battles at bridges, for everyone knew the enemy must approach by them. In military planning still, one must know the location of all the places where one can quickly form a bridge with pontoons and ships, and also places where bridges can't be made. So bridges are numinous places where one feels attacked by the devil, but where one can also cross over oneself.

The powers of good and evil concentrate on the bridge. That is why in many Catholic countries bridges have either a crucifix to protect the transition, or a statue of St. Nepomuk, the special protector of bridges. We still read sometimes in the papers of drunken people who, staggering home at night, fall from a bridge and die in the water. That happens most often only on little bridges in the country. But still, sometimes when you are walking home at midnight, heavily loaded with alcohol, on the bridge it takes you over—you become giddy.

Also, bridges seem to evoke suicidal fantasies in some people. There, evil attacks us, and we need specific protection. On the other hand, the bridge opens new dimensions. It connects us with the unconscious.

In ancient Rome the highest priest had the title of Pontifex, "bridge builder." Later, the Catholic Church took it over so that today the Pope is the Pontifex Maximus, "the uppermost bridge builder." Such a bridge builder was understood as one who builds the bridge between mankind and the godhead or the Beyond.

Thus we have to ask ourselves, "What is it that psychologically connects consciousness and the unconscious? What connects those two realms?"

It is what Jung called the transcendent function, that aspect of the unconscious which produces symbols.[73] Now, the bridge is not itself the transcendent function, for the transcendent function is a natural phenomenon while the bridge is a human construction. But I want to speak first of the transcendent function.

If one has no religious institution that mediates between the conscious and the powers of the unconscious, then we can see the transcendent function at work in that person's symbolic dreams. The unconscious produces religious symbols to unite, to make a bridge between consciousness and the unconscious. Every symbol is, in a way, a bridge, for every symbol has one base in the unconscious and one base in consciousness. It has a conscious aspect and an unconscious aspect. It *is* a bridge par excellence. But it is a nature bridge. On the other hand, the material bridge is a human achievement, and a very dangerous and difficult one it was and is!

Think of the Devil's Bridge near Göschenen, for instance, at the Gotthard: it is so numinous that even now, since the construction of the autobahn, they spent several million francs to transport the picture of the devil there in the rock off to one side, rather than give it up. This was to remind us of the saga that the devil built that bridge, and in return he asked for the first soul to walk over it. But the people of Uri were very clever and chased a he-goat over the bridge. The he-goat was the symbol of the devil himself, so he went away furious. But this bridge at that very narrow part of the Schöllenenschlucht is still called the Devil's Bridge.

With all bridges, it seems that either saints have built them or the devil has built them. They are often surrounded by legends of how they came into being, and in many countries there are festivals on bridges where one dances and drinks and has fun: they are numinous places.

Whenever a bridge was under construction, it seems the transcendent function, that mysterious life process which produces in us symbols that bridge the opposites, was encountered by human consciousness. In old Rome, the Pontifex was the builder and watcher of the bridge, of the Roman relationship to the gods of upper and lower worlds. The Catholic Church, too, was a man-made bridge that originally contained the symbols produced by the collective unconscious. It became an institutionalized bridge over which collective consciousness could get in touch with the other side. But from the parallels we see that the bridge can also be directed the other way, from the underworld toward consciousness.

The coal and the bean want to cross. They want to be recognized and accepted in consciousness. They have something creative to contribute. But the

---

[73] See "The Transcendent Function," *The Structure and Dynamics of the Psyche,* CW 8.

transition doesn't succeed because the boastful straw offers to become a bridge.

Besides representing futile nonsense, straw is also something that essentially belongs to the unconscious. It represents what one should give to the gods of the underworld, something to be burned as a sacrifice to the powers of nature. So it is a sacrilege and a blasphemy for the straw to want conscious recognition. He belongs on the unconscious side. Not understanding his own nature, he calls for a wrong enterprise. This shows us that the unconscious in its natural state is not only a source of supreme wisdom; it is also the source of utter nonsense.

Sometimes you can see this in people who are possessed. For instance, sometimes an anima-possessed man throws over a happy marriage or makes his children unhappy by running after some kind of anima illusion. He is the victim of an unconscious anima possession, and in discarding his conscious reason and moral judgment, he has permitted the unconscious to involve him in absolute nonsense.

Among the misunderstood geniuses who populate lunatic asylums, you can find some who will tell you they have invented the perpetual motion machine or have found some new explanation of the cosmos that goes far beyond Jung and Max Planck and Einstein. So you say, "Well, come on, I'm willing to listen!"— but then they just feed you with utter nonsense full of factual errors. But *they* are gripped by it; they are moved and feel like a genius. They have the world's secrets in their pocket, but with a huge inflation on top. They are tragic victims of the nonsensical side of the unconscious, which in many people is the shadow realm. I once knew a borderline woman who was in love with a man but had an affair with another. She confessed to me that the pleasure of it was that when she shut her eyes, she thought she was sleeping with the man she really loved. Imagine! But the shadow can involve a woman in just such nonsense.

So it is essential not to lose oneself. That's why Jung stresses that consciousness must have a say too; there must be a dialogue between the unconscious and consciousness. We cannot simply swallow uncritically what the unconscious says; we must also think about the level on which it wants to be realized.

You see here that the straw is a symbol of the tendency of something that wants to enter consciousness. It might even be a creative fantasy that has not yet quite enough substance or essence to be viable. In his paper on the gifted child,[74] Jung says that one has to discern in children if they are absorbed in creative fantasies or in nonsense. I think that sometimes, in certain cases, it is rather difficult to judge, but Jung does differentiate between the kind of fantasy

---

[74] "The Gifted Child," *The Development of Personality,* CW 17.

world that is just immature and fantasies that contain real creative germs.

We all have fantasies, but it is often very difficult to determine what kind of fantasies they are; we need to know how we feel about them. We cannot make judgments about them with the intellect alone; only with the help of our feeling can we determine if a fantasy has substance and creative potential, or if it is only blown-up, insubstantial nonsense.

In our story the straw stretches across the river to make a bridge and the coal. attempts to cross. The coal has a hot temperament and boldly steps onto the straw. Clearly they both have no self-knowledge: the straw doesn't know how weak he is, and the coal doesn't know how hot she is. Then suddenly, in the midst of the bridge, the coal hears the gurgling of the water and stands still; she burns right through the straw and plunges into the water.

She becomes frightened at hearing her own opposite! Water and fire are the great opposites. And therefore, if you get to the middle of the bridge that *unites* the opposites, you cannot cross it if you don't know your own opposite. That is why you cannot be changed in analysis if you don't know your shadow, if you don't know that all your ideals have a very seamy underside. Without that awareness, you can't cross into a new life. There's no transition without a confrontation of the opposites. And the silly coal, who should really know that fire and water are opposites, suddenly gets frightened when she hears the gurgling water. She stands still—that means the transition process doesn't go on. Her fire burns through the straw and both are thrown into the water of the unconscious: the transition into consciousness has not succeeded. The creative attempt of the dark world to become conscious has failed, apparently because it lacked sufficient energy and substance to make the crossing. But at least someone survives, and that is the bean.

The bean is wise. She waits to see what will happen to the others. When she sees the two drowning, since she has a good sense of humor, she laughs and laughs and laughs. We have a German proverb that says, "Pleasure at someone else's bad luck is the purest pleasure." That's what happens to the bean.

If you pay attention to your own reactions, you may notice that you feel this way usually when you perceive the other to be inflated. If someone nice is lucky and wins money at the lottery and then loses it somehow, you feel sorry for that person. But if someone wins a million and then goes around boasting and doesn't know you any more, plays the proud millionaire, and *then* loses it, you think, "Well done!" So, we can say that the bean, the straw and the coal invited trouble by their stupid and inflated behavior; by not knowing even the most elementary things about themselves, they were asking for it! The bean too does a silly thing:

she laughs too much—so much that she bursts.

We often say, "Oh, I laughed and laughed 'til I nearly burst!" One can't burst from laughter, but when one bursts psychically, it means the feeling one had was so wild that it suddenly snaps into the opposite, and afterward one finds oneself with a kind of hangover, a terrible depression. It is as if even fun and merriment have certain proper bounds. If we overstep them and become too excited, then we become dissociated. If you have a merry drunken evening but don't overdo it, then you wake up the next morning refreshed; you are at peace again with your shadow. You feel vivified and at one with yourself. But if you laugh too much, if you go too far, then you wake up the next morning feeling awful.

Also, it is well known that at meetings and festivals, mainly under the influence of alcohol, people can suddenly snap into quarrelsomeness. Sometimes people are even killed at folk feasts that begin quite happily; they are trampled down or shot in drunken arguments. The redeeming jollity, in an enantiodromian switch, snaps into dissociated destructiveness.

So you see again the close, mysterious relationship between joking, merriment, and the deepest sadness—even death. Just as at funerals one can be merry, happy festivals can end with a funeral. There is always a dangerous closeness between these two states of mind.

Schopenhauer once said that the sense of humor is the only divine quality in humans. Jung often quoted this saying. Once he told me that he made it a great point to see if his patients had a sense of humor. People who have no sense of humor are very difficult to treat, and if they are psychotic they are practically incurable. On the other hand, even severely psychotic people sometimes have a sense of humor. Of those, Jung would say, "Oh, take them, they have *such* a sense of humor. You might not cure them, but you can keep them afloat."

Once I took such a case, and whenever she showed signs of going off into a psychotic episode, I let myself sink back in the unconscious and it would give me the idea of some obscene joke. It had to be terribly vulgar, but when I merrily told it she would always laugh and become normal again. I always prayed to have the right joke because, you know, you can't think of such a joke on purpose. It has to come to you in the moment. I remember once she had already turned still as an ox. She was not making eye contact with me any more, and she was ready to storm out of the room, to do God knows what. But then, when an appropriate joke did come to me, she just sat back in her chair and laughed and laughed, and I did too, and then we had human contact again. I could bring her back from the underworld in that way; it was absolutely saving. I know Barbara Hannah once didn't want to take on a crazy old schizophrenic, but Jung said,

"Oh, for God's sake, take her! She's *so* funny. That is her redeeming quality."

You see, you get that strange taste of this closeness between madness, danger, death, and the divine sense of humor. But too much of it is inflation. The gods may laugh, like they do in Homer's *Iliad,* but one must keep one's own laughter within certain bounds, and at certain things we must not laugh at all. A god may, but we may not. We must remember our limitations and our mortality. The bean forgot; she went too far and became dissociated. But in the end it didn't matter because there was a friendly, warm-hearted tailor to sew her back together.

The profession of the tailor belongs astrologically to Mercurius, and you have in Grimm "The Valiant Little Tailor" and "The Cunning Little Tailor."[75] There you find that the tailor is always the trickster, the merrymaker, who even overcomes giants and unicorns and gets the princess. He's a bit boastful—a tiny little fellow, a man no one respects because in former times it was only the weaklings who became tailors; they couldn't follow a so-called stronger male profession.

It is by his wit that the tailor overcomes the demons and the giants and wins the princess. So the tailor is the typical trickster hero, a personification of the god Mercurius, who is the uniter of the opposites. He is death and life, the merry and the sad, the clever and the stupid. Mercurius is the transcendent function, who in alchemy is the bridge—not the blade of straw. He is the spirit of the unconscious, the transcendent function that unites the opposites. He sews up the bean with a black thread, so beans now always carry this mark. He brings the opposites together, but with a dark thread; the bean is an underworldly being, so she needs to be sewn up with a dark thread.

Now we must interpret the thread. The thread in general symbolizes a meaningful connection; when we lose that we say, "I have lost the thread." It is something very mysterious that is delivered to us by the unconscious, and when the unconscious does not want to help we lose the thread. Not to lose the thread is a gift of the Self—we forget that too often. Mercurius sews up the bean with a *dark* thread. Black means nocturnal and subterranean; the gods of the underworld are often black. A black thread would therefore be a meaningful nocturnal connection. And what would that mean?

The meaningful nocturnal connection manifests in our dream life. We have, so to speak, a logic of our daytime, waking life, and a hidden meaningfulness in our nighttime dream life. The latter is the instrument with which Mercurius sews up the bean. When we mend something our thread goes back and forth between two parts. That is how our dream life moves back and forth between the oppo-

---

[75] *The Complete Grimm's Fairy Tales,* pp. 112, 525.

sites until they come together. That, in us, is the function of the archetypal energy of Mercurius.

One must read Jung's *Psychology and Alchemy* and *Mysterium Coniunctionis* to get the whole meaning of the end. Then one can really begin to see how deep such little stories go.

Index

Studies in Jungian Psychology
by Jungian Analysts
Quality Paperbacks

Prices and payment in $US (except in Canada, and Visa orders, $Cdn)

Risky Business: Environmental Disasters and the Nature Archetype
Stephen J. Foster (Boulder, CO) ISBN 978-1-894574-33-4. 128 pp. $25

Jung and Yoga: The Psyche-Body Connection

Judith Harris (London, Ontario) ISBN 978-0-919123-95-3. 160 pp. $25

The Gambler: Romancing Lady Luck
Billye B. Currie (Jackson, MS) 978-1-894574-19-8. 128 pp. $25

Conscious Femininity: Interviews with Marion Woodman
Introduction by Marion Woodman (Toronto) ISBN 978-0-919123-59-5. 160 pp. $25

The Sacred Psyche: A Psychological Approach to the Psalms
Edward F. Edinger (Los Angeles) ISBN 978-1-894574-09-9. 160 pp. $25

Eros and Pathos: Shades of Love and Suffering
Aldo Carotenuto (Rome) ISBN 978- 0-919123-39-7. 144 pp. $25

Descent to the Goddess: A Way of Initiation for Women
Sylvia Brinton Perera (New York) ISBN 978-0-919123-05-2. 112 pp. $25

Addiction to Perfection: The Still Unravished Bride
Marion Woodman (Toronto) ISBNj 978-0-919123-11-3. Illustrated. 208 pp. $30/$35hc

The Illness That We Are: A Jungian Critique of Christianity
John P. Dourley (Ottawa) ISBN 978-0-919123-16-8. 128 pp. $25

Coming To Age: The Croning Years and Late-Life Transformation

Jane R. Prétat (Providence) ISBN 978-0-919123-63-2. 144 pp. $25

Jungian Dream Interpretation: A Handbook of Theory and Practice
James A. Hall, M.D. (Dallas) ISBN 978-0-919123-12-0. 128 pp. $25

Phallos: Sacred Image of the Masculine
Eugene Monick (Scranton) ISBN 978-0-919123-26-7. 30 illustrations. 144 pp. $25

The Sacred Prostitute: Eternal Aspect of the Feminine
Nancy Qualls-Corbett (Birmingham) ISBN 978-0-919123-31-1. Illustrated. 176 pp. $30

The Pregnant Virgin: A Process of Psychological Development
Marion Woodman (Toronto) ISBN 978-0-919123-20-5. Illustrated. 208 pp. $30pb/$35hc

FREE SHIPPING via SHOPPING CART on website: www.innercitybooks.net

Credit cards accepted. Toll-free Canada and U.S.: Tel. 1-888-927-0355

INNER CITY BOOKS, 53 Alvin Ave., Toronto, ON M4T 2A8, Canada

Tel. 416-927-0355 / sales@innercitybooks.net/ www.innercitybooks.net